Invitation to Terror

Invitation to Terror

The Expanding Empire of the Unknown

FRANK FUREDI

continuum

Continuum UK
The Tower Building
11 York Road
London SE1 7NX

Continuum US
80 Maiden Lane
Suite 704
New York, NY 10038

www.continuumbooks.com

First published 2007

British Library Cataloguing-in-Publication Data
A catalogue record for this book is available from the British Library.

ISBN 9780826499578

Typeset by Ben Cracknell Studios I www.benstudios.co.uk

Printed and bound by Cromwell Press Ltd, Trowbridge, Wiltshire

Contents

Acknowledgements

During the course of working on this project I have incurred many intellectual debts. I am grateful to colleagues on both sides of the Atlantic for sharing their insights. This study has greatly benefited from my collaboration with Bill Durodie of Cranfield University. The research was made possible by a grant (L147251003) from the Economic and Social Research Council and from the British Academy. The book is dedicated to Jacob Laszlo.

Preface
Why Do They Hate Us?

> Americans are asking, 'Why do they hate us?'
>
> (George Bush, 20 September 2001)[1]

Just a week after the momentous events of September 11, President Bush asked the question, 'Why do they hate us?' He did not suggest an answer to this question, which he posed in his address to the Joint Session of Congress. Nor has he or any major Western public figure made a serious attempt to engage with this query. At the time many writers interpreted this query far too narrowly, to mean 'Why is there such a powerful mood of anti-Americanism throughout the world?'[2] However, Western politicians on both sides of the Atlantic are still asking the same question: 'Why do they hate us?' British officials, stunned by disturbing evidence of home-grown terrorism, have never stopped asking themselves the same question. Politicians in Holland are equally alarmed and along with their EU colleagues are demanding to know 'Why do they hate us?'

Throughout Europe this conundrum is regularly repeated by opinion makers and commentators. As one populist British journalist states:

> *Since 9/11, we haven't stopped asking ourselves: why do they hate us? We've reached out more often than the Four Tops. We've picked enough fluff out of our navels to fill duvets for everyone in the Third World.*[3]

In its original inception, this book began as an attempt to engage with the question 'Why do they hate us?' However, after inspecting official statements and publications on the subject it became evident that it was far from clear who 'they' were. Even more unsettling was the realization that from the available evidence it was not at all obvious who 'us' was. Wars and conflicts can be confusing, since the main actors are by necessity secretive and duplicitous. However, despite the absence of transparency it is usually evident who are the main protagonists and what they are fighting about. Today we have a global conflict that appears so confusing that we are not even certain what to call it. The failure to conceptualize the issues at stake is demonstrated by the absence of consensus around even what words to use to describe the meaning of the present conflict and the enemy. Suddenly governments cease to speak about the *War on Terrorism* and talk about the *Long War*. The shift in terminology often betrays confusion about the issues at stake. Lack of clarity about what this war is about, who are the protagonists, its scope and duration dominates discussions on this conflict.[4] Meaningless terms often represent an attempt to evade. In this case they express confusion and the inability to make sense of life in the twenty-first century.

A fear that dare not speak its name

When one reads official statements about the terrorist threat, it is difficult to avoid the conclusion that their authors have been far too busy studying children's Harry Potter books. In these books Harry's nemesis, the evil wizard Lord Voldemort evokes so much fear that people dare not mention him by name. Consequently they refer to him as 'He Who Must Not Be Named' or 'You Know Who'. No doubt there are some very real threats out there that are causing violence in many parts of the world. But at the moment officials appear to have a lot of difficulty in engaging in a grown-up discussion about 'You Know What'. Commentators on terrorism constantly demand that we 'mind our language'. 'We strongly urge the government to abandon talk of a "War on Terror"' demands a report on the issue of home-grown terrorism in the UK.[5] The British Broadcasting Corporation appears to be continually at a loss to know when the usage of the word 'terrorist' or 'terrorism' is appropriate. 'The value judgements frequently implicit in the use of the words "terrorist" or "terrorist groups" can create inconsistency in their use or, to audiences, raise doubts about our impartiality,' states the BBC's editorial guidelines.[6]

The imprecise and incoherent manner with which the narrative of terrorism is communicated often appears as a problem of language. Questions have been raised about whether the term 'war on terror' has any precise meaning. Even supporters of the war on terror have reservations about using this term. A US senator, Rick Santorum, has remarked that to say 'we are fighting a War on Terror' is 'like saying World War II was a war on blitzkrieg'. He added that terror, like blitzkrieg, is a tactic used by our enemy, not the enemy itself.[7] Occasionally even the architects of the war on terror concede that they got their lines mixed up. 'We actually misnamed the war on terror,' conceded President Bush in August 2004. Without a hint of irony he added that 'it ought to be the struggle against ideological extremists who do not believe in free societies who happen to use terror as a weapon to try to shake the conscience of the free world'.[8] In the very attempt to rectify the 'misnaming' of a war, Bush exposes the poverty of the intellectual resources with which the battle against terror is fought. It is difficult to avoid the conclusion that the confusion lies not just with the occasional word, but the entire script.

President Bush's acknowledgement that 'we actually misnamed the war on terror' should not be seen as proof of the White House's lack of rhetorical skills. Confusion about terminology expresses a wider mood of disorientation about the very meaning of the war. One of the clearest manifestations of this problem is the constant display of verbal acrobatics shown by officials in London and Washington in their attempt to explain the significance of this conflict. Sometimes they struggle to find the right words. At times they even attempt to distance themselves from the term 'war on terror' and give the impression that they are uncomfortable with the rhetorical idioms that they invented. In December 2006, it was reported that the Foreign Office had advised government ministers, ambassadors and officials to stop using the term 'war on terror' and similar provocative terms, as 'they risk angering British Muslims and generating tensions in the wider Islamic world'.[9] That the name designated to define this global conflict could be perceived as a liability and so easily dispensed with is symptomatic of a mood of unease about progress in the war. It also indicates that for a significant section of the political elites the war on terror has little meaning.

Not long after the Foreign Office issued its favoured speech code, some government ministers fell in line. In April 2007, the Secretary of State for International Development, Hilary Benn asserted that the term 'war on terror' was a really bad idea. 'In the UK, we do not use the phrase "war on terror" because we can't win by military means alone,' he stated.[10] This less than accurate statement about the official rhetoric used during the first six years of the war seeks to evade the issues. As everyone knows, wars are rarely won by military means alone, but that does not stop the protagonists from calling it a war. If it is not a war then what is it?

To some critics the policing of language by the Foreign Office smacks of a cowardly refusal to face up to a serious threat to the West. 'Rather than identifying Islamism as the ideological enemy of democracy, government and commentators alike used "terrorism" as a euphemism to avoid naming the real threat and thus linking violent anti-westernism to elements in the Islamic community,' they argue.[11] Others are worried that the official language is already too provocative and needs to be toned down. 'But the rhetoric of war has encouraged an overreaction in which human rights and the rule of law are among the more obvious casualties' pleads a call for even greater linguistic restraint.[12] One national security adviser to former President Carter has gone so far as to state that 'The damage these three words have done', that is the 'war on terror', is 'infinitely greater than any wild dreams entertained by the fanatical perpetrators of the 9/11 attacks when they were plotting against us in distant Afghan caves'.[13]

So what is this war about? Well, it seems to be against Islamic terrorism but apparently the enemy has little to do with 'real' Islam. According to former Home Secretary John Reid, 'The aim of the terrorists is to divide the community, to pretend that this is a war between Muslims and everyone else, when it isn't'.[14] Other commentators also like to point out that the enemy is not Islam and, like Reid, also go to great lengths to avoid offering a comprehensible designation to the enemy. In April 2006, Senator Joseph Biden, the leading Democrat on the Foreign Relations Committee, acknowledged that the American political class has been singularly unsuccessful in the task of defining its adversary. He criticized the Bush Administration for defining the enemy 'too broadly and inaccurately'. However, he had the good grace to concede that the Republicans did not have a monopoly on confusion on this subject. 'I have never been able to define the threat, and my party hasn't been able to define the threat either,' stated Biden.[15] In a spirit of bipartisan solidarity, supporters of the Bush Administration are also prepared to admit that they find it difficult to define the enemy. Stephen Hadley, National Security Adviser to Bush, acknowledged that 'We have sometimes struggled to find the proper label for the enemy we face in the War on Terror – be it Islamic extremists, militant Jihadists, or Islamo-fascists'.[16]

It is a sign of the times that, almost six years after 9/11, a leading American politician can publicly acknowledge that he along with his colleagues cannot persuasively define the enemy. This is clearly no ordinary foe. Politicians in the past had no problem pointing the finger at the Germans or the Japanese or the Communists and stating with utmost clarity that they were the enemy. Through the displacement of this language of clarity with a confused and defensive sounding rhetoric, Anglo-American officials continually transmit a sense of confusion and embarrassment. Their apprehension about giving a name to the enemy is almost tangible. The very term 'war on terror' can be interpreted as a rhetorical idiom constructed to avoid naming the enemy. On occasion, even the former US Secretary of Defense, Donald Rumsfeld recognized this point. Back in June 2004 he noted that 'Terrorism is simply a technique being used by extremists' and is 'not the problem in and of itself.'[17] But terms like the 'global war on terrorism' and the equally empty phrase 'the war on extremism' continue to highlight the absence of lucidity. Nor did Bush succeed in clarifying matters when he declared that 'America's enemies are ideologues', since 'these people have an ideology' which is 'different from us'.[18]

The reluctance to give a comprehensible name to the enemy is not simply an outcome of the difficulty that the elites have in making sense of the threat they face. It is also motivated by a sense of anxiety about appearing to explicitly convey the message that identifies the enemy too closely with Islam. Time and again Western officials attempt to convince the world that although the enemy claims to uphold the banner of Islam, it isn't really the genuine article. One reason why the war is expressed through so many euphemisms is to avoid closely associating the enemy with the Muslim faith. The project of demonstrating that the enemy is not what it claims to be is constantly pursued by the Bush and Blair regimes. 'Some call this evil Islamic radicalism; others, militant Jihadism; still others Islamo-fascism,' notes Bush, before insisting that whatever it's called, this 'ideology is very different from the religion of Islam'.[19]

The confused attempts to construct a non-emotive name for the enemy can be diagnosed as an affliction of political confusion. The war against terrorism is directed at individuals who uphold Islam. That is why they are described as Islamic radicals or jihadists. But Western officials also insist that their targeting of Islamic radicals does not mean that they are fighting a religion. Time and again officials insist that their war is not against Islam. There is little doubt that Western leaders have no desire to wage a war against Islam. That is one reason why they find it difficult to name the enemy. But labels like Islamic radicalism and

Islamo-fascism and even jihadist have manifest connections with the Muslim faith, which is one reason that Western officials are often found apologizing for the language they use.

Take the guidelines issued by EU officials in April 2006 on the difficult question of what words to use to describe the enemy. The guidelines suggested that European governments should avoid the term 'Islamic terrorism' in favour of the Orwellian-sounding phrase 'terrorists who abusively invoke Islam'. The invention of this term was part of the project of cobbling together a 'non-emotive lexicon for discussing radicalisation'.[20] The authors of the guideline claimed that 'Islamic terrorism' was 'too emotive a phrase', by which they meant that it would be resented by most Muslims. Their alternative may well be non-emotive but it is also confusing and unclear. Karen Hughes, the US Undersecretary of State, also uses 'non-emotive' jargon. 'It's difficult to know what to call the ideology that we're up against because it is a perversion of Islam,' she noted. In the end she decided on the non-emotive but diffuse term 'violent extremist'. Why? 'Because I think they are extremists, they are violent, they are actually mass murderers who pervert their religion,' argued Hughes.[21]

The confusion displayed by officials about the use of language is influenced by a wider sense of defensiveness and confusion towards Islamic culture. One manifestation of this climate of disorientation was the instruction issued by Learning Teaching Scotland to pupils and teachers advising them not to stare at Muslims. 'Staring or looking is a form of discrimination as it makes the other person feel uncomfortable, or as though they are not normal' it warned.[22] Such self-conscious regulation of speech and behaviour exposes apprehensions that that are further compounded by a reluctance to acknowledge them in public.

One of the few attempts to resolve the tension between clearly naming the enemy and not wanting to offend the Muslim world came in an important speech made by Tony Blair in March 2006. Blair noted that his ministers have been advised 'never' to use the phrase 'Islamist extremists' because 'it will give offence'. Blair acknowledged this problem and attempted to overcome it by attempting to formulate a dichotomy between the extremist and the authentic version of Islam. He stated that the 'extremist view of Islam is not just theologically backward but completely contrary to the spirit and teaching of the Koran'.[23] On several occasions Blair has attempted to project himself as an admirer of the Koran whilst being an uncompromising foe of terrorism. 'To me, the most remarkable thing about reading the Koran is to understand how progressive it is,' enthused Blair.[24] The French President Jacques Chirac echoed this sentiment when he declared that 'All should be done to avoid anything that creates tension between people and religions and avoid any association between Islam, which is, of course, a respected and respectable religion, and radical Islam, which is totally different and is of a political nature.'[25] Numerous academic experts implicitly agree and have opted for the neutral-sounding term, 'Political Islam'.

The project of seeking to isolate the West's adversaries through characterizing Islamic radicals as alien to the Islamic faith is likely to result in a confusing and unhappy outcome. The very attempt to distinguish between the false and the authentic dimensions of a faith or an ideology that is not one's own is unlikely to carry conviction. Most Muslim people are not particularly interested in Tony Blair's interpretation of the Koran. Nor will they take seriously a non-Muslim's advice of who is and who isn't a true adherent of their faith. Moreover, even the slightest hint that the word 'Islam' is associated with negative connotations is likely to provoke the anger of this community. So it is not surprising that when Bush used the term 'Islamic fascism' he was attacked by the Council on American–Islamic Relations. The Chairman of this organization, Parvez Ahmed stated that although 'you have on many occasions said Islam is a "religion of peace",' in this instance 'you equated the religion of peace with the ugliness of fascism'.[26]

Another reason why the project of attempting to praise Islam while attacking its radicals is confusing is because it contributes to the avoidance of clarifying who is the enemy. It is a negative designation of what they are not. In the Cold War, Anglo-American politicians did not make distinctions between good and bad communists. During the Second World War the enemy was not Nazi extremists, or bad Nazis, but the Nazis. Clarity about who was on what side helped people make sense of the war and indicated that they possessed a language and a system of meaning that bound them together.

From time to time the consensus of hiding behind non-emotive words is punctuated by the impatient outburst of an angry politician. The American senator, Rick Santorum, has criticized 'our fear of speaking clearly, publicly, and consistently about the enemy'. He took exception to those who argue that 'We can't say or do anything that might offend Muslims'.[27] However, such expressions of impatience rarely help clarify matters, for the simple reason that the problem is not merely one of presentation, but of meaning.

It is tempting to conclude that Western leaders are only pretending not to be at war with Islam. One could draw the inference that they actually 'know' their enemy, but diplomatic considerations and pragmatism has led them to censor their concerns in public. Undoubtedly there are individual politicians, officials and generals who possess very clear ideas about the enemy. Some of them may actually believe that the enemy is Islam. But such individuals constitute an insignificant minority. From the experience of the past six years it is possible to draw the conclusion that, as a group, the Western political elites lack a web of meaning through which they can make sense of the threat of terrorism. Their silences and convoluted words do not simply represent an attempt to avoid stating what they know. They also signify a mood of defensiveness towards a threat that they neither understand nor deal with.

The enemy has acquired an increasingly diffuse and abstract character. Not for nothing does a Homeland Security Council planning scenario refer to the enemy as the Universal Adversary (UA). This is another way of saying that the enemy is the enemy. The concept of a universal adversary also conveys the idea that anyone could be the enemy. According to this scenario, 'Because the attacks could be caused by foreign terrorists; domestic radical groups; state sponsored adversaries; or in some cases, disgruntled employees, the perpetrator has been named, the Universal Adversary'.[28] The official imagination has been allowed to run wild. Virtually every form of grievance – from the grumbles of individual employees to secret conspiracies – inexorably leads towards a major terrorist attack. Uncertainty about the identity of the enemy has led to scenarios where little is left to chance and virtually anyone can be represented as a potential foe. One critic of this exercise in official fantasy construction notes that what we have here is a 'kind of satanic force whose particular human form is treated as utterly irrelevant for any exercise hoping to gain insight into its purposes or techniques'.[29] The Universal Adversary is probably best personified by 'You Know Who'. As we shall see, with enemies like that it is difficult to feel secure.

In a confrontation with a Universal Adversary, is it any surprise that the War on Terror has been gradually rebranded as The Long War? The term was first mentioned in 2004 by US Army General John Abizaid, in reference to the conflict with Al-Qaeda. President Bush adopted the term in his 2006 State of the Union speech, when he spoke about how 'our generation is in a long war against a determined enemy'. Since its adoption by the Bush Administration, official reports regularly write about a war with an indefinite time limit. 'The United States is a nation engaged in what will be a long war' states the 2006 Quadrennial Defense Review of the US Department of Defense. Sadly, a war without an end with a universal adversary is not a comic-book caricature, but, as we shall see, official rhetoric in search of meaning.

Who is 'us'?

It is bad enough that we are not sure about who 'they' are that hate us. Unfortunately there is compelling evidence that we are far from certain about who or what constitutes 'us'. Time and again we are confronted with disturbing evidence that not everything can be taken for granted on the home front. From time to time newspapers feature stories about 'Brits Who Hate Us' that draw the readers' attention to 'how young men spread poison to undermine their OWN country'.[30] The formulation of 'Brits who hate us' suggests that we cannot assume that everyone who lives in our community is part of 'us'. The title of Michael Moore's polemical book *Dude, Where's My Country?* indicates that, at least for some, what divides 'us' is more important than what binds us together.

So, what binds 'us' together? As we outline in this book, the difficulty that Western societies have in accounting for themselves constitutes the nub of the problem. Attempts to outline what constitutes 'our way of life' or what values 'we are defending' tend to have an empty rhetorical character. So, back in August 2006 Tony Blair called for an 'alliance of moderation' to combat extremism.[31] But moderation is unlikely to be able to serve as an effective focus for unity nor will it help answer the question of 'Who are we?'

Yet if we are to understand the meaning of twenty-first-century terrorism, it is essential to have a clearer grasp of who we are and how we are expected to respond to this threat. This is a book that is more about us than them, since it is our response that determines the impact of this problem. Virtually everyone agrees that terrorism is defined by its impact on the public it targets. Yet there seems to be very little open discussion about how society has responded to it and how people are affected by it. This is no small gap in our understanding of twenty-first-century terrorism. *Invitation to Terror* argues that what we need to really worry about is not what terrorists do, but our reaction to it. We agree with the other studies on this subject, which argue that the damage caused by terrorism may well be outweighed by our response to it.[32]

There is little doubt that the responses of Western societies to terrorism have been disproportionate to its threat. There is of course evidence of a real physical threat. The atrocities perpetrated in New York, Istanbul, Bali and London illustrate a nihilistic and destructive force at work. But such tragic episodes, along with the recent wave of suicide bombings in the Middle East, are not always the outcome of the same phenomenon and do not represent a threat to a way of life. In terms of their physical impact and significance these threats are relatively modest in historical terms.

The war on terror has more than its share of sceptics. Some have gone so far as to dismiss the very existence of terrorism. It is frequently represented as a dishonest construction invented by a small circle of neo-conservative war mongers. Such 'big lie' theories of history overlook the way in which the issue of terror haunts the political elites. Governments do not just practise the 'politics of fear' – they live by it and often they are consumed by it.[33] That is why, contrary to the expectation of radical critics, there is a manifest absence of a triumphant or crusading tone to the conduct of this conflict. On the contrary, as we show in successive chapters, the official response has been hesitant, defensive and sometimes even defeatist.

This book suggests that the question of 'why do they hate us?' tends to deflect attention from why society feels so uncomfortable with dealing with the threats that confront it. The existence of a physical threat of terrorism can not be denied. But the idea that terrorism represents an existential threat is the product of society's inability to give meaning to human experience. It is a symptom of a society that has lost its way and lacks the intellectual and moral resources to deal with the routine threats that it faces. When terrorism is unmasked we shall see an all-too-familiar, albeit uncomfortable face. Maybe we should be asking the question, 'Why do we hate ourselves?'

Notes

1. George W. Bush, 'Address to a Joint Session of Congress and the American People', 20 September 2001, www.whitehouse.gov/news/releases/2001/09/print/20010920-8.html.

2. See, for example, Peter Ford, 'Why do they hate us?', The Christian Science Monitor, 27 September 2001.

3. Richard Littlejohn, 'If they hate us so much, why don't they leave?', Daily Mail, 8 August 2006.

4. This shift in terminology is well described in Bradley Graham and Josh White, 'Abizaid credited with popularizing the term "Long War"', The Washington Post, 3 February 2006.

5. Blick, Choudury and Weir (2007) p. 11.

6. See 'Editorial Guidelines: War, Terror & Emergencies', www.bbc.co.uk/guidelines/editorialguidelines/edguide/war/mandatoryreferr.shtml, March 2007.

7. 'Senator Santorum Delivers Speech at the National Press Club', 20 July 2006.

8. Online NewsHour, 'Campaign Snapshots', 6 August 2004, www.pbs.org/newshour/bb/politics/july-dec04/snapshot_8-6.html.

9. 'Christmas Terror strike "highly likely"', *Daily Telegraph*, 11 December 2006.

10. *BBC Politics On Line*, 'Benn criticises "war on terror"', 16 April 2007.

11. Jones and Smith (2006) p. 1083.

12. Blick, Choudhury and Weir (2007) p. 11.

13. Zbigniew Brzezinski, 'Terrorized by "War on Terror"', *The Washington Post*, 25 March 2007.

14. 'Christmas Terror strike "highly likely"', *The Daily Telegraph*, 11 December 2006.

15. Cited in Jonathan Rauch, 'A War on Jihadism, Not "Terror"', in *reasononline*, 17 April 2006, www.reason.com/news/show/117337.html.

16. The White House, 'Remarks by Stephen Hadley to the American Israel Public Affairs Committee National Summit 2005', 26 October 2005. www.whitehouse.gov/news/releases/2005/10/20051031-4.html.

17. Department of Defense, 'Secretary Rumsfeld's Remarks at the International Institute for Strategic Studies', 5 June 2004.

18. The White House, 'President Discusses Second Term Accomplishments and Priorities', 3 August 2005.

19. 'President Discusses War on Terror at National Endowment for Democracy', 6 October 2005.

20. '"Islamic terrorism" is too emotive a phrase, says EU', *Daily Telegraph*, 12 April 2006.

21. Cited in Anne Gearen, 'Hughes: Fixing US Image May Take Years', *Associated Press*, 28 September 2006.

22. Jason Alardyce and Abul Tahel, 'Don't stare at Muslims says advice to schools', *The Sunday Times*, 15 April 2007.

23. Tony Blair, '"Clash about Civilisation" speech', 21 March 2006, www.number10.gov.uk/output/Page9224.asp.

24. Blair (2006) p. 12.

25. See interview, *Europe 1*, radio, 18 September 2006.

26. Cited in Ken Herman, 'Bush shifts rhetoric; it's now a war on "Islamic Fascism"', *Cox News Service*, 14 August 2006.

27. 'Senator Santorum Delivers Speech at the National Press Club', 20 July 2006.

28. The Homeland Security Council (2004), *Planning Scenarios, Executive Summaries; Created for Use in National, Federal, State and Local Homeland Security Preparedness Activities*, Washington DC, p. iv.

29. Lustick (2006) p. 124.

30. See 'Brits Who Hate Us', *The People*, 7 January 2007.

31. See 'Blair's multicultural stance', *The Australian*, 3 August 2006.

32. See Mueller (2006a) and Lustick (2006).

33. See Furedi (2005).

Introduction
Beyond Comprehension

Is there much point in writing another book about terrorism? Since September 2001 this topic has been the subject of ceaseless debate. Politicians, public officials and security experts are continually making pronouncements about the threat posed by terrorists. The media is constantly discussing and analysing the subject. According to my estimate, since 9/11 nearly 8000 books have been published in the English language on the subject. When I consulted the International Bibliography of the Social Sciences I found 1413 academic monographs published since 2001 that had the term 'terrorism' in their title. Yet the sheer scale of intellectual effort that has gone into investigating this problem appears to have yielded meagre results.

For a start we have very real difficulties deciding what we mean by a 'terrorist'. There is no consensus about the very definition of the term. A recent attempt to construct one notes that 'few terms or concepts in contemporary political discourse have proved as hard to define as terrorism.'[1] One study reviewed 109 definitions of terrorism that covered 22 definitional elements.[2] Walter Laqueur, a well-known expert on the subject, has counted over 100 definitions. He has concluded that the only 'general characteristic generally agreed upon is that terrorism involves violence and the threat of violence'.[3] But of course the use and threat of violence are not confined to terrorism. Angry husbands, anti-social teenage gangs, religious zealots, old-fashioned criminals and even democratically elected governments have all been known to deploy or threaten to use violence. It seems that the very expansive remit of this term threatens to deprive it of coherence and clarity.

Most serious contributions on the subject acknowledge that they have difficulty in agreeing on a working definition of terrorism. Often this difficult problem is side-stepped through attempting to enumerate a list of features that distinguish this form of crime. However the attempt to construct a list of characteristics that are specific to terrorism is undermined by the fact that different forms of political violence are not confined to terrorists. For example Wilkinson claimed that 'a major characteristic of political terror is its indiscriminate nature.'[4] The insistence that the indiscriminate quality of terrorist violence is one of this phenomenon's distinct features is accepted by many specialists on the subject. Images of the Washington snipers randomly shooting pedestrians or of pedestrians blown to bits in Tel Aviv by a hidden bomb lend weight to the argument that this form of violence is distinguished by its indiscriminate character. However as the American sociologist Joel Best argues in his *Random Violence*, many of today's high profile crimes have a capacity to scare the public precisely because they are perceived to be carried out indiscriminately. It is random violence that characterizes the acts of the serial killer, the perpetrator of road rage or the pedophile preying on innocent children.[5] Indiscriminate violence is not the sole property of terrorism. Indeed it is associated with many of the high-profile crimes that excite the public's imagination.

The absence of agreement on the meaning of terrorism is not simply an issue for academic experts. Confusion about terminology is often symptomatic of uncertainty about the constitution of the problem. Lack of precision has encouraged sloppy thinking. It has also led to a free-for-all where virtually every unpleasant phenomenon can be represented as a form of terrorism. So we have narco-terror, computer- or cyber-terror, bio-terror, agro-terror, eco-terror, apocalyptic terror, hyper-terrorism, postmodern terror, religious terror, mega-terrorism, sexual terrorism, Islamic terrorism, mass-casualty terror, cataclysmic terrorism, catastrophic terrorism, single-issue terrorism and the more straight-forward 'new terrorist'. A single concept that encompasses the destruct-ive lashing out of a small group of frustrated anti-abortionists and the global movement of jihadists is unlikely to yield great insight into the constitution of the problem. Indeed the construction of a concept that appears to account for the deployment of such a wide range of diverse types of public violence is likely to encourage a confusing if frightening perception of the threat.

Guesswork, often uninformed guesswork, represents the dominant trend in the discussion of this subject. That is why there is virtually no agreement on what motivates the terrorism. One major review of the literature found that there are almost as many theories as definitions of terrorism. It also found that the quantity of theories surpasses the number of empirically based research papers into the subject. Significantly it raised concern about how the emotional and subjective approach of researchers to this subject served as an obstacle to clarifying issues. It argued that in both the spheres of academia and counter-terrorism, 'one must acknowledge the possibility that terrorism excites passions that erode logical discourse, leading to responses that are reactive and engaged rather than proactive and analytical.'[6] In other words, most theories of terrorism are often the product of powerful emotions rather than analytical thought and lack significant empirical substantiation. Not surprisingly, as Victoroff notes, such theories have not 'been tested in a systematic way'. He adds that they are 'overwhelmingly subjective, speculative and, in many cases, derived from 1920s-era psychoanalytic hypotheses that are not amenable to testing'.[7]

And what if there is nothing to test? Victoroff acknowledges that terrorists may be far too heterogenous to be constituted by a distinct type of individual.[8] The evidence available from the small number of studies that are based on interviews with individuals imprisoned for terrorist violence suggests that there might not be a distinct type of person who becomes a terrorist. Scott Atran, whose research into suicide terrorism represents the most interesting documented contribution to the subject, argues that 'it is not possible to "profile" suicide terrorists' since 'they are just like us.'[9] What Atran means is that how an individual becomes a terrorists has far less to do with psychological dispositions than with external influences. Atran believes that attempts to profile suicide terrorists will do little to deter such attacks since they are not 'sufficiently different from everyone else'.[10] This point is also understood by many individuals involved in intelligence gathering. Back in 1999 a report written for the Central Intelligence Agency (CIA) concluded that 'unfortunately for profiling purposes, there does not appear to be a single terrorist personality.'[11] That's another way of saying that we don't really know what a terrorist looks like.

Little Intelligence

While terrorist experts speculate, public officials rely on the power of the imagination. In official publications it is difficult to extract the rare valuable nugget of fact from the layers of gossip, rumour and speculation within which it is embedded. Both the British and US governments have been caught out manipulating information and intelligence in order to strengthen the case for the military invasion of Iraq. Of course governments have always manipulated the facts to justify their foreign policy and drive to war. And how governments interpret intelligence is invariably influenced by their agenda and objectives. So too today. The accusation that the UK Government presented intelligence that was 'cherry picked' about Iraq could be made about any regime assessing its option for a future conflict. Yet there is something uniquely disturbing about these official documents.

What is striking about the UK Government's dossier on WMDs is not its manipulation of intelligence but its absence of intelligence. Nevertheless in the Foreword to the dossier Tony Blair promotes it as a unique document based on material that is 'largely secret'. Blair pointedly asserts that 'it is unprecedented for the Government to publish this kind of document.'[12] However the document reveals very few 'secrets' – almost all its content is based on information available in the public domain. Intelligence is used as a rhetorical device or as an add-on to endow the content with legitimacy. The now-discredited claim that the 'Iraqi military are able to deploy chemical or biological weapons within 45 minutes of an order to do so' is the only attempt in the document to invent an intelligence-led fact.[13] What the close inspection of the dossier exposes is something far more disturbing than the routine manipulation of information. The dossier conveys a powerful sense of confusion and disorientation, and a total absence of intelligence. It is written by authors with little intelligence to reveal. Its aim is not simply to fool the public but also its authors. It is worth noting that a couple of weeks before the publication of the dossier, US President Bush noted that 'We haven't the faintest idea what has been going on in the last four years . . . other than what we know is an attempt to carry on rebuilding weapons.'[14] Bush was not exaggerating his officials' level of ignorance. According to an official inquiry into pre-war claims about WMDs, the US intelligence community was 'dead wrong' about virtually every dimension of its assessment of Iraq's weapon capability.[15]

One intriguing dimension of the UK's Government's presentation of the threat of Saddam's WMDs was that it probably genuinely believed the story it concocted. Driven by the catastrophist imagination that characterizes our times, the report sought to render comprehensible the Government's worse suspicions. As one journalist noted, the 'intelligence community got into the habit of making worst-case scenarios and these were used to make factual claims by politicians'.[16] It is worth noting that worst-case thinking is not confined to the feverish fantasies of a handful of security analysts. As we document in chapter 4 its adoption is advocated by commanding institutional interests and influential academic experts.

The second dossier issued by the Blair Government, on 3 February 2003 – known as the 'Dodgy Dossier' – is further testimony to its formidable capacity for self-delusion. This report, billed as drawing 'upon a number of sources, including intelligence material', was swiftly exposed as a cobbled-together fantasy document based on plagiarized material.[17] What is remarkable about this fraud is not so much the attempt to manipulate the public but the attempt to represent a dossier based on widely available public-domain texts as an authentic intelligence document. Critics of Blair have raised concerns about the subordination of intelligence to a political agenda; 'intelligence was being sought to support political judgements already arrived at' observes one study of 'threat exaggeration'.[18] That's true, but what is even more significant about this episode is the obvious dearth of intelligence about a supposed threat to world peace. According to Sir Robin Butler, who was charged with inquiring into the fiasco surrounding the publication of these documents, the dossier did 'not make clear that the intelligence' on which the conclusions were based was 'very thin'.[19]

As one study of this affair notes the real problem with these dossiers was not so much that intelligence had been distorted by political pressure. Rather it was a fundamental case of 'intelligence failure'. The so-called intelligence community was so wedded to worst-case scenarios that they got Saddam's intentions and Iraq's capabilities entirely wrong. According to this study 'there was a systematic belief – almost an ideological conviction – that all militarist dictators wish to acquire WMD.'[20] This belief acquired the character of a dogma that simply did not require any proof. Instead of intelligence it was dogmatic prejudice that provided the justification for extending the 'war on terror' to Iraq.

It appears that the so-called intelligence community knew as little about its target as many terrorism experts do about their subject matter. The report of the *U.S. Commission on the Intelligence Capabilities of the United States Regarding Weapons of Mass Destruction* unequivocally highlights the collective ignorance and confusion of the Bush Administration on this topic. It concluded that:

> the Intelligence Community was dead wrong in almost all of its pre-war judgments about Iraq's weapons of mass destruction. This was a major intelligence failure. Its principal causes were the Intelligence Community's inability to collect good information about Iraq's WMD programs, serious errors in analyzing what information it could gather, and a failure to make clear just how much of its analysis was based on

> *assumptions, rather than good evidence. On a matter of this importance,*
> *we simply cannot afford failures of this magnitude.*[21]

The triumph of assumptions over evidence indicates that in fact there is very little real intelligence to be manipulated for political ends. The *Commission* acknowledged that US intelligence agencies 'collected precious little intelligence for the analysts to analyze, and much of what they did collect was either worthless or misleading'.[22]

The *Commission* also observed that 'our case studies resoundingly demonstrate how little we know about some of our highest priority intelligence targets.'[23] In other words the war on terror is being conducted on the basis of very little information about the enemy. At a time when these targets are portrayed as the greatest danger to the world, the admission that the US Government is working in the dark indicates that this is a threat that it does not understand. However the absence of information does not appear to deter political leaders from allowing their imagination to serve as a substitute for information. Speculation, opinion and even fantasy have considerable latitude to flourish. Speculation has become a driver in the construction of intelligence reports. Suspicion and apprehension about what's not known influences policy-makers and policy-making.

Recent experience indicates that the unique feature of contemporary intelligence policy is not its *manipulation* but its *invention*. In fact officials in London and Washington have had little intelligence to manipulate. Yes they needed arguments to lend legitimacy to the invasion of Iraq. But the principal challenge they faced was to convince themselves and the public that they actually possessed real facts about their opponents' intentions. In the absence of such facts, guesswork served as a substitute for informed policy-making. Subsequent experience suggests that this state of affairs continues to influence the conduct of the War on Terror. For example, less than a day before the 7 July suicide bombings in London, the Director-General of MI5 told senior MPs that there was no imminent terrorist threat to this city.[24]

Imagination in question

It is interesting to note that lack of clarity about the nature and threat of terrorism is frequently represented as a problem of imagination rather than of information. A couple of weeks after 9/11 an editorial in *The Washington Post* argued that the 'nation and government' was unprepared for the attacks 'in large part because of a failure of imagination'.[25] This argument was not confined to the opinion pages of newspapers. According to the *9/11 Commission Report*, the 'most important failure' of government was 'one of imagination'. It criticized the Clinton and pre-9/11 Bush Administrations for not treating terrorism as the 'overriding security concern' and stated that it was due to 'this failure of imagination'.[26] The *Commission*'s conclusion is echoed by retired Admiral Bobby R. Inman, former Deputy Director of the CIA, who described 9/11 as an 'intelligence failure' but one 'grounded in a failure of imagination', a situation where 'you don't know what you are looking for, you don't know where to look.'[27] This interpretation of government failure continues to influence deliberations on the subject. 'Failure of imagination still plagues us, five years later,' writes a *Boston Globe* columnist on the eve of the fifth anniversary of 9/11.[28]

British officialdom also looks to the imagination for answers. In his review of intelligence on WMDs, Lord Butler stated that 'well-developed imagination at all stages of the intelligence process is required to overcome preconceptions.' To overcome preconceptions, Butler proposed that analysts play 'Devil's advocate' and adopt 'red teaming', which is a managerial term for brainstorming and group speculation.[29]

The tendency to associate the failure to anticipate and counter the threat of terrorism with the failure of imagination provides a worrying insight into how the problem is conceptualized. The act of imagining involves the forming of a 'mental concept of what is not actually present to the senses'. As the *Oxford English Dictionary* notes, this word often conveys the 'implication that the conception does not correspond to the reality of things'.[30] Thought directed towards actions and events 'not yet in existence' can help frame important ideas. It can also encourage speculation and confusion. Whatever its outcome, the act of imagination does not serve as a substitute for knowledge-led policy responses. And imagining the threat of terrorism is not quite the same as understanding it. The focus on the imagination can obscure the far more fundamental failures of knowledge, understanding, intelligence and policy.

The constant repetition of the diagnosis of 'failure of imagination' indicates that policy-makers are reluctant to face up to their own intellectual and strategic failures. As one thoughtful study of the *9/11 Commission Report* argues 'the Commission's "failure of imagination" is more of a slogan than an argument: it sounds good but is an almost indecipherable muddle.'[31] This verdict is contested by the authors of the *Report* who prefer to interpret the failure of the US Government to contain the threat of the 9/11 attack through the idiom of imagination. According to Ernest May and Philip Zelikow, two leading figures involved with the *Commission*, those involved in his investigation:

> could not explain to themselves in other language why options that seemed so obvious on the afternoon of 9/11 – particularly that of military action against the camps in Afghanistan where Osama bin Laden was known to be training thousands of terrorists to kill Americans – had never previously, in either Bill Clinton's or George W. Bush's administration, been a subject of serious staff work. Nor could we explain in other language why there had been only desultory, low-level planning for the possibility of terrorists using airplanes as weapons. After all, it was their practice to use vehicles as weapons – cars, trucks, boats. Why not airplanes?[32]

May and Zelikow's inability to make sense of Washington's failure to anticipate 9/11 has led them to embrace a language that is both imprecise and difficult to verify. That this is the only language with which the authors of the *Report* feel comfortable is symptomatic of the confused state of official thinking.

An examination of the meaning of the term 'failure of imagination' indicates that it is often used to indict those who fail to imagine worst-case scenarios. 'We could have had perfect intelligence on all the key pieces of 9/11, but the fact is we lacked for the very best of reasons people with evil enough imaginations to put those pieces together and realize that 19 young men were going to hijack four airplanes for suicide attacks against our national symbols and kill as many innocent civilians as they could, for no stated reason at all,' wrote Thomas Friedman of *The New York Times*.[33] He added that 'imagination is on my mind a lot these days, because it seems to me that the only people with imagination in the world right now are the bad guys.' Imagining evil is presented as the medium through which understanding of the terrorist threat may be gained. As the editor of the journal of the American Academy of Actuaries argues, 'we and our leaders are going to have to embrace the imagination of our enemies.'[34] This prominence attached to the imagination betrays a mood of disorientation towards the threat of terrorism. The valorization of imagination directs attention towards the senses and intuition, encouraging a turn toward speculation and fantasy. That is why in the months after 9/11 US officials took the step of consulting people who are truly imaginative – Hollywood film directors and screen writers.

The embrace of the imaginative may well express a lack of confidence in the theories and concepts available to policy-makers for making sense of the world. Instead of confronting this intellectual malaise, officials prefer to evade the problem by pointing the finger of blame at unimaginative individuals.

But is it really the case that policy-makers lack the capacity to imagine bad things? A review of public debates during the past two decades suggests that in fact politicians and their officials are rather good at imagining worst-case scenarios. Since the 1980s American politicians and officials have possessed a very rich imaginative sense of an impending terrorist act of destruction. In the 1990s the Clinton White House ran scenarios of bio-terrorist attacks in order to plan for such eventualities. Clinton's Defense Secretary William Cohen summed up the prevailing consensus that anticipated acts of mass-destruction terrorism when he stated that 'the question is no longer if this will happen but when.'[35] Birkland has questioned the claim that the 'scale and organisation' of the 9/11 attack was 'unimaginable' to the 'expert community'. His study concludes that 'counter-terrorism experts had long considered the possibility and impacts of large-scale terrorist attacks, particularly those involving nuclear, chemical, or biological agents.'[36] Richard Falkenrath pointed out in his trenchant criticism of the *9/11 Commission Report* that 'with respect to the potential consequences of certain kinds of catastrophic terrorism, the half decade prior to 9/11 was characterized by an excess of imagination, not its deficiency.'[37] As we shall see in subsequent chapters, during the decades leading up to 9/11 the perception of the terrorist threat possessed by an all-too-imaginative official mind continually ran ahead of events.

Condemnation masquerading as analysis

It is not so much a failure of imagination but of understanding that accounts for the confusing state of public discussion on this subject. The very fact that the difficulty we have in conceptually capturing the threat of terrorism is portrayed as a problem of the imagination rather than of understanding is significant. This attitude expresses a tendency to over-look or minimize the role of research, reasoning and analytical thinking for making sense of this subject. The official exhortation to increase the capacity for imagining the threats ahead does not displace the necessity for understanding. It merely assigns understanding an unusually modest status. Why? Because many of the current versions of terrorism assume that to understand terrorism is to realize that this is a phenomenon that cannot be entirely understood. **The belief that, to some extent, the threat of terrorism is beyond understanding informs public discussion on both sides of the Atlantic.** Politicians, journalists and commentators continually signal their own sense of uncertainty and insist that terrorism represents a danger beyond understanding. After the conviction of the British Muslim, Dhirren Barot, for terrorist-related offences, an editorial in *The Times* stated that 'the threat posed by Barot is hard to envisage.'[38] A couple of days later a commentary in a London-based paper described terrorism as a 'disease beyond comprehension'.[39]

The judgment that acts of terrorism are beyond comprehension is continually asserted as a self-evident truth. After a horrific terrorist attack on a Russian school in 2004, President Bush told a press conference that the 'atrocities that took place in the school were beyond comprehension'.[40] In Australia a terrorist plot to attack Sydney's Kings Cross Station was described as a 'diabolical and uncivilised act beyond the comprehension of normal people'.[41] According to the father of a 9/11 hijack victim, the ideology of the terrorist is 'warped beyond comprehension'.[42] An editorial commemorating the fifth anniversary of 9/11 in the *Charleston Gazette* observes that 'some horrible human events are almost beyond comprehension.'[43]

There is of course something of the rhetorical in the allegation that a threat is beyond understanding or comprehension. On one level such statements are meant to signify the immoral and inhumane dimension of the threat. However the constant depiction of terrorism as a danger that cannot be entirely known is not simply a rhetorical flourish or an acknowledgement of a writer's intellectual modesty. After all it is the hidden and unpredictable qualities of terrorism that makes it so peculiarly frightening. Incomprehensibility represents the response of impotence towards foes that cannot be understood. At the same time it serves as a marker for a threat that is uniquely dangerous. The conventional fear of the unknown becomes amplified when faced with unknown forces that are known to be ready to strike and intentionally inflict harm. It continually invites the response of incomprehension. 'How can they do this?', 'Why do they hate us?', 'Who are these people?', 'What do they want and who do they want to kill?' Implicitly this response of incomprehensibility has become a dimension of the way terrorism is defined. Not only is terrorism not entirely knowable ? not being able to comprehend it is what makes it so frightening.

Even at the best of times terrorism has posed difficulties to those who seek to understand it. In the discussion of terrorism, what divides fact from fiction and information from propaganda has tended to be inexact. The inexplicable behaviour of the apparently irrational terrorists is often tenuously linked to events whose causes are not known. Incomprehensible events are readily presented as consequences of the actions of agents we do not understand. As Jenkins noted, even with the best will in the world, government officials are not in the position to inform the public of all the facts. When it comes to terrorism, official agencies 'have a powerful vested interest in not revealing the full extent of the information available to them'. Indeed, transmitting misinformation is part of the job-description of anti-terrorist agencies. 'Since so much official action involves clandestine methods or sources, even the most reputable and responsible agencies will on occasion present less than the full truth, or actively give false information in order to protect their methods or sources,' wrote Jenkins.[44]

One important reason why the discussion of terrorism is so fraught with difficulties is that it continually involves the making of value judgments. 'Terrorism' is not simply a term of description. It represents a judgment of value – a moral condemnation of an act which also serves as a political statement about an enemy. Sometimes, when the relationship with the enemy improves, the terrorist label is withdrawn and the 'ruthless terrorist leader' is recycled as a responsible statesman. Jomo Kenyatta, Robert Mugabe and Nelson Mandela are amongst the well-known leaders of their country who were once castigated as fanatical terrorists. So much confusion surrounding the definition of this term is due to the fact that it is not simply an objective analytical concept but also a moral statement on the behaviour of the terrorist. 'Thus in attempting to determine whether a specific action (or series of actions) is terroristic or not, the scholar should be aware that he is making a value judgement about the perpetrators of the alleged act, and about the circumstances of their actions,' writes Wilkinson in his classic account of the subject.[45] The normative dimension of this concept is evident in the political controversies that surround the issue of terrorism. Since debates about terrorism are so often linked to taking sides, the controversy that surrounds it is likely to be far more inflated than the kind of arguments that occur around other forms of deviant behaviour in the social sciences. The moral and political concerns that surround discussion of this subject mean that the concept is rarely used consistently and objectively.

The terrorist is frequently represented as an immoral and irrational agent whose actions are senseless. Many commentators cannot resist the temptation of using essentially moral or highly subjective categories to account for the behaviour of these individuals. Steele writes that 'when all is said and done, most men, and especially men from non-western cultures and less-developed areas, are capable of taking great pleasure in great evil.'[46] Many other observers adopt the perspective of regarding 'them' as our moral opposites. Dunlap claims that 'likely future adversaries will be unlike ourselves.' He characterizes opponents as members of 'The New Warrior Class' 'who have acquired a taste for killing, who do not behave rationally, who are capable of atrocities that challenge the descriptive powers of language, and who will sacrifice their own kind in order to survive'.[47] These are people whose behaviour defies comprehension. It appears that all that we can do is speculate about their motives.

So the term 'terrorist' is a loaded one – highly subjective, with aggressive connotations. It has acquired extremely negative associations. In the West, only the crime of pedophilia can compete with the act of the terrorist as a symbol of evil.[48] The terrorist label serves as a health warning, suggesting that those to whom it is attached are morally inferior individuals. 'To identify someone as a terrorist is to render judgment on them, not simply to make a discovery,' writes Claudia Card.[49] Frequently the attempt to represent an individual or a movement as terrorist is part of a propaganda war designed to discredit opponents. Not surprisingly official statements on terrorism are not entirely detached from the propaganda battle for hearts and minds

Often the definition of terrorism that is adopted is self-consciously designed to undermine the legitimacy of those promoting political violence. According to the RAND Corporation, the aim of its definition is to criminalize the acts it deems to be terrorist. 'In separating terrorist tactics from their political context, the intent clearly was to criminalize a certain mode of political expression.'[50] Although there is a substantial body of literature that attempts to provide an objective account of political violence, the imperative of propaganda tends to dominate the discussion. Far too often official analysis serves as a masquerade for moral condemnation. In the intense political climate that surrounds the War on Terror, such a reaction is an understandable one. However moralistic rhetoric about the evils of terrorism frequently distracts from engaging with the real issues of the day.

Far too often statements that purport to explain turn into condemnation of what is depicted as an incomprehensible evil. Speaking on this subject in the aftermath of 9/11, President Bush told the audience that 'they have no justification for their action' and 'the only motivation is evil.'[51] In the immediate aftermath of 9/11, the rhetoric of fighting evil was understandable. But unfortunately the simplistic scenario of good versus evil continues to serve as a substitute for educating the public about the issue. Sometimes even academics convey the impression that it is the threat of evil that confronts society. One American psychologist warns that terrorists 'embody "creative evil" at its worst' and therefore this 'creatively evil enemy cannot be underestimated'.[52] The problem with this approach is that the term 'evil' can at best describe someone's act or the consequences of their behaviour. It does little to explain or clarify the nature of the threat itself. Indeed the diagnosis of evil invites a moral and not a purposeful political or public response.

Moralizing statements about terrorism have a double purpose: first to condemn and stigmatize, but also to claim authority for occupying the moral high ground. It is important to note that this project has had an unusually modest success during the past five to six years. Unable to endow the conflict with meaning or even give the enemy a name has meant that the situation has become too confusing to give any of the protagonists a clear moral victory. Meaning pertains to the ultimate goals that society sets for itself. It can take a religious form – salvation – or a secular one, such as liberation or freedom. Social scientists have for long recognized that 'without the minimum of a meaningful goal', people find it difficult to make sense of the events that impinge on their lives.[53] As we argue in chapter 5, it is a lack of clarity about ends rather than a failure of imagination that may explain the difficulties that officials have in interpreting threats.

Recycling old rhetoric

The advocates of the vocabulary of good versus evil have sought to harness the familiar language of the Cold War to help render it comprehensible to the public. Terrorism is often represented as the contemporary manifestation of the kind of totalitarian ideology that led to the worst excess of Stalinist Russia or Hitler's Germany. 'We have seen their kind before,' remarked President Bush in his address to a joint session of Congress in September 2001. He added that 'they're the heirs of all the murderous ideologies of the 20th century.' Moreover by 'sacrificing human life to serve their radical visions, by abandoning every value except the will to power, they follow in the path of fascism, Nazism and totalitarianism'.[54] The White House continually portrays terrorism as the 21st-century's variant of previous totalitarian threats. So in his address to the Reichstag in Berlin, President Bush denounced the 'new totalitarian threat'.[55] It may be a new threat but Bush also insists that 'in many ways, this fight resembles the struggle against communism.' Why? Because, 'like the ideology of communism, our new enemy pursues totalitarian aims.'[56] Similarly, the former British Foreign Secretary Jack Straw indicted terrorism as the 'new totalitarianism'.

Even a cursory examination of the Cold War vocabulary used to describe the threat of terrorism exposes the fact that it is mainly empty rhetoric. The enemy is described as totalitarian, it is driven by a murderous ideology and is said to have totalitarian aims. 'We're engaged in a global struggle against the followers of a murderous ideology that despises freedom and crushes all dissent, and has territorial ambitions and pursues totalitarian aims,' declares *The President's National Strategy For Combating Terrorism*.[57] Official statements claim that the enemy is motivated by a 'new totalitarian ideology'. But this appears to be an ideology without a name or clearly discernible principles and goals. Every statement about this 'new totalitarian ideology' avoids dealing with its content and instead focuses on the means used. So the public is informed that 'its content may be different from the ideologies of the last century' but is left in the dark about how it is dissimilar. What we are told is that the new totalitarian ideology adopts means that are 'similar' to the old: 'intolerance, murder, terror, enslavement, and repression'.[58]

Official statements are characteristically evasive about what their opponents stand for and concentrate on denouncing the tactics used by them. That is why the term 'War on Terror' has been adopted as the signifier of meaning for this conflict. Many critics claimed that it makes little sense to wage a war against terror, which is a technique or tactic used to realize a particular objective. A war on terror makes as much sense as a war against kidnapping, hijacking or carpet bombing. The irrationality of the war on terror formulation notwithstanding, it is essential to realize that this focus on tactics represents an attempt to lend meaning to a conflict that officialdom does not quite get.

From the perspective of new totalitarianism, little can be learnt. Through associating the new enemy with the well-known totalitarian foe of old, the rhetoric attempts to turn the otherwise incomprehensible into something more familiar. By representing terrorism as a variant of an old familiar enemy, it can be rendered a little more understandable. Sadly, analysts and academics too have started to plunder the vocabulary of the Cold War. Too often they make do with the rhetoric that purports to explain 9/11 as 'an act of terrorism by people committed to totalitarianism'.[59]

In contemporary times the usage of the term 'totalitarianism' lacks any intellectual content. Academics and terrorist experts promiscuously embrace the label totalitarian to make sense of a threat they do not quite grasp. The motivation for virtually every political threat to Western democracies is portrayed as a totalitarian ideology. Instead of analysing it, radical Islam is rediscovered as a new guise for 20th-century totalitarian Marxism. So Paul Berman notes that the doctrine of radical Islamist Sayyid Qutb, 'was wonderfully original and deeply Muslim, looked at from one angle; and from another angle, merely one more version of the European totalitarian idea'.[60] From this standpoint the totalitarian idea transcends time and place to haunt the world. It becomes an all-purpose concept to designate movements and political actors who possess violent and extremist tendencies.

The links drawn between very different movements from very different historical periods verge on the simplistic. Berman believes that Islamists regard their religion as a 'totality', as do old-fashioned Marxists. Therefore both express a totalitarian imperative.[61] He contends that what totalitarian movements of the past and the Islamists of today have in common is an impulse to submit to a godlike authority.[62] Mandel states that totalitarianism represents the 'negation of personal freedom'.[63] Accordingly every threat to freedom can be reduced to one single enemy, totalitarianism. For Mandel it is the same old story – 'democracy's greatest nemesis today, as throughout the 20th century, is not terrorism but totalitarianism – whether it takes the form of Nazi fascism, Soviet communism, or militant Islamist fundamentalism.'[64]

Timeless theories of totalitarianism do little to illuminate the motivation and behaviour of groups and individuals who were responsible for the violence inflicted on ordinary people in New York in September 2001 or London in July 2005. Such theories merely serve as warnings about a historic threat to freedom. However by associating the danger posed by terrorism with that of Stalinist Russia and Nazi Germany such theories both confuse and disorient the public. As Anson Rabinbach notes, 'The rhetoric of fighting totalitarianism may mobilize the liberal imagination, but it can just as easily muddy the political waters, sometimes against the best of liberal intentions.'[65] Moreover it does little to explain who these people are and why they hate freedom with such venom. They may resemble old enemies but the public is still left with the conviction that the contemporary phenomenon of terrorism is still beyond comprehension.

Rendering the incomprehensible comprehensible

As we note in the chapter 'The Expanding Empire of Unknown Dangers', anxieties about global conflicts are far more focused on what we don't know than what we do. However, while incomprehensibility can serve as a response to a disturbing and dangerous threat, governments need to be able to communicate a coherent story about the enemy. In any war the public needs to have some idea about who is the enemy and what they are fighting for. The public needs to know more than that they are engaged in a global crusade to 'rid the world of evil'.

In a sense it was much easier to combat the totalitarian movements of the 20th century. These were not movements whose motives and aims could not be comprehended. These were movements with a name – communist, fascist – and with clearly formulated objectives and programmes. The opponents of these movements could explicitly counter the claims made by these movements. Indeed they self consciously describe themselves as anti-communists or anti-fascists.

But what about the War on Terror? What ideology is it targeting? Western Governments continually insist that this is neither a clash of civilizations nor a war against Islam. Indeed they continually heap praise on Islam and contend that terrorism violates the fundamental tenets of the Koran. 'While the War on Terror is a battle of ideas, it is not a battle of religions,' notes the 2006 *National Security Strategy* report of the White House.[66] Although the war is not against a religion, it is sometimes claimed that terrorists distort or exploit religion. So there is a lot of ambiguity in all this conflict. The totalitarian movements of old were not criticized on the grounds that they contradicted the otherwise unobjectionable principles of Marx or of Mussolini. There was clarity about the enemy. The very attempt to relive the current conflict through the familiar language of totalitarianism exposes an intense desire to recapture that clarity. But clarity is precisely what is lost when a leading US military officer is forced to declare 'what we're fighting is an "-ism", the first 21st-century "-ism", the way we fought communism and fascism in the 20th century.'[67]

In practice the language of the Cold War serves a public relations function that helps render the unknown a little more familiar. In reality far from regarding global terrorism as merely the contemporary manifestation of an old problem, policy-makers regard it as a radically new threat. In fact, as we shall see in the next chapter, that is why they constantly talk about the novelty of the problem.

Notes

1. Weinberg, Pedahzur and Hirsch-Hoeffler (2004) p. 777.

2. Schmid and Jongman (1988) pp. 5–6.

3. Laqueur (1999) p. 6.

4. Wilkinson (1974) p. 13.

5. See Best (199)

6. Victoroff (2005) p. 33.

7. Ibid., p. 33–4.

8. Ibid., p. 35.

9. Sharon Begley 'Likely Suicide Bombers Include Profiles You'd Never Suspect', *The Wall Street Journal*, 4 April 2003.

10. Atran (2006) p. 240.

11. Sharon Begley 'Likely Suicide Bombers Include Profiles You'd Never Suspect', *The Wall Street Journal*, 4 April 2003.

12. *Iraq's Weapons of Mass Destruction: The Assessment of the British Government*, The Stationery Office: London, 24 September 2002.

13. Ibid., p. 19.

14. Brendan O'Neill, 'Blair's Dodgy Dossier', www.spiked-online.co.uk/Articles/00000006DA63.htm

15. *Commission on the Intelligence Capabilities of the United States Regarding Weapons of Mass Destruction*, 29 March 2005, www.wmd.gov/report .

16. 'Iraq's WMD: the big lie?', 25 January 2004.

17. *Iraq: Its Infrastructure of Concealment, Deception and Intimidation*, www.number-10.gov.uk/output/Page7111.asp

18. Doig and Phythian (2005) p. 369.

19. Ibid., p. 37

20. See Aldrich (2005) 'Whitehall and the Iraq War: the UK's Four Intelligence Enquiries', *Irish Studies in International Affairs*, Vol.16, pp. 74 and 77.

21. 'Letter from the Co-Chairmen of the Commission on the Intelligence Capabilities of the United States Regarding Weapons of Mass Destruction to President of the US', 29 March 2005.

22. *U.S. Commission on the Intelligence Capabilities of the United States Regarding Weapons of Mass Destruction, Washington DC, 2005*, p. 3

23. Ibid., p. 12.

24. 'MI5 told MPs on the eve of 7/7: no imminent terror threat', *Guardian*, 9 January 2007.

25. See the editorial in *The Washington Post*, 25 October 2001.

26. *The 9/11 Commission Report: Final report of the National Commission on Terrorist Attacks Upon the United States*, 9–10, 22 July 2004.

27. 'Perspectives: U.S. Must Rebuild Its Intelligence Capabilities', Public Agenda Special Edition: Terrorism, 2005, www.publicagenda.org/specials/terrorism/terror_interview2.htm, accessed 12 October 2006.

28. Ellen Goodman 'Failure of imagination still plagues us, five years later', *The Daily Herald*, & September 2006.

29. *Report of a Committee of Privy Councillors, Review of Intelligence on Weapons of Mass Destruction, The Butler Report*, The Stationery Office: London, 2004.

30. See 'Imagination', *Oxford English Dictionary Online*, Oxford University Press, 2006.

31. Falkenrath (2004/5) p. 178.

32. May, Zelikow and Falkenrath (2005) p. 209.

33. Thomas Friedman, 'Opinion', *The New York Times*, 28 March 2004.

34. Failure of Imagination', *Contingencies*, Vol. 13, No. 6, 2001.

35. Sprinzak (1998) p. 111.

36. Birkland (2004) p. 182.

37. May, Zelikow and Falkenrath (2005) p. 210.

38. 'The face of terror', *The Times*, 8 November 2006.

39. Bob Ripley, 'Terrorism Beyond Comprehension, Cure', *London Free Press*, 9 November 2006.

40. 'President condemns terrorism in Russia', Office of the Press Secretary, September 12 2004.

41. Mary Kenny, 'High Moral Ground', *The Advertiser*, 6 November 2006.

42. Cited in *Chicago Tribune*, 24 October 2006.

43. 'Editorial', *Charleston Gazette*, 11 September 2006.

44. Jenkins (2003) p. 6.

45. Wilkinson (1974) p. 21.

46. Steele (1998).

47. Dunlap (1996).

48. See Daniel M. Filler (2003), 'Terrorism, Panic, and Pedophilia', *Journal of Social Policy and the Law*, Spring issue.

49. Claudia Card, 'Making War on Terrorism in Response to 9/11', in Sterba (2003) p. 178.

50. B.M. Jackson 'Foreword' in Lesser *et al.* (1999) p.v.

51. President Bush, 25 September 2001, 'International Campaign against Terrorism Grows', www.whitehouse. gov/news/release.

52. See Philip Zimbardo 'Opposing terrorism by understanding the human capacity for evil', *Monitor on Psychology*, 10 November 2001.

53. See for example Mannheim (1960) p. 18.

54. Transcript of President Bush's address to a joint session of Congress on September 20, 2001. http://archives. cnn.com/2001/US/09/20/gen.bush. transcript/.

55. 'In Reichstag, Bush Condemns Terror as New Despotism', The New York Times, 24 May 2002.

56. White House Press Release, Office of the Press Secretary, 6 October 2005. Bush in a speech at the National Endowment for Democracy

57. *The President's National Strategy For Combating Terrorism*, Office of the Press Secretary, September 5, 2006.

58. *The National Security Strategy of the United States of America*, March 2006, Washington DC, p. 1.

59. Mandel (2005) p. 211.

60. Berman (2004) p. 99.

61. Ibid., pp. 66–7.

62. Ibid., p. 46.

63. Mandel (2005) p. 211.

64. Ibid., p. 211.

65. Anson Rabinbach, 'Totalitarianism Revisited', Dissent, Summer 2006

66. *The National Security Strategy of the United States of America*, p. 9.

67. Cited in Bradley Graham and Josh White, 'Abizaid credited with popularizing the term "Long War"', *The Washington Post*, 3 February 2006.

CHAPTER 1

Perceptions of the Threat

The rhetoric of old-fashioned totalitarianism notwithstanding, terrorism in everyday life is presented and understood as a problem that is radically different from anything that the world has confronted in the past. Time and again the public is informed that since 9/11 the world has changed and we live in a **New Era of Terrorism**. The threat to society is frequently defined as the **New Terrorism**. In many accounts the early twenty-first century is designated as the **Age of Terror**. Indeed terms like 'age of terror' and 'new era of terrorism' are casually used as markers for defining the contemporary epoch. The premise for the thesis that ours is an age of terror is the belief that this threat has assumed an unprecedented potential for inflicting violence on a mass scale. The corollary of this perception of danger is a crisis of confidence in society's capacity to avoid acts of mass-casualty terrorism. Accounts of the age of terrorism often radiate a mood of uncertainty if not defeatism towards the capacity of society to triumph and overcome this challenge to its security.

We are also continually reminded that the age of terrorism will be with us for a very long time. Leading American military officials now refer to the current global conflict as the Long War – one with an indefinite time frame. *The National Security Strategy of the United States of America*, published in March 2006, indicates that the 'United States is in the early years of a long struggle, similar to what our country faced in the early years of the Cold War'.[1] This view was forcefully advanced in 2002 by National Security Advisor Condoleezza Rice, when she stated that 'I really think this period is analogous to 1945 to 1947 in that the events' initiated 'shifting the tectonic plates in international politics'.[2] On a more ominous note, in October 2001 Vice President Dick Cheney remarked that the war against terrorism was different to previous conflicts 'in the sense that it may never end'. He added, 'at least, not in our lifetime'.[3] Three years later Cheney was still adopting an indefinite timescale for this conflict and claimed that it could last for generations.[4] The same point is continually reiterated by British officials who insist that this war will last for at least a generation. In November 2006, Prime Minister Blair indicated that this war will take 30 years to win.[5] And a month later his Home Secretary, John Reid warned that the threat of a Christmas terror attack was not only 'highly likely' but also that the war against Muslim terrorism will last at least 30 years.[6] This projection of an indefinite timescale into the unforeseeable future lends this age of terror an epochal character. This assessment of a conflict without end is not simply a response to the chain of events unleashed by 9/11. At least since the end of the Cold War such an assessment has influenced the thinking of the US military. 'The war against terrorism will be a protracted conflict,' wrote President Clinton's Secretary of Defense in 1997.[7]

As I write this chapter in November 2006, I feel inundated with reminders about the fact that I live in an age of terror. For example, here are a few of the many examples from newspapers published in the past couple of months. One journalist advises the Democratic Party not to get too carried away with its 2006 mid-term electoral success because 'we still live in a dangerous time – an age of terror'. His colleague writes to make a case for the introduction of a tamperproof ID card, because 'this is the age of terror'. An Australian religion teacher reports on an attempt to tackle classroom prejudice in Britain 'in an age of terror'. A Jewish commentator reminds us that 'the age of terror' has turned 'every Jewish community world-wide into a target'. A Canadian observer points to the importance of humour, since it 'holds the secret of survival in an age of terror'. His Australian colleague agrees and observes that 'in this age of terror, we could all do with some more laughs'. Others adopt a more sober approach. David Brooks of *The New York Times* warns that 'in the age of terror, statesmanship means knowing how to create a sense of security'. And a group of American political scientists declare that 'in an age of terror and perpetual fear' their discipline needs to be galvanized.[8]

We are not only told that we live in an age of terror, but we are also regularly reminded that this is a period where terrorism has acquired new, novel and unique dimensions. Experts write about a **new** terrorism and a **new** era of terrorism. One former British war hero reminds us that we face a 'new era of terrorism' and that 'we're dealing with a ruthless and sophisticated enemy which is growing in confidence with every passing day'. Others insist that, in 'the new era of terrorism', no one is 'isolated from the threat of attack'. A leading British lawyer explains that 'in the new era of terrorism, there will need to be a new balance between measures needed to combat that threat and the liberties we cherish'. There is widespread agreement that the problem of security has acquired a new dimension and 'safety in this new era of terrorism is not something to be taken lightly or brushed off'. One commentator is not satisfied with simply repeating the term and writes of a 'new era of "terrorism without limit"'.[9]

To define the principal character of our age as that of terrorism signifies the importance attached to this threat. The point of departure for this approach is the perception that after 9/11 the world would never be the same. Of course in societies confronted by a major catastrophe people always tend to imagine that their world will never be same. The day after a serious disaster is often regarded as the beginning of a new era. But after the passing of time such episodes are usually interpreted as an important defining moment in their life but not necessarily as a point of radical rupture with the past. What's interesting about the subsequent perception of 9/11 is that it continues to be interpreted as the start of Year Zero. 'At 8:46 on the morning of September 11, 2001, the United States became a nation transformed', begins the report of the 9/11 Commission.[10] A similar prognosis is offered by politicians and analysts throughout the Western world. A poll taken of West European opinion makers shortly after 9/11 indicated that 76 per cent of those surveyed stated that the day represented a turning point in world history. In the Middle East and Latin America the same view was expressed by 90 per cent of the respondents.[11] Five years after the event the belief that the US became a nation transformed continues to haunt the imagination.[12] 'When the smoke cleared from the collapsed World Trade Center towers, everything had changed,' observed a journalist in the *San Francisco Chronicle*. Most editors agreed. 'The terrorist attacks on the United States is the sort of historic event that permanently changes the way people think,' echoed a Canadian newspaper.[13]

The passing of time has not diminished the conviction that 9/11 marks the beginning of a new era. On the contrary, the belief that the world has changed and continues to change on an unprecedented scale

3

informs public deliberation of the issue of global security. Tony Blair expressed this sentiment in the following terms:

> *Here is where I feel so passionately that we are in mortal danger of mistaking the nature of the new world in which we live. Everything about our world is changing: its economy, its technology, its culture, its way of living. If the 20th century scripted our conventional way of thinking, the 21st century is unconventional in almost every respect. This is true also of our security. The threat we face is not conventional. It is a challenge of a different nature from anything the world has faced before. It is to the world's security, what globalisation is to the world's economy.*[14]

According to this scenario, in a world of unconventional threats little can be taken for granted. Consequently governments perceive these unconventional threats as ones without historical precedent. These are threats for which the rules and institutional responses of the past provide little guidance for policy-makers.

The shift from conventional to what Blair characterizes as unconventional signifies a qualitative transformation in threat perception. Unconventional threats are perceived as potentially far more dangerous than conventional ones because they are difficult to detect, visualize and anticipate. By definition, unconventional threats do not subscribe to a convention or to clear rules. Some analysts argue that the emergence of this threat has rendered obsolete pre-9/11 ideas about security and military doctrine. One defence analyst believes that it has led to 'a paradigm shift in strategic planning as significant as that of 1945'.[15] Some hint that the nuclear age that followed the dropping of the atomic bomb in 1945 on Hiroshima represented less of a break with its past than the post-9/11 age of terrorism with the era that preceded it. According to a UK Ministry of Defence publication, 9/11 represents a rupture with the past as historically significant as the destruction of Minoan civilization due to a volcanic eruption in 1450 BC and the impact of the Black Death on fourteenth-century Europe.[16]

Today's unconventional threats are regularly perceived as more dangerous than those confronting humanity during the Cold War. *The National Security Strategy of the United States of America*, published a year after 9/11, claimed that although terrorists do not have the destructive power of the former Soviet Union they represent a more formidable menace to global security. It argues that 'the nature and motivations of these new adversaries, their determination to obtain destructive powers hitherto available only to the world's strongest states, and the greater likelihood that they will use weapons of mass destruction against us, make today's security environment more complex and dangerous'.[17] John Reid, the British Home Secretary, also took the view that this threat is worse than the Cold War.[18] One reason that Western military strategists perceive our era as 'more complex and dangerous' than the past is because they fear that small groups of individuals have the capacity to inflict an unprecedented scale of destruction on society. 'Now, shadowy networks of individuals can bring great chaos and suffering to our shores for less than it costs to purchase a single tank,' warns the American Government.[19] Some commentators argue that literally anyone can unleash an act of destruction of catastrophic proportions. 'Whatever happens next in the war on terror, mass destruction will remain only a mouse click, a credit card and a rental truck away,' warns a group of commentators who also believe that 'during the Cold War, we could not all be potential superpowers, but today, we are all potential terrorists'.[20]

It is believed that the individualization or privatization of the power of destruction has reinforced the dangers facing the public. Individuals and small groups do not have to operate according to institutional rules and procedures nor engage in diplomacy. Indeed the absence of any institutional affiliation between these 'non-state actors' and a nation state protects them from scrutiny. According to American security analysis, statelessness offers the 'most potent protection' for terrorists.[21] Their action is less constrained by pragmatic considerations and therefore their behaviour is likely to be arbitrary and unpredictable. Terrorists always possessed a capacity for surprise and unexpected behaviour. But today it is claimed that they have access to powerful forms of technology that significantly amplify their capacity for causing mass destruction. Time and again the public is reminded that this is an imminent threat. According to CIA Director Porter Goss, 'it may be only a matter of time before Al-Qaida or other groups attempt to use chemical, biological, radiological or nuclear weapons'.[22]

Western strategists are disturbed by the necessity for confronting 'stateless' opponents for the very simple reason that such foes appear to have little to defend and to lose. 'They have nothing to defend,' Dick Cheney noted, before adding that 'for 50 years we deterred the Soviets by threatening the utter destruction of the Soviet Union'. This is a war with no obvious targets. 'What does bin Laden value?' asked a frustrated target-seeking Dick Cheney.[23] At least for the time being, the fear of terrorism has displaced the traditional anxieties that governments possessed towards the military power of hostile nation states. Terror today 'divorces war from the idea of a nation'.[24] Centuries of statecraft and security policies that had as their premise the need to protect society from the military threat posed by competing nation states provide little guidance for confronting terrorism. That is why so many Western officials appear to believe that the threat of a new terrorism renders conventional power obsolete. Paradoxically this fear of the power of the powerless may serve to empower those inclined to engage in an act of political violence.

The perception of the threat of terrorism

Thankfully the belief that we live in a new era of terrorism that is characterized by an unprecedented threat to human security is not sustained by the experience of the past decade. As numerous experts point out, the various acts of terrorist violence, even the catastrophe of 9/11, do not add up to an age of terror.[25] It is difficult to disagree with one commentator who notes that 'terrorism is obviously a threat, and the killing of innocent civilians an outrage, but it is not a very big threat'.[26] Statistics that are used to argue that there is a sharp rise in global terrorism usually include casualties due to insurgency and civil war in places like Iraq or Afghanistan.[27] Nor do terrorist organizations possess the capability to deploy apocalyptic weapons of mass destruction (WMDs).[28] Yet the perception of an all-powerful non-conventional foe that threatens life in Western societies is widespread. So how is the public encouraged to make sense of the threat of terrorism?

The threat of terrorism is framed in objective material terms as that of mass-casualty terrorism or catastrophic terrorism. It is claimed that terrorists are interested and are likely to inflict mass destruction on their target population. To realize that objective, they are prepared to use biological, chemical and nuclear weapons on civilian targets. The threat is vividly presented by the editors of *Foreign Policy* in the following terms:

> Today, at the end of 2006, there may be no greater fear than the threat posed by nuclear terrorism. Whether it comes in the form of a suitcase bomb or something jerry-rigged from parts, the death and devastation unleashed by a nuclear blast in a densely populated city is a danger of nightmarish proportions. Is there a policy goal more important than guaranteeing that the most terrible technology does not land in the hands of those who wouldn't hesitate to use it?[29]

This rhetorical question invites the answer of an unqualified 'no'.

Government experts contend that terrorist networks are actively seeking to acquire such weapons of mass destruction. Moreover, terrorists do not regard WMDs as weapons of last resort but of choice.[30] The use of such weapons is said to be one of their immediate objectives. So for example, in November 2006 it was announced at a Foreign Office counterterrorism briefing that the British intelligence service believed that Al-Qaeda was determined to attack the UK with nuclear weapons. Officials indicated that there was 'no doubt at all' that this was the objective of the enemy. There are people for whom a devastating nuclear attack on Britain 'would be a triumph for the cause', stated a Foreign Office official.[31] There is widespread consensus that in contrast to the experience of the past these terrorists are not simply interested in inflicting terror but also want to cause mass casualties.

It is not only Britain that perceives itself as a terrorist target. The UK Home Secretary, John Reid calls terrorism the greatest threat to Europe. Russian Security Council Deputy Secretary, Valentin Sobolev is alarmed by the mix of nuclear and cyber-terrorism, while in the US Fred Ikle, in his book *Annihilation from Within*, fears the threat posed by home-grown terrorists using weapons of mass destruction.[32]

The threat represented by mass-casualty terrorism is not confined to its capacity for destruction. Public dread of this phenomenon is underpinned by the assumption that this is a threat that is unpredictable and random, and its effect incalculable. The very manner in which this threat is communicated to the public invites people to feel threatened. The approach adopted by the Office of Homeland Security in its *The National Strategy for Homeland Security* is paradigmatic in this respect. One single sentence on the first page of this report sums up the frightening dimension of the peril facing the public. It states that 'today's terrorists can strike at any place, at any time, and with virtually any weapon'.[33] Just pause and reflect. If indeed the terrorists can strike any place, any time and with any weapon, they must possess some formidable superhuman qualities. Until recent times the power to strike anywhere and at any time was associated with that of God. The manner in which this enemy is portrayed by an official government publication is historically unprecedented. Neither the Nazi hordes nor the Red Army possessed the kind of superpower attributed to small groups of terrorists. These large military machines did not have the resources or the capability to strike anywhere, any time and with virtually any imaginable weapon. The attribution of such fantastic divine powers to the terrorist endows this threat with an omnipresence that indeed entitles our age to be defined by it.

The belief that terrorism can strike any place and at any time is not restricted to periodic outbursts of official paranoia. The warning that terrorists can strike any place and any time is transmitted as if it were a fact of life in official communiqués on both sides of the Atlantic. 'Once again, we've seen the truth that terrorists can attack at any time, at any place, using any tactic', former US Defense Secretary Rumsfeld told troops at Camp Victory after a series of suicide bombings in Iraq.[34] Since September 2001, this message is regularly circulated to the public by anxious officials throughout the world. The warning that terrorists could strike at any time was issued by Canada's former Deputy Prime Minister Anne McLellan in July 2005 and by President Gloria Macapagal Arroyo of the Philippines in May 2004 and John Howard, Prime Minister of Australia in March 2003.[35]

Warnings about the omnipresence of terrorism are constantly reproduced throughout every sector of life. By their very ubiquity they give the impression that no one is safe. For example Cornell University's guidelines 'Terror Threats and Anxiety' ask rhetorically, 'Am I in Danger?' After informing students that 'the nature of terrorism is that terror groups can strike at any time in any place', it adds that 'the random nature of terrorism means that we can not say who is in specific danger at any time'. Such warnings are continually reinforced by the message that it is only a matter of time before terrorists will strike a devastating blow on unsuspecting civilians.

The very manner in which the threat of terrorism is formulated conveys a mood of helplessness and fatalism. Official alerts betray more than a hint of defeatism since they insist that unlike other violent threats to people's security acts of terrorism can not be prevented. Terrorists no longer need to boast of their prowess and power to kill when official communiqués insist that it is only a matter of time before these malcontents get their hands on a weapon of mass destruction and use it against the civilian population. The fatalistic idiom 'only a matter of time' is continually repeated by anxious officials who are determined to educate the public about the perils it faces. Sometimes it is difficult to avoid the conclusion that the constant repetition of the mantra 'it is only a matter of time' bears the hallmark of a self-serving project of pre-empting criticism of a failure to prevent such a tragic incident in the future.

What officials say about the inevitability of a terrorist dirty-bomb attack is in sharp contrast to the language they used during the era of the nuclear arms race. Throughout the Cold War, Western political leaders insisted that the use of weapons of mass destruction could be avoided. In the age of terrorism, fatalism reigns supreme. Eugene Habiger, a former four-star general who used to manage the Department of Energy's antinuclear terror programme, believes that it is impossible to prevent a terrorist with a nuclear suitcase causing an American Hiroshima. He claims that 'it is not a matter of if; it's a matter of when'.[36] David Veness, in his capacity as the London Metropolitan Police Assistant Commissioner in charge of the anti-terrorist branch, also stated that the question is 'when, not if …'[37] His views are widely shared by his former colleagues in Washington. 'It may be only a matter of time before Al-Qaeda or another group attempts to use chemical, biological, radiological and nuclear weapons,' noted CIA Director Porter Goss to a meeting of the Senate Select Committee on Intelligence.[38] His UK counterpart Eliza Manningham-Buller, the head of MI5 echoed this prognosis about the inevitability of a terrorist WMD attack. In her first public speech she concluded that 'we are faced with the realistic possibility of some form of unconventional attack' that would involve biological, chemical, nuclear or radiological weapons.[39] Referring to the proliferation of nuclear weapons, Tony Blair reinforced the official consensus and stated that 'it is only a matter of time before terrorists get hold of it'.[40] Since 9/11, 'it is only a matter of time' has become a tired idiom that is repeated without any thought to its meaning.

Western officialdom's interpretation of the threat of terrorism projects a weary mood of fatalism. It suggests that whatever the course of events in Afghanistan or Iraq, Western governments cannot stop individual terrorists from inflicting grave damage at home. As Sir John Stevens, the former Metropolitan Police Commissioner stated, 'there is an inevitability that some sort of attack will get through but my job is to make sure that does not happen'.[41] It appears that Western leaders regard the catastrophic attack of 9/11 to be a precursor of similar and possibly more destructive episodes. No one can any longer accuse them of a failure of imagination – on the contrary they enthusiastically demonstrate to the public that they are constantly capable of imagining the worst. 'America will be attacked by Al-Qaeda again, and more destructively than on 9/11,' predicts one former CIA officer.[42]

On the fifth anniversary of 9/11 President Bush told the nation that this war was 'unlike any other' that the US had previously fought.[43] But he was less than clear about spelling out the distinguishing feature of this conflict. Since the conflict has been rebranded as the Long War, it is frequently represented as a struggle that will last for generations or at least well into the unspecified future. People hearing this prognosis can be forgiven for drawing the conclusion that this may turn into a war that cannot be won. Critics of the war often misinterpret the rhetoric of the Long War. They only see flag-waving Machiavellianism. In their view this is yet another classical colonial adventure promoting an expansionist agenda. What this simplistic depiction of events overlooks is the sense of demoralization that regards the future as one of never-ending conflict.

And yet despite the constant display of official fatalism, Bush and his colleagues are regularly accused of indulging in flag-waving triumphalism. But the projection of this conflict into the indefinite future shows a sombre, even defeatist interpretation of this conflict. From this perspective the future looks utterly bleak. The future, as Deputy Secretary of Defense, Paul Wolfowitz told the House and Senate Armed Services Committee in 2001 was one 'where new enemies visit violence on us in startling ways; a future in which our cities are among the battlefields and our people are among the targets; a future in which more and more adversaries will possess the capability to bring war to the American homeland; a future where the old methods of deterrence are no longer sufficient'.[44] This is not a statement of a triumphalist and gung-ho political leader, but of an individual who is uncertain and confused about the danger that lies ahead.

It is not entirely clear why politicians and their officials have adopted such a defeatist tone about the prospect of containing the threat of terrorism. Their threat assessment seldom contains a coherent account of the enemy they face. The belief that terrorists can strike at any time and in any place is founded on the belief that they possess the formidable tactical advantage of being 'able to choose the time, place, and method of their attack'.[45] What's implicit in this interpretation of the tactical advantage enjoyed by a terrorist is the assumption that governments are powerless to disrupt or eliminate the threat they face. Of course if the terrorists genuinely possess such significant tactical advantages they have become transformed into an enemy that is impossible to defeat. That is why there is more than a hint of defeatism conveyed through official statements that fatalistically assign all the tactical advantages to the terrorists.

A terrorist public communiqué designed to terrify its target audience is likely to announce: 'You don't know when we will strike, you have no idea where we will hit you nor do you have any idea what weapon we will use – but we will get you!' This declaration of threat is frequently recycled by unthinking defensive officials when they issue alarmist press releases that echo their fears that terrorists can attack at any time at any place and with any weapon. An unfortunate illustration of how official warnings can amplify the threat of terrorism was a statement released by the British Home Office in November 2002. No sooner did the Home Office issue this statement on terrorism than it withdrew it in a rare display of embarrassment. The text released in the name of former Home Secretary David Blunkett portrayed the threat of terrorism in a language that could only incite fear and anxiety among the public. Its message was, 'Be prepared for anything'. It transmitted a chilling sense of helplessness as it noted that 'we cannot be sure of when or where or how terrorists will strike'. The only statement of certainty that this press release conveyed was that there was no doubt that terrorists will soon try to strike Britain. 'But we can be sure that they will try,' it observed.

It is far from clear what the authors of this statement had hoped to achieve. It did not specify any particular threat nor provide any useful information. Indeed it explicitly acknowledged that it lacked any hard information of an impending terrorist threat and the warnings it issued had an entirely ritualistic character. To take a few examples of this statement's unspecific and speculative warnings: 'They may attempt to use more familiar terrorist methods, such as leaving parcel or vehicle bombs in public places, or hijacking passenger aircraft,' it noted. Another idea thrown out was that 'they may try something different, perhaps as surprising as the attacks on the World Trade Center, or the theatre siege in Moscow'. Or 'maybe they will try to develop a so-called dirty bomb, or some kind of poison gas, maybe they will try to use boats or trains rather planes'. As the Home Office statement's speculation gradually morphed into a narrative of fantasy, it reminded the public that 'the bottom line is that we simply cannot be sure'. There are very few public documents that provide such an explicit statement of official helplessness – which is why it was so swiftly withdrawn.[46] However, this botched press statement is not qualitatively different from many alarmist warnings that are regularly communicated to the public. Who needs to worry about threatening communiqués issued by terrorist organizations when a Home Office statement informs the public that it is more or less helpless in the face of this threat? Or when a US Homeland official informs the public, 'Be scared. Be very, very scared. But go on with your lives'.[47] These are statements that constitute a public acknowledgement of confusion and fear. They represent an invitation to be terrorized.

Invitation to terror

Official perception of threats says as much about the attitudes of policy-makers as about the physical strength of the enemy. Such perceptions are also influenced by the confidence, authority and sense of legitimacy of the political elites. An inflated assessment of the power of terrorist organizations is frequently associated with an intense sense of vulnerability. Statements about terrorist threats also contain an implicit assessment of the public's response to them. It is from this perspective that sense can be made of anxious official declarations that regularly inflate the capacity of terrorists to do as they please. The enemy appears to be everywhere and society lacks the resources to stop a determined terrorist attack. The conviction that terrorists can strike at will expresses a surprising degree of anxiety about the resilience and capacity of society to deal with this threat. What is striking about the threat assessments made by political leaders and their officials is the lack of confidence they have in the resilience of their own institutions and people. Rather than seeing technology and prosperity as resources that can be mobilized against terrorism, policy-makers and security analysts interpret them as a source of vulnerability. This point is echoed by academic and official analysts. Writing in this vein, the German sociologist Ulrich Beck claims that 'the terrorist dangers we face expand exponentially with technical progress'.[48] The same point is asserted by the American sociologist Lee Clarke, who asserts that 'modern organizations and technologies bring other new opportunities to harm faraway people'.[49] From this perspective Western technological power serves to empower the terrorist. As the Bush Administration's *National Security Strategy* report stated, 'terrorists are organized to penetrate open societies and to turn the power of modern technologies against us'.[50]

The very fruits of human development and prosperity that were until recently seen as essential for providing society with protection and security have become a source of concern because they have the potential to serve as instruments of terrorist destruction. 'Paradoxically, progress has made key elements of the national infrastructure increasingly vulnerable,' wrote an American Secretary of Defense a decade ago.[51] Numerous contributions on this subject insist that any technology can be transformed into a terrorist weapon. From this perspective a technology has a **dual use**. It can be used for the purpose for which it was originally designed or it can be turned into a weapon. So a passenger plane can fly people to their destination or be turned into a weapon that can crash into a building. 'Attackers can use the diffusion capacity of our large critical networks and turn them against the target population so that each element of the network (e.g. every aircraft, every piece of mail) now becomes a potential weapon', argues a contribution on the dual use idea.[52] Or, as the UK's Select Committee on Defence notes in its report: 'We have been forced to recognise that, in our modern societies, many things may have the potential to be used as weapons of mass effect by terrorists'.[53] From this perspective the technological supremacy of the US provides little protection to its citizens. 'The paradox of our age is that modern technology is both the great *separator* and the great *equalizer* in military affairs,' argues a study of this dilemma.[54]

A mature, complex, technologically sophisticated society is often represented as powerless against the actions of small groups of determined individuals. It is as if the relation of power has been reversed to the benefit of those lacking economic and technological resources. Indeed it is sometimes claimed that it is the very success of Western economies that makes them so intensely vulnerable to the threat of terrorism. According to one account, vulnerability is the product of growing complexity and interconnectedness. It states that 'the advantage in this war has shifted toward terrorists'. Moreover, 'our increased vulnerability – and our newfound recognition of that vulnerability – makes us more risk-averse, while terrorists have become more powerful and more tolerant of risk'. Consequently, it is claimed that 'terrorists have significant leverage to hurt us'.[55] According to the 1997 *Report Of The Quadrennial Defense Review*, even in areas where the US enjoys a significant technological superiority such as 'space-based assets, command, control, communications, and computers; and intelligence, surveillance; and reconnaissance' could 'involve inherent vulnerabilities' that can be 'exploited by potential opponents' through attacking the nation's 'reliance on commercial communications'.[56]

Since 9/11 the predominant approach to the threat of terrorism can be described as **vulnerability-led**. A heightened sense of vulnerability has encouraged an attitude of fatalism, pessimism and a dread of terrorism. There is an almost obsessive desire to represent vulnerability as the sensibility that dominates the public imagination. It is as if the very anticipation of an act of terror serves to expose the wounds of the collective psyche. 'America the vulnerable' summed up the self-diagnosis of many Americans about their circumstances after 9/11. Bush articulated this sentiment in statements that tended to magnify the scale of destruction suffered by the US as a result of this catastrophe. In numerous post-9/11 speeches he emphasized the gravity of the threat to the US economy and to the American way of life posed by this attack. He also repeatedly stressed that Americans are 'hurting' and feel vulnerable. According to Bush, it was the very condition of an open, democratic industrial society that served to render the US vulnerable to terrorism. He stated:

> the characteristics of American society that we cherish – our freedom, our openness, our great cities and towering skyscrapers, our modern transportation systems – make us vulnerable to terrorism of catastrophic proportions. America's vulnerability to terrorism will persist long after we bring justice to those responsible for the events of September 11.[57]

Bush's association of freedom and prosperity with a disposition to vulnerability reveals a radical reversal of the way that modern, relatively open industrial societies make sense of themselves. In previous times democracy and industrial might were associated with national power. These dimensions of a modern democratic society were seen as a source of strength and flexibility. That these features of American life are now regarded as markers of vulnerability is testimony to a defensive and confused response to the threat of terrorism.

The pervasive sense of unease about the vulnerability of powerful industrial nations to terrorism also represents a cultural statement about the way a society experiences socio-economic and technological change. Take this assessment contained in the *1997 Annual Defense Report of the US*:

> Technological advances may have the unintended consequence of increasing system vulnerabilities. For example, fiber optic cables enable phone companies to use a single line to carry tens of thousands of conversations that not many years ago would have required thousands of separate copper cables. The results have been greater efficiency, better service, and lower costs; however, there is a downside. Progress has heightened infrastructure efficiency, but the resultant reduction in redundancy has produced vulnerabilities that make US infrastructure an increasing attractive terrorist target.[58]

Technological innovation and the evolution of an efficient network of cooperation are represented as a source of vulnerability rather than of prosperity and resilience. This vulnerability-led perspective tends to regard society one-sidedly as a target, and people as victims. Such an orientation tends to focus on the task of avoiding losses rather than looking for opportunities for taking the initiative. **Its defining feature**

is an inflated sense of vulnerability to risk and an exaggerated assessment of the threat it faces. Public pronouncements often take the form of an alarmist oracle. According to one commentary of Bush's post-9/11 statements, they tended to exaggerate 'the terrorist threat at every level, so that his speeches seem evidence too of a more general anxiety and vulnerability'.[59] Vulnerability has turned into the dominant idiom through which the threat of terrorism is represented and experienced. Numerous contributions insist that this threat should be addressed through an analysis of society's vulnerability. After noting how a 'handful of determined individuals' so 'greatly disrupted the world's most powerful nation' on 9/11, Paul Slovic, a leading US expert on risk perception, demanded that 'risk analysis should be supplemented by "vulnerability analysis", which characterizes the forms of physical, social, political, economic, cultural and psychological harms to which individuals and modern societies are susceptible'.[60] 'I think we haven't paid enough attention to how vulnerable we are to worst case events,' argues Lee Clarke.[61]

A vulnerability-led response to terrorism is likely to foster a climate that intensifies people's feeling of insecurity and fear. This is a response that helps magnify the impact of terrorism and encourages more attacks. 'America is full of fear from its north to its south, from its west to its east,' crowed Osama bin Laden with delight in October 2001.[62] The search for vulnerabilities invariably leads to the discovery of weaknesses that have the potential to turn virtually any institution in any place into a terrorist target. The steady proliferation of such targets inevitably follows threat assessments that are vulnerability-led. One of the unfortunate consequences of a vulnerability-led response is that virtually every dimension of social life is perceived as a terrorist target. It is as if Western societies have come to think of themselves as sitting ducks living in a state of vulnerability. According to the Office of Homeland Security, 'Our society presents an almost infinite array of potential targets that can be attacked through a variety of methods'. It claims that with so many targets the terrorists enjoy 'tactical advantages', since the reduction of vulnerability in one sphere simply encourages terrorists to look for a target somewhere else. 'As we reduce our vulnerabilities in one area, they can alter their plans and pursue more exposed targets,' it notes.[63]

Too often the vulnerability-led approach helps consolidate a mood of helplessness. Such a response can only encourage acts of terror. Bill Durodié is rightly worried that 'assuming far-fetched scenarios and acting as if these were true' has led to a situation where instead of asking 'What is?'-questions that call for specific evidence, there is a shift to 'asking more speculative or anticipatory "What if?"-type questions'.[64] 'What if they contaminate the milk supply?' 'What if a train carrying nuclear fuel is hijacked?' 'What if a toxic biological substance infects the water supply?' 'What if' thinking encourages speculation which in turn can transform previously untroubled aspects of life into targets. Such thinking distracts attention from the far more productive questions of 'What can?' and 'What is likely?' to happen.

On the defensive

Many critics have accused the Bush and Blair regimes of deliberately inflating the threat of terrorism. It is frequently suggested that these politicians dishonestly exaggerate the danger facing society in order to consolidate their authority. 'Why have the leaders of Britain and America felt driven to adopt so wildly distorted a concept of menace?' asks a leading British journalist in an article titled, 'Blair is wildly exaggerating the threat posed by terrorism'.[65] A similar accusation was made in a report published by The Joseph Rowntree Reform Trust. This report accused government ministers of 'exploiting the politics of fear' and of subordinating anti-terror policy to party political interests.[66] Others argue that that a coalition of business, media and political interests have sought to stoke up anxiety to realize their objectives. In a useful commentary on this subject, John Mueller argues that 'the most common reaction to terrorism is the stoking of fear and the encouragement of overreaction by members of what might be called the "terrorism industry", an entity that includes not only various risk entrepreneurs and bureaucrats, but also most of the media and nearly all the politicians'.[67]

There is little doubt that politicians and special-interest groups play the terrorist card in pursuit of their agenda. There is a veritable fear market in operation where competing claims-makers draw attention to the many threats we face.[68] However, the alarmist representation of the terrorist threat by politicians and their officials is not simply the outcome of an attempt to manipulate public opinion. Perceptions of threat which are underpinned by a consciousness of vulnerability contribute to the creation of an environment where the sense of feeling terrorized thrives. As we shall see throughout this book, it is difficult to avoid the conclusion that the political class on both sides of the Atlantic is genuinely on the defensive. Its alarmist management of this threat may well be a consequence of it own confusion and inability to make sense of the problem.

Often political elites recycle their own failure of nerve through attributing to the wider public a fragile and defeatist mentality. Its elevated sense of danger is expressed through a lack of confidence in the capacity of the public to deal with a terrorist attack. Gone are the days when the people are regarded as a source of strength. In the twenty-first century, policy-makers do not trust the people to respond effectively to acts of terrorism. They assume that a terrorist attack could lead to mass panic and the breakdown of social norms and civil behaviour.[69] US General Tommy Franks has stated that a 'massive casualty-producing event somewhere in the Western world' could lead American people to 'question our own Constitution and to begin to militarize the country' and risking the loss of 'what it cherishes most, and that is freedom and liberty'.[70]

According to one study, 'the perception of the public as inherently prone to panic in the face of scenarios such as a chemical, biological, radiological (CBR), or mass casualty conventional attack is pervasive'.[71] Another study speculates that the 'United Kingdom might prove to be rather brittle in the face of a CBRN attack – there might be a demoralizing sense of defencelessness, particularly if unknown and invisible agents and pollutants are used, and possibly even widespread panic'.[72] Ideas about how the public is likely to respond to a terrorist attack have an important influence on the conceptualization of this threat. And if emergency planners anticipate public panic, the gravity of the threat will become magnified.

Officials, politicians and the media appear to believe that the public lacks the resilience to cope with a violent terrorist incident. The apprehension that communities lack the capacity to bounce back and thrive after a terrorist incident continues to influence government policy. Strengthening or raising community resilience has become an important policy objective on both sides of the Atlantic. 'The importance of improving the psychological resilience of the American population cannot be overstated,' writes a supporter of the National Resilience Development Act of 2003.[73] This outlook is echoed by the UK Cabinet Office's report, *Dealing with Disaster*. It claims that the 'central government's approach to civil contingency planning is built around the concept of **resilience**'.[74] The focus on resilience or on bouncing back implicitly assumes that there is little that can be done to prevent a destructive event. As Eve Coles from The Centre For Disaster

Management at Coventry University noted, this 'choice of terminology is interesting' because it 'appears to accept an inevitability that such events will happen rather than an adoption of a proactive anticipatory crisis management approach'.[75]

In recent years, resilience has emerged as a key concept among emergency planners. It is frequently suggested that resilience underpins the policies directed at mitigating the impact of emergencies on the public. Policies focused on containing terrorism claim the promotion of resilience as a key dimension of their approach. For example, *Dealing with Disaster* (2003) argues that the 'the processes, which underpin resilience, form the fundamental elements of civil protection'. It is also claimed that the concept 'underpins' the Draft Civil Contingencies Bill.[76] But it is not evident what the processes are that underpin this concept. The report offers a very general definition of resilience. It is defined as the ability 'at every relevant level to detect, prevent, and if necessary, to handle and recover from disruptive challenges'. It is worth noting that, although this key concept is mentioned in the first paragraph, it is never referred to in the rest of the 96-page report.

UK Government officials do not have a single agreed definition of resilience. According to the *Draft Civil Contingencies Bill: Consultation Document* (2003), 'Resilience is the ability to handle disruptive challenges that can result in crisis'.[77] Even after a close examination of this text it is difficult to be sure what exactly is meant by this concept. It appears that resilience is used as a synonym for effective emergency planning. Apparently, it is also 'the ability – at every level – to anticipate, pre-empt and resolve challenges into healthy outcomes' and 'the key to resilience is agility'. It is worth noting that the reference to 'every level' refers to institutions and organizations associated with emergency planning and the State. Every level does not include the public and normal communities. In this document, as elsewhere, resilience serves the role of a 'hurrah word' that signifies aspiration rather than conviction. The everyday official usage of resilience suggests that the term is underpinned by the assumption that resilience is not a phenomenon that can be relied on to flourish by itself. **Frequently it is used as a second-order concept that implies that it is a counter-trend to the dominant state – which is that of vulnerability.** This point is rarely made explicit, but in most of the discussion around the threat of terrorism, vulnerability is perceived as the norm and resilience is presented as a potential counter-trend against it. The term resilience tends to be used in a way that presupposes the primacy of vulnerability –

resilience is the exception, the modifying factor – rather than the defining state.[78] In many accounts, vulnerability is conceptualized as both logically and chronologically prior to resilience. Indeed resilience is sometimes presented as a phase that is encompassed by a more dominant working of vulnerability:

> *While a focus on reducing risk directs attention to mitigating or containing the phenomenon causing harm to a community – whether it be fire, floods, or terrorist attacks – vulnerability encompasses the community's responsiveness and resilience in the face of loss.*[79]

With vulnerability emerging as the defining feature of existence, the impact of threats expand and encourage official overreaction. In such circumstances it is the perception of vulnerability that dictates how the terrorist threat is perceived.

In previous conflicts officials talked about the 'nation's spirit' or the 'public's morale'. Current official disquiet about resilience and the capacity of the public to deal with adversity indicates confusion about the status of the government's authority, the citizen's loyalty and support for the war. As we shall discuss in Chapter 4, the main reason for the defensive posture of Western governments may be due to their inability to provide a meaningful account of the issues at stake.

Notes

1. *The National Security Strategy of the United States Of America*, March 2006, p. 1.

2. Cited by Dobson, 'The Day Nothing Much Changed', *Foreign Policy*, September/October, p. 25.

3. Cited in *The Washington Post*, 7 October 2001.

4. 'Cheney: War Could Last For Generations', *NewsMax.com.wires*, 17 January 2004.

5. See Michael Settle, 'Struggle Against Terrorism Could "Last Another Generation"', *The Herald*, 20 November 2006.

6. 'Christmas Terror strike "highly likely"', *Daily Telegraph*, 11 December 2006.

7. Cohen (1997) Chapter 9, p. 5.

8. John Heilman, 'The Dems' Next War', *New York Magazine*, 20 November 2006; Bill O'Reilly, 'Illegal Immigration and GOP Defeat', *Fox News Network*, 13 November 2006; Keith McDonald, 'Taking religion into the classroom', *The West Australian*, 11 November 2006; 'Community's "Other Fifth" Needs Help', *The Forward*, 10 November 2006; John Terauds, 'Time to settle the score', *The Toronto Star*, 28 October 2006; Sally McCausland, 'Comedy right on target', *The Australian*, 29 September 2006; David Brooks, 'Closing of A Nation', *The New York Times*, 24 September 2006; and Richard Byrne, 'At Annual

Meeting, Political Scientists Explore
Mechanisms of Power'.

9. SAS hero Chris Ryan, 'Secret War Of
Whispers', *News of the World*, 10 July
2005; 'What price this war on terror?',
Townsville Sun, 27 August 2005; Martin
Howe QC, 'Ministers face legal
minefield over clerics', *Evening Standard*,
12 August 2005; 'Concerns on the port
problem', *The Associated Press State &
Local Wire*, 22 February 2006; and
'Opinion', *The Irish Times*, 10
November 2005.

10. *The 9/11 Commission Report: Final
Report of the National Commission on
Terrorist Attacks Upon the United States*,
9–10, 22 July 2004, p. 1.

11. The results of this poll conducted by
the Pew Research Center are cited by
William Dobson, 'The Day Nothing
Much Changed', *Foreign Policy*,
September/October 2006, p. 22.

12. See Brian Albrecht, 'Scorched Into
Our Memories', *Plain Dealer*, 11
September 2006.

13. See J. Ryan, 'Terrorists have riddled
us all with fear', *San Francisco Chronicle*,
12 September 2002; and J. Robson,
'The world changes in Manhattan',
Ottawa Citizen, 12 September 2001.

14. Blair's speech, cited in the *Guardian*,
5 March 2004.

15. Harry Laver (2005), 'Pre-emption
and the Evolution of America's Strategic
Defense', *Parameters*, Summer, 108.

16. Development, Concepts and
Doctrine Centre (2007) *The DCDC
Global Strategic Trends Programme,
2007–2036*, www.mod.uk/NR/
rdonlyres/5CB29DC4-9B4A-4DFD-
B363-3282BE255CE7/0/strat_trends_
23jan07.pdf, p. xiii.

17. *The National Security Strategy of the
United States of America*, September 2002,
p. 13.

18. See *Independent*, 1 November 2006.

19. *The National Security Strategy of the
United States of America*, September 2002,
p. i.

20. Alexis Debat and Nikolas Gvosdev,
'America the Vulnerable', *The National
Interest*, September/October 2006, p. 29.

21. *The National Security Strategy of the
United States of America*, September 2002,
p. 13.

22. Cited in Merle D. Kellerhals, 'Al-
Qaida Remains Grave Threat to United
States, FBI and CIA Say',
USINFO.State.Gov, 16 February 2005.

23. Cited in *The Washington Post*, 7
October 2001.

24. Appandurai (2006) p. 92.

25. See for example Mueller (2005a).

26. Max Rodenbeck, 'How Terrible Is
It?' *New York Review of Books*, 30
November 2006.

27. See Susan Glasser, 'US Figures Show
Sharp Rise in Terrorism', *The
Washington Post*, 27 April 2005.

28. While insurgent groups may have
the capacity to exploit biological and
chemical agents, there is little evidence
that they are able to cause mass
destruction with such weapons. There is
an unhelpful tendency to label all
weapons containing unusual materials as
WMDs. For one assessment of this
threat, see Cornish (2007).

29. The editors, 'Unknown Dangers',
Foreign Policy, November/December
2006.

30. *The National Security Strategy of the
United States of America*, September 2002,
p. 15.

31. Vikram Dodd, 'Al-Qaida plotting
nuclear attack on UK, officials warn',
Guardian, 14 November 2006.

32. See 'German, French Ministers make proposals for joint EU immigration policy', *BBC Monitoring Europe*, 30 October 2006; 'Nuclear, cyber terrorism mix greatest threat to world – Russian expert', *Russia & CIS Military Newswire*, 8 November 2006. Ikle is cited in John O'Sullivan, 'Saddam's execution won't end nuke fears', *Chicago Sun-Times*, 7 November 2006.

33. Office of Homeland Security (2002) *The National Strategy for Homeland Security*, Washington DC, p. 1.

34. 'Rumsfeld urges resolve by US Troops', *The Boston Globe*, 25 December 2004.

35. See *Sudbury Sun*, 22 June 2005, 'Philippines to set up new anti-terror force following Madrid bombings', *The Associated Press State & Local Wire*, 22 March 2004; and 'PM arrives back to criticism over Bali comments', *AAP Newsfeed*, 11 March 2003.

36. Cited in Max Boot, 'The Paradox of Military Technology', *The New Atlantis*, Autumn 2006.

37. Cited in Rosie Cowan, Andrew Clark and Richard Norton-Taylor, 'Top police officer ready to put troops on street', *Guardian*, 15 March 2004.

38. Bill Gertz, 'Goss fears WMD attack in US "a matter of time"', *The Washington Post*, 17 February 2005.

39. 'Britain; Al-Qaeda capable of unconventional attack', *USA Today*, 17 June 2003.

40. 'The prime minister's address to British ambassadors in London', *Guardian*, 7 January 2003.

41. Cited in *BBC Online*, 16 October 2006.

42. Michael Scheuer, 'Courting catastrophe; America five years after 9/11', *The National Interest*, September/October 2006, p. 20.

43. www.cnn.com/2006/POLITICS/09/11/bush.transcript/index.html

44. Rasmussen (2002) p. 329.

45. Office of Homeland Security (2002) *The National Strategy for Homeland Security*, Washington DC, p. 4.

46. See 'Text of terror warning', *BBC Politics Online*, 8 November 2002.

47. Mueller (2005a) p. 12.

48. Beck (2002) p. 260.

49. Clarke (2006) p. 34.

50. 'Terrorists are organized to penetrate open societies and to turn the poser of modern technologies against us', p. 1

51. Cohen (1997) Chapter 9, p. 2.

52. Kunreuther and Michel-Kerjan (2004) p. 4.

53. House of Commons, *Select Committee on Defence, Second Report*, paragraph 51, 18 December 2001.

54. Max Boot, 'The Paradox of Military technology', *The New Atlantis*, Autumn 2006.

55. Homer-Dixon (2002).

56. *Report Of The Quadrennial Defense Review* (1997) p. 3, www.defenselink.mil/pubs/qdr/index.html, accessed 13 December 2006.

57. Mitchell (2003) p. 64.

58. Cohen (1997) Chapter 9, p. 3.

59. Johnson (2002) p. 215.

60. Slovic (2002) p. 425.

61. Clarke (2006) p. 35.

62. 'Bin Laden Defiant', *BBC News*, 7 October 2001.

63. Office of Homeland Security (2002) p. vii and p. 4.

64. Durodié (2005) p. 46.

65. Simon Jenkins, 'Blair is wildly exaggerating the threat posed by terrorism', *Guardian*, 22 November 2006.

66. See 'Ministers exploit terror fears', *BBC News OnLine*, 13 November 2006.

67. Mueller (2005a) p. 32

68. See Furedi (2005).

69. See for example the response of Anthony Giddens to Simon Jenkins in fn 50. Goddens claims that a dirty bomb that exploded in London 'wouldn't kill many people, but it would cause mass panic'. 'The risks are real – and the response', *Guardian*, 24 November 2006.

70. Cited by Mueller (2006b) p. 45.

71. Sheppard, Rubin, Wardman and Wessely (2006) p. 220.

72. Cornish (2007) p. 3.

73. Barnett, M. (2004) 'Congress Must Recognize the Need for Psychological Resilience in an Age of Terrorism', *Families, Systems & Health*, Vol. 22, no. 1, p. 64.

74. Cabinet Office Civil Contingencies Secretariat (2003) *Dealing with Disaster*, revised Third Edition, London: Cabinet Office, para. 1.1.

75. Eve Coles (2003) 'A Systems Perspective on United Kingdom National Vulnerability: the Policy Agenda', www.corporate.coventry.ac. uk/content/1/c6/01/02/90/A.

76. Cabinet Office (2003). See www. ukresilience.info/ccbill/draftbill/ consult/4 resilience.htm

77. www.ukresilience.info/ccbill/ draftbill/consult/4 resilience.htm

78. For example, see Waller (2001).

79. Clarke, S. E. and Chenoweth, E. (2006) 'The Politics of Vulnerability: Constructing Local Performance Regimes for Homeland Security', *Review of Policy Research*, Vol. 23, no. 1, p. 12.

CHAPTER 2

New Terrorism: A
Self-Fulfilling Prophecy

As noted in the previous chapter, one of the principal justifications for characterizing the present time as an era of terrorism is the claim that this threat has become qualitatively different to how it existed in the past. The main consequence of its transformation is that it now constitutes an unprecedented danger to global stability. This claim resonates with public sentiment and, especially since 9/11, the belief that terrorism represents 'a threat of a magnitude never before faced is gaining political currency'.[1] Opinion polls frequently point out that people regard terrorism as one of the principal threats that confronts them in their day-to-day lives. A BBC survey carried out in September 2006 indicated that the threat of terrorism is the main reason that the respondents believed that Britain 'is a worse place to live now compared with 20 years ago'.[2]

Numerous accounts now write about a 'new terrorism' that represents a break with the practices of the past. Unfortunately the discussion on the new terrorism is no less confusing than the debate about the old. Indeed, the conclusion that some manifestation of terrorism is 'new' appears to be as old as the modern deliberation of this threat. One British police officer reported in 1898 that 'murderous organisations have increased in size and scope; they are more daring, they are served by the most terrible weapons offered by modern science, and the world is nowadays threatened by new forces which ... may someday wreak universal destruction'.[3] Back in 1970, after a series of domestic terror incidents the *US News and World Report* observed that 'officials and citizens all across the country are wondering if the United States is entering a new and highly dangerous era'.[4] Five years later *Newsweek* characterized 1975 as the 'Year of Terror'.[5]

'If this is an age of terror, then it has become all the more important for us to understand exactly what it is that terrorism means,' wrote American historian David Fromkin in 1975.[6] Fromkin too believed that the world was confronting a new type of terrorism, and was concerned that its 'novelty' has 'not been perceived'.[7] 'True, other ages have suffered from crime and outrage, but what we are experiencing today goes beyond such things,' he warned. As commentators do today, he pointed to the powerful technology available to the terrorists of the mid-1970s. Fromkin believed that 'the bazooka, the plastic bomb, the submachine, and perhaps, over the horizon, the nuclear mini-bomb' have led to a 'transformation' which has 'enabled terrorism to enter the political arena on a new scale'.[8] By the late 1990s the claim that terrorism had come to constitute a qualitatively new threat had become an integral part of the security doctrine of the US. The US Government's *1997 Annual Defense Report* argued that this threat had 'changed markedly in recent years'.[9]

The periodic discovery that terrorism represents a new and unprecedented danger does not mean that history simply repeats itself. Nor should the preoccupation of the twenty-first-century Western world with this threat be interpreted as simply a continuation of the way that policy-makers responded to it in the past. As this book argues, the way that contemporary society perceives, engages with and problematizes this threat and the impact of terrorism is in most respects unique to our times. Nevertheless, ideas about new terrorism are not simply a direct response to a current trend. They are based upon a cultural and historical legacy that was forged during the past 50 years. As a result, through the working of our cultural imagination, the new terrorist acquired an existence a long time before 9/11. Public concern with this danger, especially in the US, also predates 9/11. For example, during the years 1980–85, 80 per cent of Americans believed that terrorism constituted an 'extreme' danger. Yet during that period 17 people were killed by acts of terrorism in the US – that is three a year in a nation where around 25,000 people were murdered at the same time.[10]

Managing uncertainty

Commentaries on new terrorism can also be interpreted as statements of anxiety about an unpredictable future. Such contributions frequently turn out to be reflections on an uncertain world where change is experienced as threatening. It is difficult to avoid the conclusion that often anxieties about the forces unleashed through economic and technological change are indistinguishable from ones that are focused on the growing destructive potential of terrorists. There is a potent undercurrent of apprehension towards change in Western society. This sensibility finds a day-to-day expression in a phenomenon that I called elsewhere the 'Culture of Fear'.[11] The fear that science and technology are running ahead of our capacity to manage and control them often acquires shape and tangibility in relation to the threat of terror. The new terrorist personifies this fear and provides a focus for cultural anxieties regarding the trajectory of change. As Nicholas King noted, 'the bioterrorist is an active agent, a sophisticated hybrid of primitive and modern who seizes "our" biotechnology – a symbol of American modernity and economic might – and transforms it into a political weapon'. King added that 'he personifies American loss of control over not only its national borders, but also its scientific achievements'. At the same time the new bio-terrorist challenges 'the moral neutrality' of scientific achievements 'exposing what has come to be called the "dual use" dilemma: greater understanding and control over infectious diseases inevitably leads to greater opportunity for transforming those diseases into weapons'.[12]

Often it is unclear whether the focus of fear is technological development itself or the power that can be harnessed by a terrorist bent on destruction. That is why discussions on new terrorism invariably have an anticipatory and even speculative character. Over 20 years ago Walter Laqueur, one of the most widely cited experts on the subject, predicted the imminent arrival of 'postmodern terrorism'. His apprehension was that the growing power of new technologies increased the 'destructive potential' of the terrorist. He ominously warned that:

> The advanced societies of today are more dependent every day on the electronic storage, retrieval, analysis, and transmission of information. Defense, the police, banking, trade, transportation, scientific work, and a large percentage of the government's and the private sector's transactions are on-line. That exposes enormous vital areas of national life to mischief or sabotage by any computer hacker, and concerted sabotage could render a country unable to function. Hence the growing speculation about infoterrorism and cyberwarfare.[13]

Unfortunately speculation about cyber-terror often assumes the masquerade of a sober analysis. Those who have invoked this threat constantly insist that it is irresponsible to ignore such a risk. As with all speculative risks, when analysts and consultants devote time to discussing it, it soon acquires a tangible and immediate quality. In such circumstances cyber-terror can acquire a reality all of its own. But decades of animated speculation about the power of cyber-terrorists to destroy critical infrastructure helps to overlook the fact that little happened during those years. Typically the language of 'it's not if, but when' helps establish a climate where expectations of cyber-terror turn into a self-fulfilling prophecy. It challenges alienated and dissident individuals to do their worst in cyberspace.

At the same time the meaning of cyber-terror has expanded and becomes trivialized. The communication of images and messages that represent the West in an unfavourable light are not simply forms of digital propaganda – they are often denounced as weapons in the armoury of the cyber-terrorist. So when an Islamist website transmits a video praising the act of a suicide bomber it is presented as a species of cyber-terrorism. The alarmist expansion of the meaning of this term helps create the impression that the shadowy presence of this online threat is an accomplished fact. As Susan Keith notes, perhaps the 'news media's use of hazy or overly broad definition of a societal problem like cyberterrorism can contribute to the problem of feeding public fears of the unknown'.[14]

There are numerous versions of the new terrorism thesis. Proponents of this thesis claim that terrorism has become more global. Some argue that it has remodelled itself and has adopted a network form. Supporters of the thesis of new terrorism insist that the aim of these groups is often unclear and the perpetrators of violence are difficult to identify, since they frequently refuse to claim responsibility for their actions. Others point to a shift from an ideological orientation towards religion. Observers also contend that the new breed of terrorists have a far more indiscriminate attitude towards violence than their predecessors.[15] Those who adhere to this thesis argue that religious zealotry creates the 'will to carry out mass casualty attacks'.[16] Some commentators believe that the distinct feature of new terrorism is that its participants 'do not answer to any government' and 'operate across national borders'.[17] But it is not the ideological, motivational or organizational capacity of the new terrorists that really excites the imagination of commentators. They believe that it is the qualitative increase in the terrorist's capacity to inflict physical destruction that represents the principal difference with past threats. So a warning written in 1997 about the threat of nuclear terrorism acknowledges that there is a continuity of terrorist behaviour with the past. It observes that 'because extremism is an inherent element in both religious-fanatic and rogue-state terrorism, extrapolating that the detonation of a primitive nuclear weapon, or the detonation of a primitive nuclear weapon, or the use of a radiological-contamination device … represents a continuation of past behaviour, not a radical departure, is logical'.[18] According to this expert, what appears to have changed is the relative ease of accessing a 'wide range of materials and technological expertise for manufacturing biological and nuclear weapons'.[19] This point was also emphasized by former US Defense Secretary William Cohen in his 1997 *Annual Report*. 'The proliferation of weapons of mass destruction and the availability of individuals schooled in their design and construction represent another dimension that impacts fundamentally on the nature of terrorism,' he noted. Cohen feared that weapons that were hitherto the monopoly of nation states could become available to groups and individuals who were non-state actors. He reported that an 'emerging and significant threat is represented by improvised biological, chemical, and nuclear devices that exploit technologies that once were the sole preserve of world and regional powers'.[20]

Cohen's warning about the emergence of a new species of non-state actors who could access and master technologies of mass destruction represents an important theme in the conceptualization of the new terrorists. From this perspective, the uncertainties of a changing world were amplified by powerful actors who were not subject to the rules of international relations. Unlike nation states who could be held to account, small groups of zealots operating across national boundaries could not be managed through the traditional conventions of international relations. The threat they represent can not be contained within the prevailing framework of deterrence. That is why the terrorist with a 'nuclear suitcase' and non-state groups have been viewed with such alarm since the 1950s.

Whatever the difference in emphasis, most versions of the thesis that the world has entered a new phase of terrorism are based on a common premise, which is that terrorism has become qualitatively different and more dangerous than in the past. Why? Because there is a lot more dangerous technology available for a terrorist intent on mass destruction. According to one pre-9/11 account, the problem is that terrorists 'may gain access to weapons of mass destruction, poison gas weapons, and even computer viruses'.[21] Almost without any conceptual effort the word 'may' is implicitly transformed into a statement of certainty. Fantasy trumps evidence-based policy. None of this speculation is based on empirical evidence. As Gearson noted, these ideas are influenced by the notion that 'though there was no evidence for such capabilities as yet, it was inevitable that they would be utilised eventually'.[22] This fatalistic assessment towards the utilization of weapons of destruction is often justified by the claim that terrorist groups already possess the capacity to undertake such acts. And yet despite the absence of evidence that they possess such expertise the claim that 'contemporary terrorists possess the technological capacities' to inflict large-scale destruction has been regularly reiterated since the 1970s.[23] Today it has acquired the status of a conventional wisdom within official opinion.

Waiting to happen

The devastating attack that occurred on 11 September 2001 is often presented as convincing proof of the challenge of the new terrorist to global stability. 'The attacks confirmed warnings from experts that a new breed of terrorist would transform available technologies into weapons of enormous destructive power' is a frequently repeated assessment of officials and experts.[24] And yet it is worth noting that those responsible for the attacks of 9/11 adopted relatively ordinary low-tech instruments and not high-technology weapons of mass destruction. The act of crashing an aeroplane into an office building is an option that was available to dissident fanatics 20, 40 or 60 years ago. Nor is the arrival of the mass casualty terrorist an unexpected phenomenon. Since the 1950s security experts and officials have been constantly concerned about the imminent arrival of the nuclear terrorist. It is almost as if by its morbid fascination with this subject society has issued an official invitation to be terrorized.

Almost from its inception the US nuclear energy industry was anxiously anticipating the arrival of the 'new terrorist'. As early as 1951, the CIA's *National Intelligence Estimates* was contemplating scenarios that involved the smuggling of an atomic bomb through customs or of terrorists using civilian aircrafts to launch a clandestine attack. It acknowledged that there was no plan in place for 'the detection and prevention of the smuggling of atomic weapons into the US at secluded points' and concluded that until such a plan is put into operation, 'the US will remain vulnerable to this threat'.[25] Apprehension about a clandestine nuclear attack intensified in the aftermath of the Cuban Missile Crisis of 1961 and President Kennedy encouraged the CIA to formulate proposals for countering this threat. With the emergence of a large number of terrorist organizations in the 1970s, this presentiment of danger acquired greater force. It was in the 1970s that the CIA's long-term preoccupation with a clandestine nuclear attack became linked with a new subject of anxiety – that of the non-state terrorist.

Concern with the risk of nuclear terrorism grew in October 1970, after officials in Orlando, Florida received a note that threatened to blow up the city with a hydrogen bomb unless a million dollars ransom was paid. Officials could not dismiss this threat as a bluff and considered paying the ransom until the police discovered that this was a hoax perpetrated by a 14-year-old high-school student. Although the incident was a hoax, it was interpreted as a harbinger of perils to come. According to an important study of the history of policy making of this threat, 'within a short time, the possibility that nuclear materials used for the production of nuclear power could fall into the hands of terrorists or criminals became a public issue'.[26] In April 1974, an internal Atomic Energy Commission (AEC) memo warned about the danger of nuclear material reaching the hands of terrorists or criminals. It argued that 'the potential harm to the public from the explosion of an illicitly made nuclear weapon is greater than that from any plausible power plant accident, including one which involves a core meltdown'.[27] It is worth noting that at this time there were still sober voices that cautioned officials from overreacting. Concerned about costs, the nuclear industry in particular counselled against new security regulations. One industry executive asserted that nuclear power plants were not ideal terrorist targets and stated that the AEC was 'making mountains out of molehills'.[28]

Official nervousness towards this threat was fuelled after the killing of 11 Israeli athletes at the 1972 Munich Olympics by the perception that international terrorism had become a global problem. It was in the aftermath of this event that international or trans-national or, in today's language, global terrorism was represented as a distinct and novel phenomenon. It was also at this time that ideas about the proliferation of technologies of mass destruction and their availability to what two decades later will be called the new terrorist took form. According to a 1976 CIA estimate, the 'prospect of nuclear-armed terrorist can, in fact, no longer be dismissed'.[29] A year later the Pentagon conducted a week-long exercise to evaluate how it should respond if terrorists succeeded in obtaining a nuclear weapon and using it to hold the government to ransom.[30] By this time the media was regularly briefed about official concerns about nuclear terrorism. For example, in 1977 *The Washington Post* reported that federal experts have 'concentrated on developing elaborate plans to cover any contingency that might arise from a nuclear terrorist attack'. The report put forward the following scenario:

> *A report comes in of a theft of weapons-grade uranium from a nuclear plant. A short while later a message arrives from an unknown group claiming responsibility and threatening to detonate a crude nuclear bomb in a crowded area if demands aren't met. The FBI, local police and quite possibly the military would be mobilized. Suspects might be rounded up on the street and forcibly interrogated.*[31]

The report raised concerns that such a massive threat to the security of the nation could provoke a frenetic clampdown on civil rights in a desperate attempt to prevent a nuclear catastrophe. A recurring idea implicit in these reports is that the public could not be expected to cope with such an attack. Since the 1970s, the assumption that a nightmarish terrorist attack would force the authorities to withdraw traditional civil rights has gained force. Such anxieties about the underlying fragility of democratic institutions have been rarely questioned since they were first raised over three decades ago.

Concern about nuclear terrorism also migrated across the Atlantic and became an issue in Britain during the 1970s. At the British Association meeting in 1972, Sir Frank Blackaby 'hinted at the nightmare possibility of a terrorist group seizing control over a nuclear device and attempting to blackmail government and society'.[32] This sentiment was echoed by one of the most influential British studies of terrorism of the time, which asserted that 'a surprising lacuna in strategic studies of revolutionary terrorism is the absence of a full treatment of weapon availability and supply and of the implications of new weapon technology for terrorism'. The author warned that the 'rapid proliferation of nuclear expertise and the recently announced American development of a "pocket" nuclear device make this threat considerably more credible'.[33]

By the mid-1970s a new breed of terrorism experts were actively promoting alarmist accounts about the risk of nuclear terrorism.[34] They successfully harnessed public anxieties towards nuclear energy to gain widespread recognition for the threat of terrorism. In October 1975, a paper on this subject by the MITRE Corporation asserted that nuclear plants and the transportation of nuclear materials represented a major security problem. The report served as a catalyst for the eruption of a series of spectacular media headlines. 'Fear A-plant Terror Raids Would Peril Millions – US Study' screamed the headline of the *Chicago Daily*

News.[35] Analysts also anticipated that the disintegration of the Soviet bloc would create new opportunities for nuclear terrorism. A year later, one senior US Government analyst, who discounted the threat of nuclear war in the 1980s, argued that nuclear terrorism was the 'growing' problem. Government analysts stated that it was the 'psychotic, anarchical groups' whose behaviour was 'entirely unpredictable' who now constituted the main danger.[36] Throughout the 1970s the conviction that nuclear terrorism posed a clear and present danger gained strength. David Rosenbaum, a prolific and influential expert on this subject, suggested that 'nuclear terrorism' could turn into 'one of the most important political and social problems of the next 50 years'. He added that it would 'remain a serious problem no matter what we do'.[37]

Lacking any empirical evidence that could support warnings about the perils of nuclear terrorism, experts mobilized rumours and hoaxes to raise awareness about the issue. The 1970 Orlando hoax threat was gradually transformed into a cautionary tale of the risk of what could happen. For example, a major survey about 'the risk of gunmen' laying 'hands on atomic triggers' referred to the hoax as evidence of the threat. It noted that 'it was a hoax; there was no bomb', but the reader was left with the implication that it could just as easily have been an act of nuclear terrorism.[38] This story was frequently rehashed by journalists attempting to demonstrate the gravity of this threat. The Orlando bomb hoax was used by ABC television's 20/20 program in 1978 to transmit what one critic called 'lip-smacking sensationalism' about nuclear terrorism.[39]

Officials too regarded hoaxes as merely a milder version of the bona fide nuclear terrorist threat. In 1974, a note threatened that a nuclear device would be exploded in Boston unless a ransom of $200,000 was paid. It turned out to be a hoax. Nevertheless alarmed by this incident, security officials decided to establish the Nuclear Emergency Search Team (NEST), a special team to deal with the detection of nuclear terrorists.[40] During the first six years of its existence NEST responded to 'more than' 20 threats of nuclear blackmail. It spent most of its time unwrapping packages that came with notes saying they contained radioactive substances, but which turned out to be dirt.[41] Such hoaxes were represented as a form of nuclear terrorism, regardless of whether or not any radioactive materials were involved. They were frequently used as illustrations of the risks confronting the nuclear industry. Officials and opinion-makers tended to regard such hoaxes as irrefutable evidence of the danger ahead. That is why in 1982 there was little opposition to a Bill that aimed to contain nuclear terrorism. On a vote of 359 to 9 the Bill was passed by the House of Representatives.[42] The issue of nuclear terrorism transcended the conventional political divide in the US. Hardened Cold War warriors were joined by environmentalists and anti-business advocates who regarded the 'specter of nuclear terrorism' as validation of their suspicion of the nuclear industry.[43]

Anxieties about nuclear terrorism escalated after the end of the Cold War and the break-up of the Soviet Union. Loss of control of the Soviet nuclear arsenal was a dominant theme of the worst-case scenario drawn up by the CIA. This anxiety haunted the official imagination in the 1990s. Louis Freeh, Director of the FBI, stated that the smuggling of nuclear weapons constituted 'the greatest long-term threat to the security of the United States'.[44] And a key report, *Terror 2000: The Future Face of Terrorism*, circulated in the Pentagon in 1993, predicted that terrorists would use weapons of mass destruction because they now had 'easy access to biological, chemical and nuclear technologies'.[45] The linkage of nuclear weapons with terrorism endowed this threat with a qualitatively new destructive dimension. According to an interesting interpretation of this development, this linkage helped to construct an image of terrorism as one that was 'uniquely threatening'. Its association with the nuclear arms race also helped it to be 'represented as an international issue'.[46] Not surprisingly, in the post-9/11 era, the belief that nuclear terrorism is a very real threat is even more widespread.[47]

As in the 1970s, warnings about the threat of nuclear terror today are constructed through the medium of worst-case scenarios, which are often packaged as a public service docudrama. Take the following scenario, proposed by Graham Allison, a leading proponent of nuclear alarmism:

> On a normal workday, half a million crowd the area within a half-mile radius of New York City's Times Square. If a terrorist detonated a 10-kiloton nuclear weapon in the heart of midtown Manhattan, the blast would kill them all instantly. Hundreds of thousands of others would die from collapsing buildings, fire, and fallout in the hours and days thereafter.[48]

Just in case the reader is not sure what to make of this scare story, Allison adds, 'My best judgment is that based on current trends, a nuclear terrorist attack on the United States is more likely than not in the decade ahead'.[49] Such contributions are rarely constrained by the dictates of factual evidence. As one French proponent of worst-case scenario thinking writes after warning of a kamikaze attack with a full load of kerosene on a nuclear installation, this 'is only one possibility among a whole series of scenarios that have now become "actually imaginable"'.[50]

The capacity to fantasize about wild cataclysmic nuclear terrorist scenarios continues at a feverish pace. Take the following scenario, dreamt up by Fred Ikle, who has a reputation for being 'one of America's foremost strategic thinkers':

> *An aspiring dictator who is an insider endowed with political charisma and extraordinary strategic vision might have his henchmen obtain a couple of nuclear weapons. With a carefully timed use of these weapons the sudden nuclear devastation would cause great shock and widespread despair. The morning after, the new dictator could exploit this despair and political crisis to grab total power – much like Lenin exploited the misery and chaos of war-ravaged St Petersburg.*[51]

That it sounds like a plotline straight out of a children's comic book does not mean that it is dismissed as rambling fantasy by policy-makers. Thirty years previously, Ikle was inventing very similar spooky scenarios involving terrorists smuggling an A-bomb in the US. 'Would we be driven in desperation to establish a police state, in an effort to prevent nuclear terrorism here?' he asked.[52]

The dramatization of security

Accounts of nuclear terrorism, like contemporary representations of new terrorism, are influenced by uncertainty about the future, a mood of vulnerability regarding unspecific threats and worst-case scenario thinking. Pronouncements about the future threat of terrorism invariably have a hypothetical character. As one American nuclear industry insider noted, 'speculation took hold with an extrapolation that said that nuclear terrorism was a natural tool of international terrorists'.[53] Such threat assessments frequently erode the distinction between what has happened and what could happen. They often assume the character of a fictionalized account of security threats to come. At the very least they presuppose that a leap of imagination provides a valid signpost towards the dangers that lie ahead. That is why so much of the writing on this subject resembles more a docudrama than objective analysis. During the past three decades leading experts have habitually resorted to the 'imagine this scenario' approach to win the attention of policy-makers and the public. Characteristically such contributions are introduced with a 'short story' or a series of vignettes pointing to different scenarios involving terrorists priming their infernal machines. One of the most influential experts on nuclear terror in the 1970s, David Rosenbaum, begins his contribution with the following hypothetical story:

> *On September 14, 1981, 100 kilograms of plutonium are hijacked en route from a plutonium storage area in France to a fuel fabrication plant in Italy. In order not to alarm the public, the French and Italian governments decide to keep the incident secret while they try to recover the plutonium. On October 20, after more than a month of fruitless search, the other governments of NATO are informed of the theft. They all agree to keep the information secret to avoid public panic.*
>
> *On December 24, the White House and major newspapers and broadcasting networks receive a letter stating that the World Peace Brigade will explode a nuclear weapon within the next two days. No one has heard of the World Peace Brigade.*
>
> *On Christmas, a nuclear explosion of approximately seven kilotons explodes on the crest of the Blue Ridge mountains sixty miles west of Washington DC.*[54]

As the story unfolds, the author continually highlights the vulnerability of the United States to the peril posed by a handful of nuclear terrorists. As in a cautionary tale written for children, the reader is left in no doubt of the risk they face unless they adopt the helpful advice of the storyteller. Three decades after this story was published, the terrorist with a nuclear suitcase continues to excite the imagination. Dramatic accounts of catastrophes caused by the acts of malevolent characters which continue to be transmitted through television programmes like *24* often shape the public presentation of the threat of terror.

Compelling fictional accounts appear to displace the need for compelling arguments in the post–9/11 publication, *The Four Faces of Nuclear Terrorism*. In this book the reader is told that 'disturbing developments' point towards four 'faces' of nuclear terrorism. These range from the theft and explosion of a nuclear device to the construction and detonation of a dirty bomb. Almost imperceptibly these imaginative stories are turned into practical and immediate problems with dire consequences. The public is informed that:

> *Consequences stemming from a terrorist-detonated nuclear weapon in an American city would emanate beyond the immediate tens or hundreds of fatalities and massive property and financial damage. Americans who were not killed or injured by the explosion would live in fear that they could die from future nuclear terrorist attacks. Such fear would erode*

public confidence in the government and could spark the downfall of the administration in power. The tightly interconnected economies of the United States and the rest of the world could sink into depression as a result of a crude nuclear weapon destroying the heart of a city.[55]

Typically this warning of the catastrophe to come is constructed through making an imaginative leap to what 'could' or what 'would' happen. The explosion 'would' impact beyond the immediate fatalities, Americans 'would' live in fear and the event 'could' result in a global depression. Elsewhere the reader is reminded that groups 'with nuclear capability could assume a quasi-state nature'.[56] A British contributor also alarms us with his 'coulds' and 'woulds'. He informs us that 'terrorists could target a reactor', and that it is 'hard to think of a terrorist attack' which 'could' be 'more catastrophic than an attack on the plutonium stores at Sellafield'. Again, such an attack 'would cause considerable fear, panic and social disruption'.[57]

In passing it is worth noting that this type of worst-case thinking always inflates the potential impact of a terrorist attacks. Its authors are always convinced that the public will panic and that economic life would dive into a tailspin. At the same time, such a complex scientifically challenging terrorist operation is casually represented as the outcome of child's play. 'The ease with which terrorists could build and detonate' dirty bombs 'or use radioactive material for other harmful purposes' is 'especially concerning', warns *The Four Faces of Nuclear Terrorism*. 'It is a sobering fact that the fabrication of a primitive nuclear explosive' does not require 'greater skill' than that possessed by the group responsible for a sarin attack on the Tokyo subway in 1995, writes a British scientist.[58]

Speculation about what 'could' happen easily mutates into a statement about 'unavoidable danger' through an effortless rhetorical adjustment. One interesting analysis of the media's use of the term cyber-terrorism before 9/11 concludes that articles that wrote about it as a likely threat as opposed to one that already occurred 'may have created a scarier definition of "cyber-terrorism" than was implicit in articles that suggested that cyber-terrorism had already occurred'. The hypothetical language pointing to an impending disaster 'may have left a more frightening impression than would have the suggestion that cyber-terrorism, though already a fact, is survivable'.[59]

In the early 1980s, a docudrama titled *Special Bulletin* adopted a TV news format to entertain the audience about the drama surrounding nuclear terrorism. It won critical acclaim and an Emmy Award.[60] Since that time, the plot involving the threat of fanatical nuclear terrorists has become a regular feature of popular culture. Many officials and media commentators are conscious of the entertainment-driven framing of the issue of WMD terrorism. As the December 2001 House of Commons Select Committee on Defence reported, 'a terrorist group in possession of nuclear weapons has long been a favourite scenario of thriller writers'.[61] So an *Associated Press* briefing on security planning reported that officials have 'planned for a variety of problems that would strain even novelists – nuclear terrorism, germ warfare, suicide pilots'.[62] It appears that officials took such works of fiction very seriously. In 1983 it was reported that Oliver Revell, the FBI's assistant director for criminal investigation and responsible for keeping an eye on nuclear-related incidents, kept a copy of the novel *The Fifth Horseman* in his office. The plot of this novel, written by Larry Collins and Dominique Lapierre, focused on a group of terrorists who threatened to detonate a nuclear bomb unless world leaders agreed to the establishment of an independent Palestinian state.[63] Another novel, *The Sum of All Fear* by Tom Clancy, also preyed on the imagination of officialdom. In this novel an Arab terrorist group plots a nuclear attack on the Super Bowl in Denver. By the 1990s this scenario was rarely dismissed as just a work of fiction. According to one of the early attempts to give coherence to the newly invented term, 'catastrophic terrorism', 'long part of the Hollywood and Tom Clancy repertory of nightmarish scenarios, catastrophic terrorism has moved from far-fetched horror to a contingency that can happen next month'.[64]

The dramatization of security acquired an unprecedented momentum during the Clinton presidency. During this period apprehension towards the threat of nuclear terrorism expanded to encompass the dangers of chemical, biological and cyber-weapon attacks. According to presidential adviser Sidney Blumenthal, Clinton became 'virtually obsessed with the dangers of bioterrorism'.[65] In June 1995, his administration issued a Presidential Decision Directive on terrorism whose aim was to contain the threat posed by weapons of mass destruction. It is from this period onwards that catastrophic worst-case thinking becomes normalized and the process that Ehud Sprinzak described as the 'Great Superterrorism Scare' becomes institutionalized.[66]

According to several accounts, Clinton's preoccupation with WMD terrorism, particularly bio-terrorism, was further stimulated by his reading Richard Preston's novel, *The Cobra Event*. This thriller depicted a bio-terrorist attack on New York with a genetically engineered virus.

Clinton decided to read this book after a dinner party in 1997, where he had a conversation with Dr J. Craig Venter, then head of the Institute for Genomic Research. According to reports, Clinton asked Venter if it was possible to develop a bio-weapon for which there was no known defence. Venter noted that it was possible to produce a virus through recombinant technology such as the one highlighted in *The Cobra Event*. It appears that a day after this conversation Clinton asked Venter to help put together a panel of experts to advise him on germ warfare.[67]

Critics of Clinton's embrace of the super-terrorist hypothesis claim that this president manipulated the fear of this threat in order to legitimate his foreign policy.[68] However, whatever policy objectives influenced Clinton's counter-terrorist initiatives, there is little doubt that he and his officials were genuinely disturbed by the horrific narratives of suspense writers. Their imagination was no less at work than those of the pulp fiction writers who were busy producing new myths about WMD terrorism. That is why there is such a striking overlap between texts produced by official policy-makers and novelists. *The Cobra Event* serves as a paradigmatic example of the dramatization of security. Preston represents his book not simply as a work of fiction, but as the product of serious research. He boasts of having interviewed over 100 senior people in government, military and scientific communities. According to his publisher's webpage:

> *The details of this story are fictional, but they are based on a scrupulously thorough inquiry into the history of biological weapons and their use by civilian and military terrorists. Richard Preston's sources include members of the FBI and the United States military, public health officials, intelligence officers in foreign governments, and scientists who have been involved in the testing of strategic bioweapons. The accounts of what they have seen and what they expect to happen are chilling.*[69]

The language used to promote *The Cobra Event* continually interweaves claims about facts with the promotion of its suspenseful literary qualities. It is described as a 'dramatic, heart-stopping account of a very real threat'. This combination of drama and reality endows the new terrorist narrative with a chilling force.

The publicity material advertising *The Cobra Event* frequently represents the text as a major contribution to public debate. The novel is portrayed as a valiant attempt to raise public awareness about a catastrophic threat facing the United States. In the introduction to this thriller, the author writes that 'experts are reluctant to talk too freely' –

a problem which *The Cobra Event* sets out to rectify, since the 'public must be told'! For his part, Richard Preston was more than happy to adopt the role of the novelist/terrorism expert. He carefully cultivated the persona of an important authority who possessed a privileged access to information of vital national importance. He flaunted his expertise to a Senate Judiciary Committee on terrorism in 1998 and informed this body that he had 'spent the past six years researching and writing about viruses and biological weapons'. Preston added that President Clinton, Defense Secretary William Cohen and Speaker Newt Gingrich 'have all read with interest' his books and with a touch of modesty noted that 'in the course of learning from a wide range of experts, I have become an expert myself'.[70]

What is fascinating about the response to *The Cobra Event* is the manner in which a work of fiction was effortlessly converted into an expert narrative which scientists and security professionals had to take seriously. This dramatization of security was lent authority by officialdom and by non-official scientific and advocacy publications who deemed *The Cobra Event* worthy of review. For example, a review in *Public Health Reports* adopts a congratulatory tone and praises Preston for providing 'an accurate and readable history of modern bio-weaponry, which alone is reason enough to read this book'.[71] With the passing of time this novel became transformed into an expert statement that advocacy organizations used to promote their crusade. So a review published by the *Genome News Network* in 2002 is concerned that, despite the warnings issued by *The Cobra Event*, the issue of biological weapons is ignored. It rhetorically asks if the 'events of this novel' could 'happen in real life' before citing 'bioterrorism expert Steven Block' who confirms that *The Cobra Event* is 'one of the most carefully researched fictional works you'll find anywhere'.[72]

The erosion of the line between fact and fiction typified by *The Cobra Event* was not simply the artefact of media influence through cleverly constructed pseudo-documentaries. Like the imaginatively constructed intelligence reports on sightings of WMDs discussed previously, such narratives speak to elite uncertainties about the future. Worst-case thinking continually attaches itself to any evidence of threats to come. And when at the end of his second term Clinton was reported to believe that within the next ten years there was a 100 per cent chance of a chemical or biological attack on the US, he was simply giving voice to a narrative that was constructed by an alliance of security officials and dramatists.[73]

After 9/11, this alliance between the imaginative outlook of cultural creatives and hard-nosed policy-makers acquired a more elaborate institutional form. In the aftermath of 9/11, Hollywood's creative imaginations (and those least constrained by reality) were sought out by the US army for help in waging the anti-terrorist campaign. Senior military personnel have held discussions with filmmakers dreaming up scenarios of possible future terrorist attacks.[74] *Die Hard* screenwriter, Steven E. de Souza, and *Delta Force One* and *Missing in Action* director, Joseph Zito, were amongst those attending brainstorming sessions with officials. At the time Robert Lindheim from the Institute of Creative Technologies (ICT) observed that the military 'wants to think differently'. He stated that 'the reason I believe the army asked the ICT to create a group from the entertainment industry is because they wanted to think outside the box'. It was reported that around 16 scenarios were cobbled together and dispatched to Washington.[75]

According to a report published on this meeting, 'it was no secret' that for some time 'Hollywood executives and video-game creators had paired up with the military to create lifelike, virtual-reality simulations intended to help soldiers train for combat on foreign soil'.[76] The ICT, which received a major grant from the American Army to develop such technology, is upbeat about the contribution that the entertainment industry can make to the war against terrorism. It described the people at the brainstorming session as a 'great group of people', who are doing something 'that actually has value, that can actually save lives'.[77] The ICT was widely praised for their 'Full Spectrum Warrior' project, which was created as a training tool for the US Army, but which also turned into a video game for the X-Box. Two years after 9/11 it was reported that the CIA's Counter-Terrorism Center (CTC) was working with the ICT to design an anti-terrorist video game that would help the US military to think like the enemy. It appears that the game provides different scenarios for analysts to play a variety of roles in the war against terror. 'We don't call them games; we call them computer-based training aids,' commented a CIA spokesman.[78]

In the nineteenth century, writers of science fiction such as Jules Verne excited the public with their stories of unknown dangers. But their influence was confined to the domain of popular culture. Today the producers of popular culture are readily absorbed into the sphere of public debate and influence perceptions of future threat. Their role in the war against terror is not confined to the provision of propaganda. Officials invite their contribution precisely because they do not think like analysts or experts. Cultural creatives are welcomed because they can 'think outside the box'. According to one account, unlike 'military and scientific planners' who 'tend to be linear thinkers', Hollywood people can work in a multidimensional manner.[79] As we shall see in the next chapter the freeing of officialdom's imagination from what is known from facts provides the cultural prerequisite for worst-case thinking. It also provides the imperative for the dramatization of security.

So what is 'new' about new terrorism?

There is very little that is genuinely 'new' about terrorism. Those devoted to the pursuit of political violence have always sought to use the latest technologies in order to maximize the destructive impact of their operation. More than three decades ago, in 1972, a group of terrorists belonging to a right-wing sect called the Order of the Rising Sun were arrested after they were found to be in possession of a large quantity of epidemic typhus pathogens with which they wanted to poison the water supplies of cities in the Mid-West of the US.[80] Nor is there anything new about official concern about the proliferation of WMDs. For almost a half a century officials have been discussing how to deal with a catastrophic terrorist attack. In all this time there is little empirical evidence of a qualitative transformation of this threat.

The one event that promoters of the new terrorism constantly allude to as proof of the arrival of a new era of terrorism was the attempt by members of the Japanese cult Aum Shinrikyo to launch a sarin attack on the Tokyo subway in March 1995. Although this millenarian sect sought to inflict mass casualties on Tokyo commuters, fortunately due to its inability to design an effective delivery system only 12 passengers lost their lives. In one sense the failure of the release of the nerve agent sarin to cause mass casualties can be interpreted as a good news story. It points to 'the difficulties in developing, producing and deploying biological agents'.[81] It is worth noting that although Aum was a relatively sophisticated organization with access to scientific expertise and significant financial resources it still failed to realize its objectives. One important assessment of this experience concluded that 'the probability of a major biological attack by either a state or a sophisticated terrorist group seems remote'.[82]

Nevertheless this incident was quickly seized upon as the harbinger of a new era of catastrophic terrorism. In the United States the Senate Armed Services Committee launched its own inquest into the sarin attack on the Tokyo subway. Leading American politicians treated the incident as one that threatened the US itself. Senator Richard Lugar stated that Americans had 'every reason to anticipate acts of nuclear, chemical, or biological terrorism'. Subsequently, numerous studies insisted that this attack represented the 'crossing of a previously unthinkable line' or that it showed that WMDs were 'within the technical reach of sophisticated terrorist organisations'.[83] Gearson notes that after this incident, 'the way in which terrorism was understood changed for ever' and 'terrorists had achieved the unthinkable and were now able to pose threats to states that previously only other states had'.[84] After Tokyo, terrorism 'was said to have made a qualitative leap', since for the first time a terrorist organization was prepared to discharge materials of mass destruction.[85] But more than a decade after this event it is evident that this assessment still has an anticipatory character. The evidence so far indicates that those oriented towards inflicting violence on civilians appear to choose more conventional weapons to create mass casualties.

Superficially, the experience of 9/11 can be interpreted as confirmation of the catastrophic terrorism thesis. Yet one of the principal defining features of the new terrorism − the use of WMDs − was conspicuously absent during this event. As Mueller wrote:

> Not only were the 9/11 bombings remarkably low-tech, but they were something that could have happened long ago: both skyscrapers and airplanes have been around for a century now. In addition the potential for destruction on that magnitude is hardly new: any time a band of fanatical, well-trained, and lucky terrorists could have sunk or scuttled the Titanic and killed thousands.[86]

In retrospect, it is evident that the destruction of the World Trade Center was the consequence of tactics that have been deployed by terrorists for a very long time. As Gearson observes, 'instead of technologically sophisticated weapons of mass destruction, the super-terrorists of 11 September utilised the long-established terrorist approach of careful planning, simple tactics and operational surprises to effect the most stunning terrorist "spectacular" in history'.[87]

One of the most persuasive arguments used to distinguish the new from the traditional form of terrorism is the claim that today it is far more brutal, destructive and indiscriminate in its attitude to human life. Specialists on this subject frequently counterpose the traditional terrorist who was relatively selective in choosing targets to today's perpetrator of catastrophic acts of mass casualty. However, this argument has been repeatedly restated since at least the 1970s. After noting that insurgent

groups were historically selective in their choice of targets, a commentary
written in the aftermath of the Palestinian attack on passengers at the
Lod Airport reported that 'most "revolutionaries" now, however, seem
to consider indiscriminate slaughter a primary tactic and one of which
they are proud'. The author added that 'it is clear that such groups
would not be deterred from nuclear terrorism by the fact that thousands
of innocent and uninvolved people might die'.[88]

Acts of apparently indiscriminate violence have a long history. As
Alexander Spencer noted, 'indiscriminate mass-casualty attacks have
long been a characteristic of terrorism'. He enumerates examples such
as the simultaneous bombings of the US and French barracks in Lebanon
in 1983, which resulted in the death of 367 people, the destruction of
Pan Am Flight 103 over Lockerbie that killed 270 people and the
bombing of an Air India plane by a Sikh group that resulted in 329
deaths.[89] Another characteristic attributed to new terrorism is the motive
of religious fanaticism. Yet from the Sicarii of the Jewish Zealot
movement of biblical times there have been numerous violent sects
who were inspired by religious and millenarian impulses.

At first sight it is far from evident what has changed about terrorism.
Virtually every characteristic that is associated with this new breed of
destructive behaviour has been linked with terrorism in the past.
However, the very fact that contemporary terrorism is perceived as
very new, uniquely dangerous and the greatest threat to global stability
renders it a distinct phenomenon. What's important about terrorism as
a social phenomenon is how society responds to it. And the more
dangerous that terrorism is perceived to be, the more dangerous it
becomes. It is the normalization of the expectation of catastrophic mass-
casualty events that transforms terrorism into a 'threat of a magnitude
never before faced'.[90] As Zimmermann argues, 'the fearful expectation
of ever more destructive mass casualty attacks involving ABC weapons'
makes today's terrorist 'more dangerous than before'. Perversely the
growing tendency to portray threats in catastrophic terms puts potential
terrorists 'under increasing pressure to reify the popular nightmare of
mass casualty terrorism'.[91] Paradoxically the significance attached to this
threat by Western political elites serves as an invitation to be terrorized.
It is difficult for anyone sensitive to Western obsessions with terrorism
to overlook the symptoms of insecurity, defensiveness and fear. The
predictions of WMD terrorism constitute something of a self-fullfiling
prophecy. 'Due to the weight currently attached to the threat scenarios
in private, public and government circles of sub-state actors seeking to

acquire ABC weapons, the actual threat itself may well become a self-fulfilling prophecy according to the dictates of the dynamic of reciprocal threat perception,' notes Zimmermann.[92]

It is of course possible to argue that decades of obsessive terror-phobia actually represented an astute anticipation of an event like 9/11. A survey of policy documents and analyses could lead to the conclusion that they successfully anticipated today's war on terror. Certainly statements like the US Government's 1997 *Report Of The Quadrennial Defense Review* have a distinct twenty-first-century feel about them. It warned that 'increasingly capable and violent terrorists will continue to directly threaten the lives of American citizens' and that their attacks 'will threaten Americans at home in the years to come'.[93] However, as we now know, such warnings are products of a fertile cultural imagination and have little to do with hard intelligence. The terrorist with a nuclear bomb in a suitcase is imaginatively but neither logically nor empirically linked to the perpetrators of 9/11. Three decades of fantasy warnings did not make the world a more secure place – on the contrary they may well have served to alert non-state actors of the US's intense sense of vulnerability to a terrorist attack.

What's significant about the three-decades-long anticipation of WMD terrorism is what it says about Western political elites. Throughout these decades the absence of evidence of such expertise has not deterred analysts and officials from thoroughly internalizing worst-case thinking. Gearson's remark that the super-terrorism debate of the 1990s revealed 'more about ourselves than the terrorists' is no less apposite for making sense of the current situation.[94] The conceptual inflation of terrorism is principally a by-product of important developments in Western culture. One of these is the West's sense of estrangement from modernity. Indeed the harnessing of new technology by the 'super-terrorist' expresses a loss of control over modernity. As we shall discuss in the next chapter, radically new attitudes towards risk and uncertainty have created a situation where the destructive potential of new technology overwhelms the imagination. It is as if, through its innovation and development, Western society provides the means for its own destruction.

Today's political elites readily associate global instability with the acts of malevolent agents. One consequence of this troubled outlook is the growing disposition to interpret and reinterpret events as symptoms of terrorism. As Matthew Carr notes, 'the perception that the world has entered an "age of terrorism" was partly due to the increasing attention given to the subject by Western governments' and partly an outcome of a 'new tendency to identify disparate acts of violence as manifestations of the same phenomenon'.[95] It was this change of elite perception and interpretation rather than the objective transformation of terrorism that encouraged the formulation of the new terrorist thesis. As a result a series of disparate events were re-categorized as terrorist incidents. For example, the dispersal of salmonella bacteria in a salad bar in Oregon by the Bhagwan Shree Rajneesh cult in 1984, which led to 751 cases of diarrhoea, was not depicted at the time as an instance of terrorism or bio-terrorism. The representation of this incident as a warning of bio-terrorism to come did not emerge until the 1990s.[96]

The one dimension of terrorism that is genuinely 'new' is the way it is conceptualized. On the one hand, this is very much the case of reinterpreting old concerns and rebranding them as existential threat. On the other hand, the meaning of terrorism has expanded and is used to account for a variety of threats. As noted previously, in recent decades a growing range of global threats have been assimilated into a narrative of new terrorism. The conceptual inflation of terrorism has been noted in an important study by Crelinsten, who remarked that the 'tendency to place disparate phenomena into the same security basket' is 'reflected in recent analyses of terrorism'.[97] A key development in this conceptual inflation was the shift from perceiving terrorism as a specific local phenomenon to one that was globally connected and therefore constituted a worldwide threat. During the 1970s a variety of disparate terrorist incidents in the West and in the Third World were interpreted as an integral part of a common global threat. 'All these events were increasingly incorporated into a single overarching narrative of "international terrorism",' notes Carr.[98] One consequence of the perception of terrorism as an international phenomenon is that it becomes uprooted from any historical, cultural and social context. As an international phenomenon it exists in its own right and terrorism can be readily interpreted as a standalone problem of apocalyptic dimensions.

Notes

1. Burnett and Whyte (2005) p. 2.

2. This survey is published on *BBC News*, 4 September 2006.

3. Cited by Rose (1999).

4. 'Behind The Terror Bombings', *US News and World Report*, 30 March 1970.

5. *Newsweek*, 5 January 1976.

6. Fromkin (1975) p. 692.

7. Ibid., p. 684.

8. Ibid., p. 683.

9. See Chapter 9 of *1997 Annual Defense Report*, www.dod.mil/execsec/adr97/toc.html

10. Zulaika (1998) p. 106.

11. See Furedi (2006).

12. King (2003) p. 438.

13. Laqueur (1996) p. 35.

14. Susan Keith (2005) 'Fear-mongering or fact: The construction of "cyber-terrorism" in the US, UK, and Canadian news media', paper presented at *Safety and Security in a Networked World: balancing cyber-rights and responsibilities*, Oxford Internet Institute, 8–10 September 2005, Oxford, p. 5.

15. For a summary of these views see Bergesan and Han (2005) pp. 135–6.

16. See Chapter 9, p. 2 of Cohen (1997).

17. Rose (1999).

18. Foxell (1997) p. 98.

19. Ibid., p. 98.

20. Cohen (1997) Chapter 9.

21. Carter, Deutch and Zelikow (1998) p. 80.

22. Gearson (2002) p. 19.

23. Waugh (1986) p. 287.

24. 'Prologue' to Martin (2004) p. 1.

25. See 'Soviet Capabilities for Clandestine Attack against the US with Weapons of Mass Destruction and the Vulnerability of the US to Such Attack', CIA, NIE-31, 4 September 1951, cited in Zenko (2006) p. 90.

26. Walker (2001) p. 113.

27. Cited in ibid., p. 107.

28. Ibid., p. 122.

29. Cited in Zenko (2006) p. 94.

30. Ibid., p. 95.

31. Bill Richards, 'Nuclear Plant Security Poses Civil Liberties Dilemma', *The Washington Post*, 21 November 1977.

32. Willkinson (1974) p. 135.

33. Ibid., p. 135.

34. For example, in 1977 a group of 200 Australian scientists signed a statement that stated that the dangers of nuclear terrorism outweighed the benefits of nuclear power. See *Facts on File World News Digest*, 8 January 1977.

35. *Chicago Daily News*, 28 November 1975, cited by Walker (2001) p. 125.

36. See 'In the Next Decade – Breakup of Communist World', *US News & World Report*, 9 August 1976.

37. Cited by Walker (2001) p. 130.

38. See Arthur Gavshon, 'Terror', *Associated Press*, 28 July 1977.

39. Betsy Carter, 'Thrash News', *Newsweek*, 26 June 1978.

40. See Richelson (2002) p. 38.

41. Judith Valente, 'Nuclear Threat', *The Washington Post*, 21 June 1983.

42. 'Bill to deter Nuclear Terrorists Passed', *Associated Press*, 21 July 1982.

43. Frederick Crane, 'Plant security: The costs to the nuclear industry', *American Nuclear Society Nuclear News*, August 1983.

44. 'Nuclear Smuggling Called a Grave Threat', *Kansas City Star*, 13 August 1994.

45. Cited in Zenko (2006) p. 98.

46. Zulaika (1998) p. 105.

47. For example, see Bunn and Wier (2005).

48. Allison (2006) p. 36.

49. Ibid., p. 38.

50. 'The threat of nuclear terrorism: from analysis to precautionary measures', by Mycle Schneider, Director WISE-Paris, 10 December 2001, www.wise-paris.org.

51. Cited in 'Annihilation Omens', *The Washington Times*, 10 October 2006.

52. Cited in Arthur Gavshon, 'Terror', *Associated Press*, 28 July 1977.

53. Frederick Crane, 'Plant security: the costs to the nuclear industry', *American Nuclear Society Nuclear News*, August 1983.

54. Rosenbaum (1977) p. 140.

55. Ferguson and Potter (2004) p. 3.

56. Ibid., p. 21

57. Frank Barnaby, 'The Risk of Nuclear Terrorism', *Scientists for Global Responsibility Newsletter no. 28*, November 2003, p. 8.

58. Ibid., p. 8.

59. Keith (2005) p. 15.

60. 'TV Whiz Gets into Cable', *The Washington Post*, 8 November 1984.

61. House of Commons, *Select Committee on Defence, Second Report*, paragraph 67, 18 December 2001.

62. Tim Ahern, 'BC cycle', *Associated Press*, 28 July 1984.

63. Judith Valente, 'Nuclear Threat', *The Washington Post*, 21 June 1983.

64. Carter, Deutch and Zelikow (1998) p. 80.

65. Blumenthal (2003) p. 656.

66. Sprinzak (1998), William Cohen statement about WMD terrorism: 'the question is no longer if this will happen but when' sums up the mood of the time.

67. See Miller, Engelberg and Broad (2001) for an account of this discussion.

68. For example, this point is argued by Carr (2006) p. 279.

69. www.randomhouse.com/catal;og/display.pperl?isbn=9780345498137&view=print, accessed 19 September 2006.

70. Senate Judiciary Committee, 'Statement for the Record by Richard Preston Before the Senate Judiciary Subcommittee on Technology, Terrorism and Government Information and the Senate Select Committee on Intelligence on Chemical and Biological Weapons Threats to America: Are We Prepared?', 22 April 1998, http://judiciary.senate.gov/oldsite/preston.htm, accessed 19 September 2006.

71. Tara O'Toole, 'Death in Gotham' in *Public Health Reports*, March/April 1999, Vol. 114, p. 186.

72. *Genome News Network*, 2 February 2002.

73. Rasmussen (2002) p. 361.

74. 'Hollywood on terror', Australian Broadcasting Corporation, 21 October 2001.

75. Peter Huck, 'Hollywood goes to war', *The Age*, 16 September 2002.

76. See Robert Wilonsky, 'Reel War', *East Bay Express*, 17 October 2001.

77. Ibid.

78. Cited in Audrey Hudson, 'CIA criticized for video game', *The Washington Times*, 30 September 2003.

79. Peter Huck, 'Hollywood goes to war', *The Age*, 16 September 2002.

80. See Spencer (2006) p. 19.

81. Durodié (2004) p. 1.

82. Parachini (2001) p. 5.

83. See 'First Anniversary of Tokyo Subway Poison Gas Attack: Is the US Prepared for a Similar Attack?', *News Advisory September 1996*, Chemical and Biological Weapons Nonproliferation Project and Tucker (2000) p. 1

84. Gearson (2002) p. 7.

85. Zanders (1999).

86. Mueller (2006a) p. 14.

87. Gearson (2002) p. 7.

88. Rosenbaum (1977) pp. 147–8.

89. Spencer (2006) p. 15.

90. Burnett and Whyte (2005) p. 2.

91. Zimmermann (2003) pp. 47–8.

92. Ibid., p. 56.

93. *Report Of The Quadrennial Defense Review* (1997) p. 2, www.defenselink.mil/pubs/qdr/index.html, accessed 13 December 2006.

94. Gearson (2002) p. 8.

95. Carr (2006) p. 206.

96. On this point, see Lipschutz and Turcotte (2004) p. 1.

97. Crelinsten (1998) p. 390.

98. Carr (2006) p. 198.

CHAPTER 3

The Expanding Empire of Unknown Dangers

Twenty-first-century ideas about terrorism are influenced by prevailing cultural attitudes towards the nature of danger and risk and about the capacity of society to deal with unanticipated threats. This chapter argues that one reason why terrorism appears so new and menacing is because of cultural influences that call into question humanity's capacity to know and deal with future threats. The belief that we lack the knowledge to deal with threats like terrorism is not confined to small groups of marginal critics. Government officials and their experts constantly express a strikingly defensive and hesitant approach in their threat assessments. As we argue, their response to terrorism is inspired by their self-acknowledged ignorance rather than knowledge-based threat assessments. These policy responses are anything but evidence-based! It is also underwritten with a radically novel conception of risk. Back in October 2001, the CEO of CAN Financial Corporation observed that 'the events of September 11 have changed the very definition of risk'.[1] In the intervening period the day-to-day usage of the concept of risk has come to bear less and less resemblance to its classical definition. The implications of this shift in thinking about risk in general, and the risk of terrorism in particular, are explored in this chapter.

The qualitative distinction drawn between the old and the new age of terrorism is also underwritten by powerful cultural forces that insist that we live in a world that is far more dangerous than in the past. Some experts and academics claim that these new dangers are so overwhelming that we can no longer even insure against them. One of the most prominent academic proponents of this alarmist scenario argues that the 'boundaries of private insurability' have simply dissolved.[2] In a similar vein, Lloyd's of London warned that climate change could destroy the insurance industry. It counselled insurers to increase prices so as to avoid being 'swept away' by a sea of claims. 'If we don't take action now to understand the changing nature of our planet we will face extinction,' observed Lloyd's Director, Rolf Tolle.[3] The insurance industry has become addicted to representing the future as one where it becomes helpless in the face of global calamity. After 9/11 the focus was on terrorism. At the time, Rodger Lawson, the president of the Alliance of American Insurers, stated that 'terrorism is an uninsurable act'.[4] The claim that society cannot insure individuals and businesses against a particular threat constitutes a very serious problem. To state that a threat is uninsurable is to acknowledge that society can do little to protect its citizens. The disintegration of insurance – an institution of risk sharing – would send out the signal that everyone is on their own and left exposed by the inability of society to manage the threat they face.

To claim that a phenomenon is uninsurable is to say that it is beyond human management or control. The idea that society is incapable of managing certain risks through insurance signals a powerful mood of defeatism towards the dangers ahead. It elevates terrorism into an existential threat; one where human survival is constantly at stake. An inflated consciousness of the dangers that lie ahead encourage an apocalyptic style of engagement with the future. It is worth noting that human survival is fast becoming an overused category and terrorism is only one danger among the many that are said to threaten existence. 'Life on Earth is at the ever-increasing risk of being wiped out by a disaster, such as sudden global warming, nuclear war, a genetically engineered virus or other dangers we have not yet thought of' notes the famous scientist Stephen Hawking.[5]

A catastrophic vision of the future is not confined to the threat of terrorism. It is frequently recycled in relation to global warming, the Aids epidemic, obesity and avian flu, to name just a few of the publicized perils facing human civilization. As one astute commentator noted, 'It is striking how such visions are being generated by the elites on the right and left' of the political divide.[6] The assertion that there 'has been a progressive increase' in new crises and threats enjoys the status of a self-evident fact.

In line with an inflated sense of disaster consciousness, there is also a manifest tendency towards expanding the range of events that can be characterized as a disaster. 'These days, disasters may result in modest levels of harm, and perhaps relatively straightforward tasks for the emergency services and yet still they are called "disasters",' notes Tom

Horlick-Jones.[7] In line with contemporary crisis consciousness, often the line between misfortune, accidents, adversity and disaster have become blurred. According to the philosopher Marcio Seligmann-Silva, the definition of catastrophe has altered. Instead of representing it as an 'unusual, unique, unexpected event', it is increasingly seen as an everyday event.[8] Such assertions are often accompanied by the suggestion that the threat posed by disasters has qualitatively changed. 'In every domain there seems to be a deep schism with the past types of crisis, be it in the field of environment, global climate, public health, technological risks, social dynamics, international relations, or violence,' argues a French contributor on crisis management.[9] These new threats are interpreted as more than just dangerous – they possess considerable potential for the realization of acts of apocalyptic dimensions.[10]

In academic and official publications, as well as in popular culture, the world is constantly presented and frequently perceived as a significantly more dangerous place than it was back in the twentieth or nineteenth centuries – and not just because of catastrophic terrorism. Of course, throughout modern times there have been professional soothsayers who constantly warned that the world had become a far more dangerous place than in previous times. However, today such warnings are not only more frequent: they have succeeded in overwhelming modern society's optimistic belief in the capacity of human beings to contain future dangers. Terrorism is only one of an innumerable number of threats whose effect is described as incalculable and unimaginable. Crisis managers are encouraged to expect 'radical surprises, potential global domino effects, real time dynamics, and the destruction of ultimate references'. Apparently, new threats are depicted as 'increasingly serious, with qualitative jumps in severity, speed, frequency, complexity'.[11] Some academic analysts believe that such worst-case scenarios are now 'normal' and that 'disasters are normal parts of life'.[12]

Catastrophic terrorism is only one variant of the numerous forms of catastrophe that haunt people's imaginations. Indeed, some disaster researchers regard the experience of 9/11 as a paradigmatic example of the many global threats. 'What happened on 9/11 is certainly the most spectacular, but certainly not the only incident, which projected the world into a new and profoundly unstable orbit as far as crises are concerned,' argues one analyst.[13] These days terrorism serves as a benchmark from which other threats are evaluated. It was in this vein that the scientist Stephen Hawking described climate change as a greater threat to the planet than terrorism.[14] Bill McGuire of University College London's Hazard Research Centre concurs he believes that climate change compares to terrorism in the way a 'huge festering sore compares to a pimple'.[15]

However, the dread of terrorism possesses one distinct dimension. Unlike other dangers, the threat posed by terrorism is intentional. Most catastrophes are the unintended consequences of natural or technological process. Not terrorism. It regards the fear of catastrophe as a realization of its ambition.

A catastrophic sensibility towards terrorism is continually reinforced by a powerful trend towards the institutionalization of threat amplification. Frequently the dangers we face are framed in sensationalist and epochal terms. Terrorism holds no monopoly over the public's sense of dread. That is why it is now common to hear that the threat of terrorism is less worrying than other far more menacing dangers that lie ahead. A report, *Global Risks 2006*, published by the World Economic Forum, indicated that bird flu was the global threat that most concerns business leaders. It claimed that the deadly H5N1 bird flu virus could 'disrupt our global society and economy in an unprecedented way'.[16] In the same vein a report discussed by the UK Cabinet Office rated avian flu as among the greatest threats facing the country and as much of a danger to Britain as terrorism.[17]

Twenty-first-century Western society feels ambivalent about its impressive technological achievement. While it continually looks to new technology to solve the many problems it faces, it also possesses a sense of foreboding towards its achievements. A mood of suspicion and apprehension towards science and technology is constantly conveyed through popular culture, and particularly through the environmental movements. Pessimism about the accomplishment of modernity and science has a direct bearing on how the threat of terrorism is perceived. Many believe that the destructive power of technology intensifies the threat of terrorism. As noted previously, many influential commentators insist that modern science and technology not only fail to make the world safe, they also provide terrorists with access to new powers of destruction. Numerous social scientists are sceptical about the promise of modern science and claim that we are back to where we started in the Dark Ages: 'to the horrors of incalculable, unpredictable evil, striking at random'.[18] According to Zygmunt Bauman, one of Europe's leading sociological thinkers, the threats we face call into question the survival of the human race.

What threatens a planet now is not just another round of self-inflicted damage ... and not another of the long string of catastrophes ... but a catastrophe to end all catastrophes, a catastrophe that would leave no human being behind to record it, ponder it and derive a lesson from it, let alone learn and apply that lesson.[19]

From this perspective it is evident that we do not merely live in an age of terrorism, but in an era that faces unprecedented catastrophic threats.

At first sight it is far from evident why contemporary threats are so easily converted into catastrophic risks which are endowed with such epochal significance. The discussion surrounding the potential destructive consequence of a bird-flu epidemic soon sounds like a script for a low-budget disaster movie. 'It is like a combination of global warming and HIV/Aids', noted a UN health official, before predicting that up to 150 million people could be killed by a bird-flu pandemic.[20] Such alarmist claims contradict what we know about our successful attempt to contain the recent outbreaks of Ebola, SARS and West Nile virus. But, in an important sense, what we know matters little. Why? Because increasingly the dangers that lie ahead – terrorism, global warming, a viral epidemic – are interpreted and experienced as threats that are far worse than we suspect. They are also portrayed as threats about which in reality we know very little and about which we are not in a position to know very much.

Far from living in an optimistic age of triumphalism, twenty-first-century society possesses an unusually modest account of its intellectual capacity and potential. Despite impressive scientific achievements, contemporary culture appears sceptical about society's ability to know very much about the future. In fact we appear to think that we know less about the future than during the past century. Western culture has lost some of its confidence in the capacity of science and knowledge to anticipate future problems. Doubt about society's capacity to engage with future problems encourages a mood of apprehension towards the world that lies ahead.

The expanding empire of the unknown

The dominant models of threat assessment insist that contemporary risks are qualitatively more dangerous than previous ones because we don't know very much about them. There is a growing body of opinion among academic risk experts and risk managers that suggests that what we have to worry about is not simply a future that is unknown, but one that is unknowable. Throughout history, societies have tended to be apprehensive about uncertainty and feared the unknown. But the way that communities respond to uncertainty fluctuates in line with how much at ease a society is with itself and how confident it feels about its future. Historically the consciousness of uncertainty expresses the realization that it is not possible to know what will happen in the future. Although experience and knowledge provide insights about likely developments and outcomes, the future always contains an element of the unknown.

How people respond to the unknown is subject to historical and cultural variations. There are times when people's response to the unknown is one of excitement, curiosity, inquisitiveness or eager anticipation. These are moments in time when people adopt a robust and optimistic sensibility towards the unknown. European sailors setting out to discover an unknown world and enthusiastic space travellers in the 1960s embraced the challenge of turning the unknown into the knowable. From this standpoint uncertainty served as a stimulus to the positive act of discovery. At other times communities respond with anxiety to uncertainty and regard the unknown as merely a threat to avoid rather than as an opportunity for discovery. In these circumstances, fear and dread express the dominant mood towards uncertainty. Today this response to the unknown has acquired an unprecedented significance.

One of the defining features of our times is that anxiety about the unknown appears to have greater significance than the fear of known threats. Often politicians and campaigners darkly hint about the grave challenge posed by threats that are perilous precisely because they are unknown. These are threats to which as yet we can give no name and whose trajectory cannot be calculated. Bauman gives voice to this vision of unnamed threats when he states that 'by far the most awesome and fearsome dangers are precisely those that are *impossible* or excruciatingly *difficult* to anticipate, the *un*predicted, and in all likelihood *unpredictable* ones'.[21]

Bauman's analysis is closely based on the work of the German sociologist Ulrich Beck, who argues that technological development has created a world where society simply cannot understand the destructive consequences of human intervention. Beck stated that 'through our past decisions about atomic energy and our present decisions about the use of genetic technology, human genetics, nanotechnology and computer science, we unleash unforeseeable, uncontrollable, indeed even *incommunicable* consequences that threaten life on earth'.[22] The formulation 'incommunicable consequences' is used to highlight the claim that humanity lacks the intellectual resources with which to interpret future trends. Consequently empirical evidence or analysis can provide little assistance in this quest, since contemporary experience has little to say about an imagined or radically different future.

Time and again the public is informed that the most dreadful dangers are not just ones that we can not predict or anticipate, but ones about which we cannot say anything because they are literally unknown. Security analysts and military planners often refer to such threats as 'unknown unknowns'. It was the former Defense Secretary Donald Rumsfeld who brought the concept 'unknown unknowns' to the attention of a wider public. At a press briefing in February 2002 he astounded those in his audience when he stated:

> *Reports that say that something hasn't happened are always interesting to me, because as we know, there are known knowns; there are things we know we know. We also know there are known unknowns; that is to say we know there are some things we do not know. But there are also unknown unknowns — the ones we don't know we don't know.*[23]

At the time many commentators responded with a mixture of incredulity and hilarity to what they interpreted as Rumsfeld's convoluted attempt to avoid accounting for the absence of information or evidence regarding Iraq's alleged weapons of mass destruction programme. Others treated it as yet another example of dishonest double-speak. However Rumsfeld's comments convey an orientation towards the problems of the future that is widely shared by political and cultural elites on both sides of the Atlantic.

As far as Rumsfeld is concerned, the problems of the future fall into three categories: first they are ones that we know and understand (known knowns), second they are ones that we know that we don't know nor understand (known unknowns) and third they are ones that we don't even know that we don't know and understand. These are the unknown unknowns. The burden of Rumsfeld's argument is that in the war against terrorism it is the unknown unknowns that constitute the greatest threat. From this standpoint the problem is not simply the absence of intelligence about a specific terrorist threat. It is a more fundamental quandary of not even possessing the capacity to know what the intelligence that is lacking should be about. The very frequency with which Rumsfeld and his colleagues use the prefix *un-* is testimony not only to a lack of facts, but of meaning. A palpable sense of disorientation is transmitted by Rumsfeld when he states that 'our challenge in this new century is a difficult one: to defend our nation against the unknown, the uncertain, the unseen, and the unexpected'.[24] Rumsfeld's three-fold categorization of risks also informs the work of the Office of Homeland Security. One of its risk managers defines unknown unknowns as 'risks of which there is no awareness at the present time of their existence and effect'. Apparently one can do little to anticipate these risks other than put a 10 per cent contingency aside 'without knowing exactly where this reserve will be applied'.[25]

An examination of official deliberations on the subject of terrorism indicates that the unknown has taken on a life of its own. The term does not simply mean strange, unfamiliar or unidentified. It signifies a state or a condition. Indeed it is treated as a distinct sphere of existence, a kind of parallel world that can not be grasped through the workings of the human mind. Take the UK's *Intelligence and Security Committee Report into the London Terrorist Attacks on 7 July 2005*, for example. One of this report's sections is actually titled 'Reassessing "the Unknown"'. For the authors of this report, the unknown does not refer simply to the dearth of intelligence about a specific group or threat. The unknown has been transformed into a world for which we have no mental map. At several points the authors of the report are lost for words as they attempt to conceptualize the unknown. They note that the July 2005 bombings had 'sharpened the perception of how big "the unknown"' was, since the government knew next to nothing about home-grown terrorism. They go on to acknowledge that the July attacks emphasized 'how much was unknown by the police and the Security Service about ideologically motivated extremist activity at the local level'.[26] What the report's threat assessment could not accomplish was to provide a strategy for dealing with a problem that is unknowable. All that it could offer was to exhort the intelligence services to embark on a journey into the unknown. It reported with approval that 'the Director-General of the Security Service told the Committee that the main lesson learned from the July attacks was the need to get into "the unknowns" – to find ways of broadening coverage to pick up currently unknown terrorist activity or plots'.[27]

Increasingly the unknown has ceased to serve merely as a rhetorical idiom connoting uncertainty. It is imagined as a place that people are exhorted to 'get into'. This is dangerous, unmapped territory containing threats of which people are unaware until they strike. Although it is only in recent times that unknown unknowns have become a subject of public attention, concern about this type of threat has been growing for some time. In one sense history was unfair to Rumsfeld when he became the target of widespread ridicule for his remarks about unknown unknowns. What many observers overlooked was that this manner of interpreting uncertainty about danger had become well established in the previous two decades.

An examination of the online newspaper database *LexisNexis* indicates that by the late 1970s the idiom 'unknown unknowns' was widely used by professionals in engineering and the aerospace industries. It was also reported that the US military sometimes referred to technological problems that were overlooked as 'unk-unks'; that is, unknown unknowns.[28] The term was used to highlight concerns about unknown technical influences creating uncertainty in the missile race with the Soviet Union.[29] In 1981, *The Washington Post* reported that 'sceptics predict that Stealth would not be ready until well into the 1990s, given all the technical "unk-unks" – the term for unknown unknowns'. [30] In 1982 it was reported that the airline industry takes 'unk-unks' very seriously and a year later it was observed that this industry 'says you can plan for the unknowns, but the unk-unks – the unknown unknowns – will sabotage you every time'.[31]

One commentator drew attention to a 'new language of space defense' that relies on the vocabulary of science fiction and from books and movies that 'depict imaginary space battles and often describe "unk-unks" – the "unknown unknowns" that no one can predict but seem likely to occur'.[32] Evidently the usage of the term was no longer confined to deliberations about uncertainty surrounding the workings of technological process. By the mid-1980s, the term had become a metaphor that signified uncertainty and risk in a variety of settings. *The Harvard Business Review* used the term in association with the risks facing high-tech companies.[33] Business leaders used the term to underline the difficulty of financial forecasting.[34] And managers were advised to 'have a feel for the "unknown unknowns"'.[35] With the emergence of new technology and information technology in the 1990s, the idiom quickly attached itself to this industry. One Harvard professor was quoted to say that the unknown unknowns were 'the inevitable products of any technological revolution'.[36] NASA used the term to describe the uncertainties of space travel.[37] Sections of the US defence industry claimed that it is 'the need to discover and solve the "unknown unknowns" that distinguishes defense-oriented research from its commercially oriented cousin'.[38]

Rumsfeld was by no means the first public official to associate the uncertainties of military conflict with the problem of unknown unknowns. During the First Gulf War the idiom was often used by American officials. At the height of the Persian Gulf crisis, Michael Darby the Undersecretary of Commerce told a news conference that it was difficult to come up with sound economic scenarios since 'there are always unknown unknowns'. The difficulty of knowing Saddam Hussein's nuclear capability was the unknown unknown preoccupying the intelligence community according to Frank Gaffney, a former Pentagon official.[39] A few years later, William Cohen, Secretary of Defense in the Clinton Administration raised the hope that 'it may be that forensic science has reached a point where there will be no other unknown-unknowns in any war'.[40]

The gradual expansion of the cultural significance attached to the idiom received a powerful boost through the writings of the US environmentalist Norman Myers. In a series of articles between 1992 and 1995 Myers sought to represent the 'horror that might lie ahead' through warning that the world was facing environmental problems that were as yet unknown. 'So what new unknown unknowns are waiting to leap out?' asked Myers, as he ominously hinted of catastrophes to come.[41] This representation of the unimaginable as a predator ready to ambush unsuspecting victims succeeded in infusing uncertainty with a powerful sense of catastrophism. As he reels off a long list of future dangers it is evident that Myers's use of the idiom is entirely rhetorical, for in reality he knows the problems that he wants the public to do something about.

The appropriation of the idiom 'unknown unknowns' by the environmentalist movement helped transform a term connoting technological insecurity into an apocalyptic invitation to feel alarmed. Therefore it is not surprising that the term comes into its own during the anxiety-ridden deliberation about the impending doom brought by the millennium bug. Industry experts, public officials and politicians perceived the Y2K bug as the very embodiment of unknown unknowns. They regarded the 'unknown unknowns out there' with dread, and frequently used the term to highlight the apocalyptic dimension of humanity's transition to the twenty-first century. 'The full impact of the year 2000 has always been and is now wrapped up in the domain of unknown unknowns,' claimed a leading computer scientist.[42]

According to this perspective, the problem was not simply an outcome of the absence of intelligence or of knowledge. It was represented as a by-product of routine human behaviour. 'There is an understanding that of the unknown unknowns, public behaviors are perhaps among the highest risk category.'[43]

By the time that Rumsfeld popularized the notion of unknown unknowns, the sensibility that risks are increasingly incalculable and difficult to anticipate had gained widespread currency. The cultural imagination that feared unknown unknowns jumping out at the unsuspecting represented an acknowledgement of the failure of the human imagination to anticipate problems. Just as 'designers can't imagine problems that appear when the aircraft enters service', so the 'unknown unknowns of global warming are mind-boggling'.[44] For Rumsfeld the failure to know what challenges confronted his nation accounted for the US military's poor intelligence on the enemy. For others the incalculability of the risks confronting society compels them to fear worst-case scenarios. The shift of emphasis from what we can know to what we cannot encourages the public to expect the worst. The signals transmitted through this orientation to the problems we face constitute an acknowledgement of the fact that we lack the resources to make sense of the future. They also represent an invitation to be terrorized.

The insistence on the salience of the unknown unknown is symptomatic of a trend where a growing range of experiences are deemed to be beyond knowledge. This perspective reverses that attitude towards the power of knowledge that characterized modernist thinking. Since the rise of modernity, the unknown was conceptualized as a gradually diminishing territory. Modernist thinkers believed that the expansion of knowledge would gradually illuminate the many aspects of life that were at the time beyond comprehension. In recent times this orientation has been reversed and the territory of the unknown has expanded. Not knowing – particularly the consequences of human behaviour for the future – has helped foster a mood of defensiveness towards what lies ahead. So whereas throughout most of modernity the known expands into the domain of the unknown, today this pattern has been reversed. At a time of unprecedented expansion of scientific knowledge – the mapping of the human gene, advances in biotechnology and nano-technology – the perception of an expanding empire of the unknown appears perverse. As we note in the next chapter it suggests that the mood of confusion reveals the absence not of knowledge, but of meaning.

Critics of Rumsfeld's verbal gymnastics overlook the fact that the problematization of unknown unknowns resonates with our time, and that a similar approach has been widely pursued by fear entrepreneurs in a variety of settings. Numerous environmentalist advocacy organizations adopt the tactic of warning people about invisible and boundless threats to the environment whose consequences are irreversible and unknown. And people's anxiety about the unknown future is often celebrated and politicized as the responsible way to engage with uncertainty. One British academic and former chair of Greenpeace UK concerned with this problem, Robin Grove-White, claims to be frustrated that 'unknown unknowns are not acknowledged since unanticipated consequences lie at the core of current public unease'.[45] Acknowledging unanticipated consequences sounds like an exercise in responsible behaviour. But what does it mean to acknowledge what you can't anticipate? It either has an entirely ritualistic or rhetorical character, or represents an exercise in accommodating to ignorance. Neither of these responses constitutes responsible behaviour. In contrast, responsible risk managers proceed by developing their grasp of human experience in order to make knowable the different dimensions of the unknown.

The framing of unanticipated consequences through the prism of unknowns lends risk a peculiarly intimidating character. A similar approach was adopted by IT consultants who were hyping up the threat facing the world in the new millennium. 'When dealing with the year 2000 and its consequences, whether in our personal or business lives, we must be prepared to deal with the whole spectrum, from the known knowns to the unknown unknowns,' wrote one of them.[46]

The objectification of the unknown creates a new species of threat that enhances the danger of terrorism. Security experts frequently contend that it is this dimension of the threat that society should really worry about. 'The greatest threat is from Al-Qaeda cells in the US that we have not yet identified,' argued Robert Mueller, Director of the FBI. Without a hint of irony he could also state that 'I remain very concerned about what we are not seeing'.[47] Of course what we are not seeing invites us to exercise our imaginations, and increasingly the imagination of the expert plays an important role in the construction of a species of unknown, but for all that very real threats. As Lipschutz stated:

The production of truths and narratives of fear are ... based not only on what is known but also on what is not; what is knowable and what cannot be known. These truths and narratives emerge from the relative ease of extrapolation and extension, by so-called experts who 'know' of such things, from incidents that have taken place and those that, as yet, can only be imagined.[48]

A narrative of fear based on the unknown authorizes the act of speculation and imagination as a legitimate form of threat assessment. The admission of ignorance about threats to a nation's security no longer discredits officials and their experts. Instead it serves to underline the seriousness of the threat. The acknowledgement that 'we don't know' communicates the signal that there is something very dangerous going on. As Lipschutz observes, 'paradoxically, confessions of ignorance can also reinforce narratives of fear'.[49]

In current fear narratives ignorance is represented not so much as a problem, but as a marker of the gravity of a threat. From the perspective of some environmentalists the greater the scope of a problem the more likely we are to be ignorant about it:

It should be kept in mind that there also will be what have been called 'unknown unknowns'. These allude to cases where we are not even able to state the questions as we are unable to picture the possible effects. Examples of such cases cannot be supplied for the very good reason that we really do not know.[50]

An inability to know what question to ask and ignorance about what is likely to occur is not dismissed as the irrelevant rambling of an alarmist mind. On the contrary, it is embraced as a realistic and honest assessment of the insignificance of people's capacity to understand. This approach is praised by a report commissioned by the Environmental Agency of the EU:

No matter how sophisticated knowledge is, it will always be subject to some degree of ignorance. To be alert – and humble about – the potential gaps in those bodies of knowledge that are included in our decision making is fundamental.[51]

No doubt ignorance is part of the human condition. However, it is only in recent times that ignorance is treated as a stable fact of life. In the very act of diminishing people's potential to know, the danger of the unknown threat becomes inflated.

A new kind of threat

The normalization of the idea that the threats we face are qualitatively different to those of the past, and that we do not know very much about them, is paralleled by a fundamental re-conceptualization of the traditional meaning of risk. Throughout modern times risk has been interpreted through the language of probability. From this perspective the outcomes associated with risks are expressed as probabilities. Consequently, the term 'risk' refers to the probability of damage, injury, illness, death or other misfortune associated with a hazard. Risk management involves the calculation of probabilities. However, if all the facts about a threat are unknown it becomes impossible to calculate the probabilities of a certain outcome. And the growing belief that society lacks knowledge about the unknown serves to undermine the premise of risk management.

Imperfect knowledge of the outcomes of future threats is not a distinctive feature of contemporary times. Since its conception, risk analysis had to engage with uncertainty. However, what has changed is that the current sense of apprehension about uncertainty has called into question the use of probability theory to make sense of risks. According to a report published by the European Environmental Agency; 'under the conditions of **uncertainty**, as formally defined, the adequate empirical or theoretical basis for assigning probabilities to outcomes does not exist'. It therefore concludes that 'conventional risk assessment is too narrow in scope to be adequate for application under conditions of uncertainty'.[52] Since by all accounts uncertainty is a constant fact of life, from this perspective it logically follows that the analysis of probabilities has only a minimal relevance. Accordingly the traditional idea of risk is displaced by Rumsfeld's unknown unknowns or by the European Environmental Agency's concept of ignorance. The latter argues:

> Once it is acknowledged that the likelihood of certain outcomes may not be fully quantifiable, or where certain other possibilities may remain entirely unaddressed, then uncertainty and ignorance, rather than mere risk characterises the situation.[53]

From this perspective, certainty is only rhetorically distinguished from ignorance. The conflation of these two concepts serves to weaken the case for calculating risks. This inflation in the status of ignorance contributes to a dramatic redefinition of the relationship between present knowledge and the future. Yet not knowing is not the same as ignorance.

And, as the experience of modern times demonstrates, imperfect knowledge can represent the point of departure for exploring the probabilities and impact of a hitherto unknown hazard.

The recent tendency to disparage probability based risk analysis is particularly striking in relation to so-called catastrophic risks. For example, it seems that 'terrorism is to some extent a "risk beyond risk", of which we do not have, nor cannot have, the knowledge or the measure'.[54] The unknown unknowns of terrorism are linked to a wider mood of uncertainty about the unpredictable and unanticipated workings of the world. The term 'uncertainty' does not fully capture the problems thrown up by new types of threats. Uncertainty no longer means a temporary prelude to certainty. It does not mean a deficiency of '*knowledge within known and specifiable parameters*'. What it points to are the 'more chronic conditions of inevitable *ignorance* and *lack of capacity to imagine* future eventualities'.[55] Beck claims that humanity has entered a 'world of *uncontrollable risk*'; one where 'we don't even have a language to describe what we are facing'.[56] This idea of uncontrollable risk has nothing to do with the traditional notion of risk, which is focused on the probability and not the inevitability of adverse outcomes. Beck recognizes that the idea of uncontrollable risk contradicts the classical meaning of risk, but nevertheless embraces the idea that developments have created a situation where risk calculation is contradicted by the reality of 'non-quantifiable insecurity'.[57]

The claim that non-quantifiable insecurity dominates the human condition calls into question classical notions of risk management. Such threats are likely to overwhelm most communities because their impact can only be represented in science-fiction terms. By definition, uncontrollable risks cannot be managed since they are beyond human control. And if terrorism is indeed such a unique threat, then it is difficult to understand how its destructive impact can be neutralized. Catastrophic risks that are said to have effects that are incalculable are in effect rendered apocalyptic through the claim that their consequences are **irreversible**. That's what Bauman means when he writes of a 'catastrophe to end all catastrophes'. Such a scenario draws attention to a species of risk that bears unanticipated and unknown consequences and which therefore cannot be managed. It points to a process of destruction whose malevolent consequences are irreversible. This view of unanticipated risks is not confined to a handful of exceptional threats. Increasingly the very idea of risk is associated with 'unknown, unintended and dangerous outcomes'. Such an interpretation of events has been fuelled by anxieties about the impact of technological and scientific innovation on the environment. Moreover, it is frequently claimed that irreversible damage is routinely inflicted on the environment:

> This question of unanticipated consequences, encapsulated in the notion of possible 'unknown unknowns' which will reveal themselves at some later stage of irreversible process, is familiar in principle to most of us – not simply from the BSE/CJD saga, but also from a succession of earlier environmental issues such as DDT, CFCs and the ozone layer, nuclear power and low-level radiation, and fossil fuels and climate change.[58]

This interpretation associates unknown unknowns with outcomes that cannot be remedied or repaired. They are not only destructive, but the damage they cause is irreversible. From this perspective the normal hazards of technological progress are rendered even more destructive through the action of terrorists.

It seems that every hazard can become a terrorist weapon that can cause mass destruction. Beck claims that the 'terrorist dangers we face expand exponentially with technical progress'. He adds that 'with the technologies of the future – gene technology, nanotechnology and robotics – we are opening a new Pandora's Box'.[59] These dystopian projections of technological development are acutely sensitive to its potential negative unintended consequences. They are even more concerned about the destructive outcomes of the deliberate harnessing of new technology to an act of terrorism.

Risks whose impact is unknown and incalculable, and whose effect is irreversible, are strictly speaking not risks, but hazards. Since the probability of such threats cannot be calculated, it is inaccurate to refer to such phenomena as risks. The management of risk allows for the calculation of the probability outcomes. However, in a world which is apparently afflicted by unknown catastrophic dangers the concept of risk can have little relevance. Bauman claims that 'what makes our world vulnerable are principally the dangers of *non-calculable* probability, a thoroughly different phenomenon from those to which the concept of "risk" commonly refers'.[60] The kind of risks that are said to be beyond calculation should be characterized as **speculative risks**. Speculative risks are not the same as theoretical risks. Faced with uncertainty, theoretical risks are oriented towards exploring the probabilities and impact of a hitherto unknown hazard. Speculation is not so much the theoretical exploration of the unknown, but an exercise of the imagination. Of course many of the risks faced by twenty-first-century society are difficult to evaluate with precision because of a lack of previous experience with them. But in the end it is relying on the rigorous evaluation of experience rather than on the realm of fantasy that will yield insights about future risks.

Speculation encourages the tendency towards perceiving uncertainty with apprehension. That is why, rather than an exception, many experts insist that incalculability is a distinct feature of the way that contemporary threats present themselves. Indeed, advocates of this new idea of uncontrollable risk believe that not knowing and not being able to calculate are now the norm. According to the sociologist, Brian Wynne:

> The latter half of the 20th century saw a succession of man-made technological disasters – Challenger, Bhopal, Chernobyl, BSE, World Trade Center being the tip of the iceberg – which branded into popular awareness an uncomfortable reality that, for all the formidable powers and benefits of modern science and technology, lack of full control is normal, including lack of intellectual control, that is, unpredictable consequences.[61]

The tendency to normalize the state of not knowing and of not being able to know represents an important statement about the status of science and knowledge. It suggests that science can provide little insight when confronted with a new species of catastrophe. Although sometimes referred to as a new paradigm of risks, these incalculable threats are not risks. From the vantage point of this paradigm, the probable occurrence and consequences of these events cannot be calculated. It is worth noting that, before this species of threat was identified with terrorism, it was already part of the discourse of environmentalism.[62]

The thesis of the new risks of unknown unknowns and the proposition that human knowledge lacks the capacity to understand global threats were initially developed through environmentalist thinking. 'The environment was the first area where catastrophic events were possible and not scientifically provable,' argue Aradau and van Munster.[63] However, it is through the rethinking of the risk of terrorism that this devaluation of the status of science and knowledge has acquired a truly frightening dimension. The very lack of understanding of the workings of the threat of terrorism amplifies its dangers. The absence of foresight and knowledge of 9/11 is now portrayed as a damning statement about the limits of science:

> The events of September 11th illustrate some of the shortcomings in our knowledge about the world we live in. Despite some of the most sophisticated models, monitoring systems, and science in the world, we were unable to effectively anticipate and predict the series of cascading impacts rendered by the attacks, nor were we able to completely understand and articulate the root causes of such actions.[64]

In accounts such as this, the project of constantly downsizing the status of knowledge is pursued with the zeal of a crusader. The diminished role assigned to science and knowledge legitimates the sense of fatalism and powerlessness projected by the author on the canvas of the future.

The emergence of dangers that are beyond knowledge transforms them into a new kind of threat. According to a new consensus that encompasses officials, policy-makers, security analysts and academic risk experts, these new threats are rooted in the workings of a new global environment or world risk society.[65] It is this perception of an unbounded and unimaginable new type of threat that provides the cultural underpinning of the thesis of new terrorism. The super-terrorist is the personification of the existential threats that haunt humanity. As Mythen and Walklate argue, 'it is evident that the global dimensions of the risk-society perspective dovetail neatly with current conceptualizations of new forms of terrorism'.[66]

Those who contend that we live in the era of the unknown unknowns regard threats like environmental degradation or terrorism as qualitatively different to the problems they presented in the past. The conceptual leap from the unknown unknowns to the new terrorist is a simple operation. Beck, the foremost proponent of the world risk society thesis, states that the 'concept "terrorist" is in the end also misleading with respect to the novelty of the threat it represents, since it pretends a familiarity with the motives of national liberation movements that does not at all hold true for the perpetrators of suicide and mass murder attacks'.[67] From this perspective, the 'novelty of the threat' is closely linked to a lack of familiarity with the motives of the 'new' terrorist. Absence of familiarity with a new species of (self-) destructive terrorist is but a variant of a widely experienced intellectual distance from the many other dangers that threaten the world. The intense sense of powerlessness which accompanies the consciousness of ignorance about the future works to empower terrorism.

The consolidation of 'what-if' thinking

The unprecedented sensitivity of Western society to unknown dangers is strikingly reflected in a radically new orientation towards how risks are perceived and managed. The traditional association of risk with probabilities is now under fire from a growing body of opinion that believes that humanity lacks the knowledge to calculate them. Numerous critics of **probabilistic thinking** call for a radical break with past practices on the grounds that we simply lack the information to calculate probabilities. Environmentalists have been in the forefront of constructing arguments that devalue probabilistic thinking. They claim that the long-term irreversible damage caused to the environment can not be calculated, and therefore a probability-based risk analysis is irrelevant. 'The term "risk" is very often confused with "probability", and hence used erroneously,' writes an opponent of genetic modification.[68] Of course, once risk is detached from probability, it ceases to be risk. Such a phenomenon is no longer subject to calculation. Instead of risk assessment the use of intuition is called for.

The emergence of a speculative approach towards risk is paralleled by the growing influence of 'possibilistic' thinking. Possibilistic thinking invites speculation about what can possibly go wrong. In our culture of fear, frequently what can possibly go wrong is confused with what is likely to happen.

The shift towards possibilistic thinking is driven by a powerful sense of cultural pessimism about knowing, and an intense apprehension about the unknown. The cumulative outcome of this sensibility is the routinization of the expectation of worst possible outcomes. The principal question posed by possibilistic thinking, 'What can possibly go wrong?', continually invites the answer, 'Everything'. The connection between possibilistic and worst-case thinking is self-consciously promoted by the advocates of this approach. The American sociologist Lee Clarke acknowledges that 'worst-case thinking is *possibilistic* thinking' and that it is 'very different' from the 'modern approach to risk', which is 'based on probabilistic thinking'.[69] However, he believes that the kinds of danger confronting humanity today require us to expect the worst and demand a different attitude towards risk. He claims that:

> *Modern social organization and technologies bring other new opportunities to harm faraway people. Nuclear explosions, nuclear accidents, and global warming are examples. We are increasingly 'at risk' of global disasters, most if not all of which qualify as worst cases.*[70]

Warning us about 'how vulnerable we are to worst-case events', Clarke concludes that 'we ought to prepare for possible untoward events that are out of control and overwhelming'.[71]

Politicians and their officials have also integrated worst-case thinking into their response to terrorism and other types of catastrophic threat. Appeals to the authority of risk assessment still play an important role in policy making. However, the prevailing culture of fear dictates that probabilistic-led risk management constantly competes with and often gives way to possibilistic-driven worst-case policies. As an important study of Blair's policy on terrorism notes, he combines an appeal to risk assessment with worst-case thinking. David Runciman, the author of this study, observed that, in his response to the threat of terrorism, 'Blair relied on expert risk assessment and on his own intuitions'. Runciman added that Blair 'highlighted the importance of knowing the risk posed by global terrorism, all the while insisting that when it comes to global terrorism the risks are never fully knowable'.[72] In practice, the co-existence of these two forms of threat assessment tends to be resolved in favour of the possibilistic approach. The occasional demand for a restrained and low-key response to the risk of terrorism is overwhelmed by the alarmist narrative of worst-case scenarios.[73]

The swing from probabilistic to possibilistic thinking is closely linked to changing society-wide attitudes and perceptions of the future. Increasingly the future is perceived as predetermined and independent of present human activities. It is an unknown world of hidden terror. The amplification of threat and of fear is inextricably linked with possibilistic thinking. As Lipschutz argues, the 'paradox of unknowability' leading to 'worst-case analysis' reinforces the 'narratives of fear' of terrorism.[74] The future of the world appears to be a far darker and more frightening one when perceived through the prism of possibilities rather than probabilities. Probabilities can be calculated and managed, and adverse outcomes can be minimized.

In contrast, worst-case thinking sensitizes the imagination to just that – worst cases! Clarke acknowledges the contrast between these two ways of perceiving the future. He notes that 'if we imagine the future in terms of probabilities, then risks look safe', but 'if we imagine the future in terms of possibilities, however, horrendous scenarios appear'.[75] While it is simplistic and inaccurate to suggest that probability analysis works towards portraying the future as safe, it is definitely the case that worst-case thinking strives to highlight the worst. Possibilistic interpretation of problems works to normalize the expectation of worst possible outcomes and fosters a one-sided and fatalistic consciousness of the future. Why? Because it minimizes the potential for understanding a threat. Since understanding is a precondition for countering a problem, the declaration of ignorance intensifies a sense of impotence, which in turn augments the threat. That is why alarmist campaigns that warn of unbounded dangers tend to embrace possibilistic thinking. 'Consequential, possibilistic thinking has been commonplace among antinuclear activists and other environmentalists for years,' writes Clarke.[76] One could also add the counter-terrorism industry among its advocates.

Probabilistic thinking has become an anathema to fear entrepreneurs because it offers a problem-solving and positive orientation towards calculating and managing risks and securing safety. Those who regard uncertainty with apprehension, and dread experimentation and innovation, depict probabilistic thinking as irresponsible and dangerous. This rejection of probabilities is motivated by the belief that the dangers that we face are so overwhelming and catastrophic that we simply cannot wait until we have the information to calculate their destructive effects. From this standpoint the procedure of acting on the basis of the worst-case scenario makes more sense than waiting for the information necessary to weigh up probabilities. In any case, it is argued that since so many of the threats are unknown there is little information on which a realistic calculation of probabilities can be made. One of the many regrettable consequences of this procedure is that policies designed to deal with threats are increasingly based on feelings and intuition rather than on evidence or facts. For example, a discussion paper published by Greenpeace is sceptical about using probabilistic thinking. It argues that 'risk-based approaches simply equate "absence of evidence" of an impact with "evidence of absence" of that impact'. Yet they claim 'all too often the absence of evidence flows simply from the limits of available scientific evaluation techniques'.[77] According to critics of probabilistic thinking, the absence of evidence regarding human impact on the environment should not influence decision-making based on worst-case thinking.

The scepticism that some environmentalist thinkers express towards the authority of evidence is echoed by proponents of a pre-emptive strike against potential enemies. It is worth noting that, after his pronouncement on unknown unknowns, Rumsfeld responded to a question about whether he had any evidence about Iraq supplying weapons of mass destruction to terrorists by stating that 'the absence of evidence is not an evidence of absence'.[78] From the worst-case perspective, military action does not require authentication of evidence. For Rumsfeld, ignorance or not knowing can be a spur to action. And the very absence of evidence served as a valid clue of a hidden invisible military threat which justified military action.

Since possibilistic or 'what-if' thinking presents the future through the prism of worst-case scenarios, it creates a demand for immediate action. From this catastrophic perspective there is no time to wait for evidence. The unknown quality of the threat is itself proof of the danger ahead. That is why, instead of properly evaluated evidence, worst-case thinking is often the driver of anti-terrorist policy. The anticipation of catastrophic consequences continually demands that something should be done. As Durodié explained, 'act now, find the evidence later' is the imperative driving this form of thinking.[79] The logic of worst-case thinking is used by the US Government to justify its adoption of its pre-emptive security strategy. According to this doctrine, 'the greater the threat, the greater is the risk of inaction – and the more compelling the case for taking anticipatory action to defend ourselves, even if uncertainty remains as to the time and place of the enemy's attack'.[80] US officials frequently argue that they cannot wait until they have proof of some catastrophic threat, since by that time action would be too late. As President Bush argued, 'America must not ignore the threat gathering against us … we cannot wait for the final proof, the smoking gun that could come in the form of a mushroom cloud'.[81] And he added that 'we have every reason to assume the worst, and we have an urgent duty to prevent the worst from occurring'. Anticipating the worst rather than weighing up the risks also informed the approach of the Blair regime. 'This is not a time to err on the side of caution; nor time to weigh the risks to an infinite balance,' declared Blair.[82]

The security policies associated with possibilistic thinking have been accurately interpreted as the application of the precautionary principle to terrorism by a group of critical scholars.[83] Advocates of the possibilistic approach, such as Clarke, explicitly endorse the precautionary principle. He believes that 'we may find that the precautionary principle is most useful for urging policy-makers to try to think about unexpected interactions and unintended consequences'.[84] The precautionary principle, which Clarke characterizes as 'quintessentially worst-case thinking', claims action should be taken to protect the environment, even if there is no evidence of harm. The precautionary principle, which has been adopted by the EU, states that when confronted with uncertainty and possible destructive outcomes it is always better to err on the side of caution. As Stern and Wiener explain, 'The Precautionary Principle holds that uncertainty is no excuse for inaction against serious or irreversible risks' and the absence of evidence should not bar preventive action.[85] This perspective informed the approach of the European Environment Agency, when it insisted in January 2002 that 'forestalling disasters usually requires acting before there is strong proof of harm'.[86] The translation of this approach in the 'war against terrorism' is pre-emptive warfare, justified by Bush's claim that the US cannot hold back military action until there is 'the final proof'.

In their discussion of the legitimating role of the precautionary principle for justifying the war in Iraq, Stern and Wiener show the similarity of the language used by advocates of EU environmental regulation and American supporters of the war on terror. Bush's warning that if 'we wait for threats to materialize, we will have waited too long' echoes the EU's Environment Commissioner, Margot Wallstorm's statement that 'if you smell smoke, you don't wait until your house is burning down before you tackle the fire'.[87] In both cases the language of caution is used to minimize the status of evidence. The intuitive conclusion that that the threat is far too great to wait leads to the exhortation for immediate action.

The precautionary approach does not necessarily encourage cautious behaviour. In its search for worst-case scenarios it continually raises the stakes and fuels the demand for action. If, as in the case of terrorism, we fear the worst then swift action is called for. As Aradau and van Munster note, the precautionary principle 'priviliges a politics of speed based on the sovereign decision of dangerousness'.[88] In the domain of security policy it promotes a highly interventionist and pre-emptive approach.

Jessica Stern has characterized the interventionist imperative contained within the precautionary approach as that of 'action bias'. She argues that perversely the 'precautionary approach as applied to Iraq, has made the world more dangerous and more uncertain'.[89] The institutionalization of worst-case thinking through official policy is constantly defended on the grounds that the stakes are so high that something must be done. 'The greater the threat, the greater is the risk of inaction,' observes the US Government's *2002 National Security Strategy* assessment. It also notes that 'if we wait for threats to fully materialize, we will have waited too long'.[90] Outwardly this call for military action bears all the hallmarks of an aggressive militarist ethos. But a close examination of the doctrine indicates an intense sense of defensiveness and anxiety towards a threat of catastrophic dimensions.

The precautionary approach towards the danger of terrorism is justified on the grounds that it represents a threat to our existence. In light of such a grave threat, policy-makers feel entitled to abandon traditional forms of evidence-based policy making. As Runciman writes,

> *The trouble with the precautionary principle is that it purports to be a way of evaluating risk, yet it insists that some risks are simply not worth weighing in the balance. This could only make sense if it were true that some risks are entirely off the scale of our experience of danger.*[91]

However, if the threat of terrorism is perceived as being beyond society's capacity to manage it has come close to triumphing over its targets. One of the unfortunate consequences of the worst-case approach is that it inflates the power of terrorism. And once terrorism is depicted as a threat of such cosmic proportions, then every precautionary act becomes justifiable. As Stern argues, one disturbing consequence of this perspective has been 'the temptation to imagine that the threats we face are so extreme that ordinary moral norms and laws do not apply'.[92]

The philosophy of the fear entrepreneur

Possibilistic thinking succeeds in transmitting the philosophy of fear entrepreneurs in a coherent form. This coherence is not based on its internal logic, but on its success in capturing and expressing the dominant mood of cultural pessimism. In the name of directing the public's attention to its worst fears, it adopts a cavalier stance towards the authority of knowledge and of evidence. A philosophy which objectifies the idea that the absence of evidence is not an evidence of absence conveys the proposition that acting on the basis of an absence of evidence is as valid as evidence-based action. Indeed, this proposition provides the rationale for the sentiment that it is precisely the absence of evidence that constitutes the proof that precautionary action needs to be taken. This enthronement of ignorance has been described as 'you never knowism' by two critics of worst-case thinking. Friedman and Sapolsky explain that 'you never knowism earns its name from its insistence on planning around what we do not know rather than what we do'.[93]

The significance that precautionary anti-terrorism attaches to the empire of the unknown has the pernicious consequences of systematically devaluing the status of knowledge. It exhorts society to take what we don't know as seriously as what we do. Furthermore, by suggesting that many future threats are unknowable, it fundamentally calls into question people's capacity to reason and understand. Not knowing, or ignorance, becomes as much driver of policy as hard-earned evidence. What is unknown is not an obstacle to action. Apprehension about the unknown continually invites action that is oriented towards the worst case.

Worst-case thinking encourages society to adopt fear as of one of the dominant principles around which the public, its government and institutions should organize their lives. It institutionalizes insecurity and fosters a mood of confusion and powerlessness. Through popularizing the belief that worst cases are normal, it incites people to feel defenceless and vulnerable to a wide range of future threats. In all but name it constitutes an invitation to terror. The elevation of terrorism into an existential threat is one of the disturbing accomplishments of precautionary-driven policies. Once the threat of terrorism is perceived according to the possibilistic paradigm, real live terrorists do not have to do very much to achieve their objectives. Societies that are wedded to fantasizing about worst cases soon learn to live them.

Commentators often associate current military action and anti-terrorist policies with a narrow neo-conservative agenda promoted by Bush and a small circle of ideologues. However, what this analysis overlooks is that these policies draw on cultural resources that influence attitudes towards uncertainty and risk in general. Fear entrepreneurs promoting campaigns around public health issues, child safety or global warming are equally responsible for encouraging the expansion of the empire of the unknown. The devaluation of knowledge and the enthronement of ignorance are systematically conveyed through policy statements and popular culture. Speculation and worst-case thinking resonate with a cultural imagination that feels so uncomfortable engaging with uncertainty. Indeed the readiness with which today's elites are prepared to defer to the unknown is evidence of a pervasive sense of cultural pessimism. In such circumstances relatively minor acts of disruption can provoke society to feel terrorized.

Notes

1. Bernard Hengesbaugh, cited in *Insurance Day*, 6 November 2001.

2. Beck (2002) p. 42.

3. Cited in 'Lloyd's tells members climate change could destroy insurers', *Guardian*, 6 June 2006.

4. 'President's message on terrorism insurance on target; AAI urges Senate to act', *Insurance Journal*, 10 April 2002.

5. Cited in http://apnews.myway.com/article/20060613/D817ADB81.html, 13 June 2006.

6. Brad Allenby, 'Duelling Elites and their catastrophic visions', *GreenBiz.com*, www.greenbiz.com/news, accessed 10 January 2007.

7. Horlick-Jones (1995) p. 304.

8. Seligmann-Silva (2003) p. 143.

9. See Quarantelli, Lagadec and Boin (2006) p. 17; and Lagadec (2006) p. 490.

10. Aradau and van Munster (2006) p. 11.

11. Lagadec (2006).

12. Clarke (2006) p. 24.

13. Lagadec (2006) p. 492.

14. Cited in *The Times*, 16 January 2007.

15. McGuire is cited by Jonathan Freedland, 'There is now no doubt that global warming is a security threat to us all', *Guardian*, 18 April 2007.

16. Report cited in 'Study: Bird Flu bigger threat than terrorism', *Associated Press*, 26 January 2006.

17. 'Bird Flu Pandemic "As Grave A Threat As Terrorism"', *Independent*, 25 June 2005.

18. Bauman (2006) p. 63.

19. Ibid., p. 72.

20. Cited in Furedi (2006) p. ix.

21. Bauman (2006) p. 11.

22. Beck (2003) p. 257.

23. US Department Of Defense, Department of Defense News Briefing, 'Secretary Rumsfeld and Gen. Myers', www.defenselink.mil/transcripts/2002/t02122002_t212sdv2.html.

24. Remarks as prepared for Secretary of Defense Donald Rumsfeld, the National Defense University in Washington DC, Thursday 31 January 2002, www.defenselink.mil/speeches/2002/s20020131-secdef.html.

25. Jiang (2002) pp. 31 and 43.

26. HMSO (2006) pp. 30 and 36.

27. Ibid., pp. 35–6.

28. See 'Synthetic fuels; Think of a number', in *The Economist*, 30 June 1979.

29. See letter 'Imaginary problems of ICBM', *The New York Times*, 20 September 1981.

30. See George Wilson, 'US Faces Critical Weapons Decision', *The Washington Post*, 14 June 1981.

31. See Christopher Lehman-Haupt, 'Books of The Times', *The New York Times*, 28 July 1982; and 'Super tall Buildings', in *Engineering News-Record*, 3 November 1983.

32. '"Unk-Unks" and "Golden Arches": The New Lingo of Star Wars', *US News & World Report*, 9 December 1985.

33. See Fred McMahon, 'High Tech Teams Up', *Financial Post*, 18 January 1988.

34. Peter Coombes, 'Understanding The Asia-Pacific Market', *Chemical Week*, 24 April 1991.

35. Jean-Louis Barsoux, 'Why a manager must trust his instinct', *The Times*, 5 November 1992.

36. Katherine Fullerton, 'The Anxious Journey of a Technophobe', *Columbia Journalism Review*, November/December 1993.

37. Patrick Greenlaw, 'Funding for NASA Called to Question in Face of Failures', *Science & Technology Week*, 4 December 1993.

38. Jed Babbin, 'Real Defense Conversion Requires Tax Relief for R & D', *Aviation Week Forum*, 8 August 1994.

39. 'News Conference about the 4th Quarter GNP, with Michael Darby, Undersecretary of Commerce', *Federal News Service*, 25 January 1991 and *The MacNeil/LehrerNewsHour*, 28 June 1991, Transcript #4105.

40. 'Remains of Airman Michael Blassie will be buried this month in St Louis cemetery', *CBS This Morning*, 1 July 1998.

41. Norman Myers, 'Environmental alarms; unknown unknowns: ominous hints of catastrophe', *The Gazette*, 14 May 1994.

42. 'A Global View of the Year 2000 Crisis', *Federal News Service*, 13 October 1999.

43. Ibid.

44. Lee Ting Ting, 'Adapting to the unknowns of new markets', *New Straits Times*, 4 April 2001; and 'The Baltimore Sun Jay Hancock Column', *The Baltimore Sun*, 12 September 2005.

45. Grove-White (2001) p. 470.

46. 'Diary of a Y2K Consultant: Bracing for the Millennium', *Computer*, January 1999.

47. Cited in Mueller (2006a) p. 3.

48. Lipschutz (1999) p. 11.

49. Ibid., p. 17.

50. Meyer, G., Folker A. P., Jorgensen, R. B., Kyare von Krauss, M., Sandoe, P and Tveit, G. (2005) p. 237.

51. European Environment Agency (2002) 'Late Lessons From Early Warnings', p. 169, http://reports.eea. europa.eu/environmental_issue_report_2001_22/en

52. Ibid.

53. Ibid.

54. Aradau and van Munster (forthcoming) p. 11.

55. Grove-White (2001) p. 471.

56. Beck (2002) p. 39.

57. Ibid., p. 257.

58. Grove-White (2001) p. 470.

59. Beck (2003) p. 260.

60. Bauman (2006) p. 98.

61. Wynne (2002) p. 459.

62. Aradau and van Munster (forthcoming) p. 11.

63. Ibid., p. 11.

64. Cutter (2003) p. 1.

65. See for example Beck (2003).

66. Mythen and Walklate (2006) p. 386.

67. Beck (2003) p. 259.

68. Professor Terje Traavik, 'GMO risks and hazards: Absence of evidence is not evidence of absence of risk', Third World Network, www.twnside.org.sg/title/terje-cn.htm.

69. Clarke (2006) p. 5.

70. Ibid., p. 35.

71. Ibid., p. 35.

72. Runciman (2006) p. 11.

73. For an example of a call for restraint in policymaking, see Sir Ken MacDonald QC's speech, cited in 'DPP warning over "war on terror"', BBC News, 23 January 2007, http://news. bbc.co.uk/1/hi/uk/6292379.stm.

74. Lipschutz (1999) p. 17.

75. Clarke (2006) p. 42.

76. Ibid., p. 42.

77. Johnston and Santillo (2006) p. 2.

78. See 'Transcript: Defense Department Briefing', 12 February 2002, www.globalsecurity.org/military/library/news/2002/02/mil-020212-usia01.htm.

79. Bill Durodié, 'Life, liberty and politics after 9/11', www.spiked-online.com/index.php?/site/printable/1602.

80. *The National Security Strategy of the United States of America*, September 2002, p. 15.

81. 'President Bush Outlines Iraqi Threat', White House Press Release, 7 October 2002, www.whitehouse.gov/news/releases/2002/10/20021007-8.html.

82. Blair, cited in the *Guardian*, 5 March 2004.

83. See Stern (2004); Aradau and van Munster (2006); and Runciman (2006).

84. Clarke (2006) p. 181.

85. Stern and Wiener (2006) p. 2.

86. European Environment Agency (2002) 'Late Lessons From Early Warnings', http://reports.eea.europa.eu/environmental_issue_report_2001_22/en

87. Both are cited in Stern and Wiener (2006) p. 6.

88. Aradau and van Munster (2006) p. 15.

89. Stern (2004) p. 1117.

90. *The National Security Strategy of the United States of America*, September 2002.

91. Runciman (2006) p. 59.

92. Stern (2004) p. 1122.

93. Friedman and Sapolsky (2006) p. 4.

CHAPTER 4

A Threat Beyond Meaning

This is a chapter about meaning. It argues that the confused orientation towards the problem of terrorism – apparently poor intelligence, the claim that it is a problem beyond comprehension, the devaluation of the status of knowledge – are expressions of the problem that Western culture has in knowing what it stands for. Lack of clarity about what is the way of life it defends is matched by confusion about defining the nature of the enemy. As we have noted, the narrative of terrorism is opaque, confused and imprecise. The absence of consensus on the definition of terrorism is indicative of the incoherent story that is communicated to the public. Time and again officials inform us that we lack sound intelligence about this phenomenon. The public is advised that nevertheless this is a threat beyond our imaginations and that what we should really worry about are the threats that are not visible to the eye – the unknown unknowns. Frequently used allusions to the unknown, uncertain, unseen and unexpected highlight the fact that we lack a grammar of meaning through which it is possible to interpret this threat. It is essential to note that it is not the absence of facts or information or knowledge that accounts for the lack of clarity of the problem. Rather, what is at stake is the difficulty that Western societies have in interpreting the facts and giving them meaning.

As we noted previously, there is widespread confusion about who the enemy is, what motivates them and just how much of a threat they represent. Many Western leaders go so far as to claim that they represent a threat to the survival of the West. 'The object of terrorism is to try to force us to change our way of life, is to force us to retreat, is to force us to be what we're not,' stated Bush in October 2001.[1] Others insist that the threat of terrorism is all in the mind. A substantial group of critics claim that the threat of terrorism is a malevolent invention of a power-hungry cabal of American neo-conservatives. Sceptics like Michael Moore compound the confusion of officialdom by declaring that 'there is no terrorist threat'.[2]

Observers sometimes mistakenly ascribe the poverty of the intellectual resources available for accounting for the war as a consequence of personal failings of its authors. Other commentators believe that these difficulties are due to the emergence of a radically new and complex global environment, whose features cannot be captured through the language of the twentieth century. They have internalized the narrative of the unknown and the unimaginable and suppose that we simply lack a language with which to represent the incomprehensible character of the threat of global terrorism. The thesis that asserts that language lacks the capacity to make sense of the events of 9/11 is forcefully argued by Beck. According to his interpretation, 9/11 symbolizes the 'silence of language'. He believes that '11th September stands for the complete collapse of language' and that 'ever since that moment, we've been living and thinking and acting using concepts that are incapable of grasping what happened then'.[3] The premise of this interpretation of the collapse of language is that we lack the conceptual tools with which to grasp the new, unprecedented and complex dimensions of an elusive phenomenon. This interpretation also influenced the analysis of Sir David Omand, the former UK Security and Intelligence Coordinator. He takes the view that 'we even lack language with which to describe the essential features of the threat and its ideology'. His concern with language is compounded by the concern that the narrative of terrorism risks 'giving offence to Muslims around the world'. That is why he too feels obliged to opt for what he calls the British Government's preferred euphemism –'international terrorism'.[4]

If indeed we lack a language to interpret contemporary reality, it has consequences that go way beyond linguistic difficulties. Language is the most important source of symbolic meaning in everyday life. And if we are genuinely lost for words it has serious implications for our ability to interpret experience as a society.

However, the linkage between 9/11 and the collapse of language may be misplaced. Indeed, Osama bin Laden pointed to this problem back in March 1997, when he described what his opponents call terrorism as a 'message with no words':

> The hearts of Muslims are filled with hatred towards the United States of America and the American president has a heart that knows no words.

A heart that kills hundreds of children definitely, knows no words. Our people in the Arabian Peninsula will send him messages with no words because he does not know any words.[5]

Bin Laden's threat is made all the more menacing through a message that consciously cultivated incoherence and ambiguity. Through his statement he recognizes that for some time before 9/11 Western society has found it difficult to capture through concepts the realities of an apparently ever-changing and complex word.

The acknowledgement of verbal confusion on all sides and the absence of 'words' should not be interpreted as testimony to a problem that is primarily a rhetorical one. Language is entirely adequate for describing an event. It can provide a factual account of what happened but not its meaning. The fault lies not with language, but with the inability of the prevailing system of meaning to make sense of the conflict. This is shown through official reports of terrorist incidents which demonstrate an inability to interpret and understand the significance of episodes such as 9/11 or the 7/7 bombings in London. These reports provide an outline of chronology and facts but say very little about causes and meaning.[6] Debates about how to describe the war, make sense of the threat or give a name to an enemy are different expressions of the same underlying problem of meaning. At its worst the problem of meaning is experienced through the state of **meaninglessness** – 'a feeling of "confusion or vagueness about what one ought to believe or about the criterion for making important decisions"'.[7] In relation to most problems of everyday life people are far from experiencing such a state of meaninglessness. But on the really big questions – ultimate values, purpose of society, what the nation stands for – the criterion for making important decisions is far from clear. This point is implicitly recognized by some leading counter-terrorist experts. According to one such source, 'we are still at a relatively unsophisticated stage in our thinking of how to present internationally and domestically what will be a long campaign'.[8]

Problems of meaning

Frequently, 'unknown unknowns' are represented as the outcome of a failure of intelligence or lack of information about global threats. 'You can't analyze intelligence that you don't have – and our case studies resoundingly demonstrate how little we know about some of our highest priority intelligence targets,' concludes an official report into the intelligence capability of the US.[9] However, the problem of unknown unknowns should be seen not so much as a failure of intelligence as the absence of a capacity to interpret or make sense of the problems facing society. Western societies do not know less than they did before 9/11. But knowledge – past and present – cannot be used effectively without a framework of meaning. That is why Western elites appear to have lost faith in the existing stock of human knowledge to help interpret events and to throw light on the problems facing society. It was not a rhetorical question when President Bush asked 'Why do they hate us?' in his speech to the US Congress in September 2001. Although the question has been reiterated by thousands of people since 9/11, it is far from evident what is being asked.[10] Who are 'they'? As we noted, questions raised in the post-9/11 era, like 'Why do they hate us?' or 'What do they want?' or 'How can they be so evil?' betray a degree of cultural naivety but they also serve as testimony to the difficulty that people have in endowing contemporary events with clarity and purpose. As we shall see, not only does contemporary culture have difficulty making sense of who 'they' are, it also finds it troublesome to give a clear account of who 'we' are. From the standpoint of the traditional vocabulary of public life, many events today do not readily make sense.

The doubts raised regarding the status of knowledge about threats in general and terrorism in particular continually highlight Western society's uneasy relationship with uncertainty and the future. The apparent failure of language to make sense of global threats, the succession of intelligence fiascos and the embrace of the fatalistic perspective of unknown unknowns are all symptoms of a crisis of meaning afflicting Western societies. Events like the destruction of the World Trade Center force society to account for the incomprehensible. Such a catastrophe demands an explanation of what happened, who is to blame and how people are expected to cope. The clarity with which these questions are answered contributes to the way the threat is perceived and the degree of resilience with which a community copes with the violent disruption to its life. How society makes sense of such an unexpected catastrophe contributes to its impact.

Research carried out on disasters indicates that fear and the intensity with which it is felt are not directly proportional to the physical impact of a specific threat. From the outset this research found that 'how a community reacts to disaster is probably determined by its culture, its morale, its leadership'.[11] In another words adversity, acts of misfortune and threats to personal security do not directly produce a certain quantity of fear. The conversion of a response to a specific event is mediated through cultural norms that inform people about what is expected of them when confronted with a threat and how they should respond and feel. Through a system of meaning provided by culture, people learn to make sense of everyday problems. A web of meaning assists people to discover what binds them together, what society expects of them and guides them in how to manage uncertainty and deal with acts of misfortune. A solid sense of meaning helps a society to believe in its way of life and is itself an important dimension of its power. In the past century societies as diverse as Nazi Germany, Stalinist Soviet Union and the United States were able to project a robust sense of meaning and this helped them achieve global prominence. The Blitz spirit of a beleaguered Britain also provides testimony of how the authority of shared meaning helps people deal with uncertainty and adversity.[12]

Twenty-first-century society's relationship to the future is characterized by an intense consciousness of rapid change which is paralleled by a sense of disorientation about knowing how to interpret it. The sensibility that the future is an unrecognizable place that we can not comprehend is often represented through the media and popular culture. As Zaki Laidi argues in his important study of this problem, 'Our feeling of an exceptionally strong change in world order after the fall of the Berlin Wall is coupled with our equally enormous inability to interpret it to give it meaning'.[13] Laidi's work is mainly focused on the rapid disintegration of assumptions, conventions and practices associated with global order that was unleashed by the end of the Cold War. But his diagnosis of the loss of an explanatory framework for interpreting global events is if anything even more relevant in the twenty-first century. His observation that 'the need to project ourselves into the future has never been so strong, while we have never been so poorly armed on the conceptual front to conceive this future' provides the context for understanding the impoverished intellectual resources with which the issue of terrorism is addressed.[14]

What Laidi characterizes as 'the world crisis of meaning' has important implications for the current problematization of the issue of terrorism. How threats are perceived and how society deals with them are inextricably linked to the web of meaning that binds people to one another. The way an act of terror is interpreted is not directly proportional to its destructive power. How the public makes sense of such an unexpected catastrophe contributes to its impact. For example, a number of commentators suggest that America's reaction to 9/11 can not be explained by the scale of the physical damage it caused. They question the historic significance assigned to this event and in particular interrogate the attempt to draw a parallel between the war on terror and the Second World War. One American journalist writes:

> *Imagine that on 9/11, six hours after the assault on the twin towers and the Pentagon, terrorists had carried out a second wave of attacks on the United States, taking an additional 3,000 lives. Imagine that six hours after that, there had been yet another wave. Now imagine that the attacks had continued, every six hours, for another four years, until nearly 20 million Americans were dead. This is roughly what the Soviet Union suffered during World War II, and contemplating these numbers may help put in perspective what the United States has so far experienced during the war against terrorism.*[15]

This attempt to place 9/11 into a wider historical context is not designed to belittle this terrible tragedy. The journalist recognizes that 9/11 was a 'horrible act of mass murder', but questions whether those who inflicted this terror represent an existential threat to the United States. The argument that America may have overreacted is also pursued by the political scientist John Mueller, in his book *Overblown*.[16]

Some commentators take the view that the Bush Administration has consciously inflated the threat of terrorism during the aftermath of 9/11. They point to statements made by Bush that stated that 9/11 threatened the US economy and way of life. According to one critic, Bush's statements involved 'exaggerating the terrorist threat at every level, so that his speeches seem evidence too of a more general anxiety and vulnerability'.[17] However, an examination of these statements indicates that they were not simply disproportionate responses to the scale of the threat. They also express a degree of bewilderment and insecurity that approximates the state of meaninglessness.

Focusing on the proportionality of the reaction to 9/11 may distract attention from the significant role of meaning in the shaping of the response to it. As Laidi insists, meaning makes the exercise of power and force comprehensible. Laidi's statement that **'power is nothing when it has lost meaning'** helps illuminate the current predicament of the only global superpower.[18] If America finds it difficult to explain to itself what it stands for and what threats it faces, its ability to engage with unexpected challenges will be compromised. Its power counts for little without meaning. This insight gains symbolic significance through the frequently cited post-9/11 idiom: 'America the vulnerable'. It is the diminished system of meaning, and not a loss of material power, that accounts for this sensibility of vulnerability as well as the conviction that the US faces a war for its survival. That is why terrorist incidents can gain such significance in the contemporary cultural imagination. That is why it is more appropriate to make sense of this response through the term 'disorientation' rather than 'overreaction'.

The role of meaning in influencing the unprecedented significance attached to terrorism becomes evident when comparing the way it was interpreted at the beginning of the twentieth century with today. Walter Laqueur, one of the most prolific contributors on the subject of terrorism, has drawn attention to a spate of assassinations of European royals and politicians including one American president (McKinley) at the turn of the twentieth century. After pointing to this phenomenon, he concludes that 'if in the year 1900 the leaders of the main industrial powers had assembled, most of them would have insisted on giving terrorism top priority on their agenda, as President Clinton did at the Group of Seven meeting after the June bombing of the US military compound in Dharan, Saudi Arabia'.[19] But is that really the case?

It is always tempting to rediscover our problems in the past. However, it requires an exercise in reading history backwards to draw the conclusion that the problematization of terrorism at the turn of the twentieth century bore a serious resemblance to that of today. That President Clinton gave terrorism top priority even in the pre-9/11 era is testimony to the confusions that erupted in the post-Cold War global order. This was a period when the fact that the United States found it difficult to give a name to its enemy actually intensified its sense of national insecurity. This is a world that is very different to the one that prevailed around 1900. It is worth noting that, despite a number of significant high-profile assassinations of political leaders around the turn of the twentieth century, at that time terrorism was not conceptualized as either a global or an existential issue. As a concern, terrorism paled into insignificance compared to the theme of national rivalries, economic competition, domestic tensions, anxieties about the rise of Japan or the influence of socialism. Yes, there was global disorder but, to use Laidi's phrase, this was not 'a world without meaning'. In contrast to the present, twentieth-century societies possessed significant cultural resources for dealing with unexpected acts of terrorism.

As the response to 9/11 indicates, Western societies feel uncomfortable when confronted with the unexpected. Since 9/11 public officials and strategists have been preoccupied with the question of why

America was caught so unawares by a surprise attack. A study carried out by the Center for the Study of the Presidency compared the experience of the unanticipated attack on Pearl Harbor in December 1941 with that of 9/11 to find out the 'mindsets that made such surprises possible'. It concluded that 'while we clearly need to cultivate the art of agile thinking, we also need to foster the creation of the structures and cultures that encourage us to think beyond the horizon' and cultivate 'innovation and imagination'.[20] The author notes that neither event can be blamed entirely on a massive intelligence failure, since there were many warnings of the impending catastrophes. The problem was not simply the quality of intelligence, but also its interpretation. His remedy for overcoming such failure of the imagination is the institutionalization of thinking 'outside the box', which is another way of saying 'more imagination'. The problem with this approach is that the encouragement of focusing on the unexpected fosters a climate of promiscuous speculation. In this vein, the Schlesinger Working Group on Strategic Surprises, a group of American experts devoted to thinking 'outside the box' drew up an impressive list of 'strategic surprises' that could face the US in the future.[21] Unfortunately, real surprises are not scenarios waiting to be discovered. They are as much the outcome of the pursuit of deception as they are of its intended and unintended consequences and the response to them.

The experience of history demonstrates that chance, surprise and being caught off-guard are an integral part of conflict and warfare. Troy fell because its defenders did not think outside the box when the wooden horse arrived at the city doors. As one study of this subject notes, 'Most major wars since 1939 have begun with surprise attacks.'[22] The French paid a heavy price for unimaginatively concentrating their troops on the Maginot Line in May 1940. Most of Europe was stunned by the German Blitzkrieg, as was Japan by the devastation of Hiroshima. Nor is 9/11 the first time that the US has been caught off guard by the unexpected. History is inherently unpredictable. Seven years after Pearl Harbor, American policy-makers were caught napping by the victory of the Chinese Revolution. In January 1968, the US military was shocked by the Vietcong's Tet offensive. The car bombing of the US Marine barracks in Lebanon in 1983 was a bolt out of the blue, which exposed the vulnerability of the most powerful military machine to such acts.

The problem facing societies is not the arrival of the unexpected, nor the physical impact of an unanticipated catastrophe. People and communities can live with the unimaginable if they can make sense of their experience. In circumstances where communities are bound together by a shared system of meaning, people are able to demonstrate formidable resilience in the face of terror. This thesis was most forcefully argued by Fritz, who claimed that 'disaster-struck communities and societies naturally develop therapies that quickly and effectively overcome the losses, traumas, and privations of disaster – without the intervention of mental health professionals'.[23] In advancing this argument Fritz drew on the experience of the Spanish Civil War and the bombing of Britain and of Dresden and Hiroshima during the Second World War. In all these cases something akin to the local equivalent of the Blitz spirit emerged and the communities affected by mass destruction demonstrated a formidable capacity for resilience and succeeded in adapting to their new circumstances remarkably swiftly.[24] Societies can live with unexpected acts of violent destruction and can even thrive if they possess a robust system of meaning through which they can interpret their experience.

Values without meaning

Western leaders do not only have difficulties in naming their foes, they also find it difficult to explain what they stand for. Indeed this is probably the principal problem confronting the authors of the anti-terrorist campaign. Clarity about what one stands for is even more important than understanding the enemy. The precondition of the public's support is that it believes that there is something worth fighting for. Historically people have been prepared to confront violent threats to their lives and make heroic sacrifices if a conflict had an important meaning for them. That is why wars are not just simply about military action; they also involve a battle for ideas. The problem of meaning discussed above finds its clearest expression in the difficulty that the West has in expressing what it stands for and in engaging in the battle for hearts and minds. It appears that the unknown is what society stands for, and not simply the threat it faces.

It is interesting to note that since 9/11 the West feels strangely confused and defensive about its image. In contrast to the experience of the Cold War it has not been able to establish itself on the moral high ground. Indeed it feels internally insecure and is concerned that it does not enjoy domestic legitimacy for its military action. These concerns are the continual focus of discussion amongst security experts.

The absence of genuine commitment and enthusiasm for the conduct of the war in the US is symptomatic not simply of war weariness, but also of the lack of meaning the conflict has for the public. In such circumstances it is not surprising that there is even an absence of consensus about the facts surrounding 9/11 and the events that surround it. Even responsibility for the tragic events of 9/11 is questioned by a significant section of the American public. A survey of 1,010 adults found that 36 per cent of the US public suspect that federal officials assisted the 9/11 attacks or took no action to stop it so that the US could go to war in the Middle East. According to this Scripps Howard/Ohio University poll, a significant proportion of the respondents are not prepared to believe the official version of events.[25] That more than a third of the US public accept some form of conspiracy theory to explain 9/11 illustrates the crisis of meaning afflicting the Western societies in the post-9/11 world. Today, as in the past, the embrace of conspiracy theories is motivated by a sense of incomprehension towards the workings of the world. Typically it represents the loss of a sense of causality regarding who is responsible for what. It also signifies the erosion of official authority.

Lack of clarity about what the West stands for influences events in Iraq and Afghanistan. If soldiers are to pursue their campaign with success they need to know what they are fighting for. If this is 'unknown' a military campaign can become fatally flawed. That is why it is not surprising to discover that in June 2006 it was announced that coalition troops in Iraq would get 'values training' in 'core warrior' values. Peter Chiarelli, the then number two US general in Iraq, observed that it was important that troops took 'time to reflect on the values that separate us from our enemies'.[26] If the experience of the past three decades is anything to go by, it is unlikely that training courses will do very much to enlighten coalition troops about their core values. Indeed 'diversity training', 'the citizenship curriculum', 'sensitivity courses' and other values-oriented schemes that flourish in our institutions have an entirely symbolic and ritualistic existence. They symbolize the absence of common purpose and value and advertise the fact that in Western societies people gain their values through training courses rather than through the experience of life.

Probably the most significant and unexpected legacy of 9/11 is the decline of the moral authority of the West. Since 9/11 the West feels self-consciously defensive and discredited. In contrast to the experience of the Cold War it has not been able to establish itself on the moral high ground. Indeed it feels internally insecure and lacks domestic legitimacy for its action. As one report on the state of British public diplomacy noted, 'effective policies for dealing with these new security challenges are quite different from those of the Cold War, and publics require much more active persuasion'. It added that 'responses to the threat of nuclear war or Russian invasion had much broader and less questioning support than do responses to the threat of terrorist attack, which are coloured by deep popular scepticism about pre-emptive wars and about the principle of regime change for "terrorism-sponsoring" states'.[27] The relatively weak public support for the war against terrorism suggests that for a variety of reasons this conflict has not encouraged national solidarity.

The inability of the Western elites to give meaning to their global policies means that they are losing the battle of ideas with their own public. This development is most evident in relation to its estrangement from the Muslim populations that inhabit Western societies. Surveys continually highlight the feeble influence of secular and liberal values on Europe's Muslim population. Despite the numerous initiatives at 'dialogue' and 'multiculturalism', a global survey indicates that Muslims in Britain are the most anti-Western in Europe.[28] According to critics of Blair, this response is the result of Britain's involvement in Iraq. However, what this criticism overlooks is the wider mood of animosity towards the West that prevails throughout most of the Islamic world.

For a brief moment numerous observers believed that 9/11 would represent a rallying point and provide the West with a sense of mission. However, in the absence of a coherent system of meaning the West struggles to promote a positive account of its own values. Instead it relies on tawdry advertising and marketing. In October 2001, advertising executive, Charlotte Beer was appointed Secretary of State for Public Diplomacy and Public Affairs. Her mission was to gain the assistance of Madison Avenue public relations firms to help rebrand and sell the US to a hostile Muslim world. The focus on improving their image indicated that the US was not able or prepared to engage in a serious battle for ideas. In Britain too, impression management is the order of the day. British public diplomacy relies on loyal moderate Muslim leaders to curb the extremists. According to the former British Foreign Minister, Lord Triesman, 'International Islamic scholars are undertaking a series of roadshows to towns and cities with important Muslim communities to counter the extremist message'.[29] This outsourcing of the fight against the extremists indicates that there is little appetite for the project of promoting a positive vision of Western society. Back in February 2003

Rumsfeld asked, 'Are we capturing, killing or deterring and dissuading more terrorists everyday than the madrasses and the radical clerics are recruiting, training and deploying against us?'[30] There is overwhelming evidence that the response to this question is a resounding 'no'. Experience shows that without a message the techniques of advertising used by Western officials are likely to prove ineffective.

The US Government is acutely aware of the ideological dimension of the war. Its counter-terrorism strategy documents frequently allude to the priority of 'winning the war of ideas'. It regularly denounces the 'murderous ideology' of its foe and attempts to gain moral authority through upholding the banner of freedom. However, it finds it difficult to give a compelling content to the values it claims to uphold and often its message has a predictable and rhetorical character. Take the declaration made in *The President's National Strategy for Combating Terrorism*:

> Not only are we fighting our terrorist enemies on the battlefield, we are promoting freedom and human dignity as alternatives to the terrorists' perverse vision of oppression and totalitarian rule.[31]

Declarations that read as if they were copied from a template to a mission statement are unlikely to galvanize domestic opinion. Such vacuous rhetoric has a general and abstract quality that fails to provide US citizens with a sense of meaning and purpose about the nature of this war.

Sometimes officials gravely hint that that the terrorists are attempting to turn Americans into something that they are not, but without spelling out what they are. 'The object of terrorism is to try to force us to change our way of life, is to force us to retreat, is to force us to be what we're not,' stated Bush in October 2001.[32] The cumulative impact of vague statements such as this is to lend the rhetoric of war a tired and meaningless character.

One of the questions that haunted Tony Blair was, as he put it, 'Why are we not yet succeeding?' Forced to recognize that 'many in our countries listen to the propaganda of the extremists, and accept it', Blair has called on the public to engage in the battle for ideas. His answer to the question 'Why are we not yet succeeding?' is, 'We are not being bold enough, consistent enough, thorough enough, in fighting for the values we believe in'.[33] Blair's acknowledgement of the fact that the war on terror lacks meaning for the British public has led him to shift the focus on values. However, the very attempt to engage in what is in effect a propaganda war raises the question of what values to promote. It is far from evident whether the 'values we believe in' can carry conviction and meaning. It is worth noting that after his call for boldness in 'fighting for the values we believe in', all that Blair managed to do was to offer a list of fashionable global causes. Support for development in Africa, peace in the Middle East, fair migration, dealing with climate change and international institutions 'fit for task' were put forward as examples of British values. But the very manner in which this shopping list of issues was cobbled together betrays its makeshift and artificial character. It smacks of an exercise in public relations. These are a caricature of values and certainly hold little meaning for the British public.

Experience shows that values work best when they are not self-consciously paraded and explained. In previous times, terms like 'I am proud to be American' or the 'British way of life' worked because they conveyed taken-for-granted assumptions about the conduct of life. Their meanings were readily understood by the public who used them in a commonsense way to inform behaviour and action. If today these terms have a diminished capacity to inform behaviour, it is because they are experienced as less real by people. As numerous observers have noted, most traditional taken-for-granted and national identities have been called into question. Very few truths have survived the loss of certainties that have dominated the end of the twentieth century.[34]

It seems that every attempt to initiate a debate about values exposes their absence. In Britain, Sir Ian Blair, Commissioner of Police of the Metropolis, has sought to draw attention to his belief that the war on terror is very much linked to a 'war of ideas'. As far as he is concerned, 'getting the message right is vital'. But what is this message? Listening to the Commissioner it becomes evident that the message does not yet exist. It is something that needs to be built and invented. This is what he meant when he declared that 'I therefore absolutely back the United Kingdom Government's intent to build a clear narrative of "Britishness", based on values of tolerance, fairness, inclusivity and respect for the traditions and faith of others'. Note the words 'intent to build'. This is a narrative that is still being worked on. At present it is merely a declaration of good intentions that has yet to be turned into a script. A 'clear narrative of Britishness' represents an aspiration rather than reality. This is a point recognized later in his speech when after insisting that 'getting the message right is vital', Ian Blair asserts that 'we need the narrative of Britishness, we need to be able to confront the terrible ease with which it can be claimed that disagreement over foreign policy can justify murder'.[35] The speaker's emphasis is very much on what we need – that is on a narrative that is still conspicuously absent. It was in this vein that Sir David Omand pleaded that we 'badly need a counter-narrative that will help groups exposed to the terrorist message make sense of what they are seeing around them'.[36]

Moral defensiveness – losing the battle for ideas

In November 2006, in a rare public appearance, Dame Eliza Manningham-Buller, the former head of MI5, provided a downbeat pessimistic account of the threat from home-grown British terrorists. According to her assessment, young Muslims are being radicalized on an unprecedented scale. 'More and more people are moving from passive sympathy towards active terrorism through being radicalised or indoctrinated by friends, families, in organised training events here and overseas, by images on television, through chatrooms and websites on the internet,' she warned.[37] Manningham-Buller was particularly concerned about the estrangement of the youth from British society. She observed that 'it is the youth who are being actively targeted, groomed, radicalised and set on a path that frighteningly quickly could end in their involvement in mass murder of their fellow UK citizens'.

Official anxiety about the growing threat of home-grown extremism represents a radical departure from the way that terrorism was conceptualized in the past. Today terrorism is understood not merely as a physical threat. It is not simply the capacity of the terrorist to wreak mass destruction that worries society, but also the concern about the moral and ideological power that terrorism is able to exercise over significant sections of the domestic population. The influence that the cause of the terrorist is able to exercise over the minds of sections of the public endows this threat with unparalleled danger. Sir David Omand goes as far as to state that 'the most effective weapon of the terrorist at present is their ideology'.[38] The model of a terrorist as an effective purveyor of ideas represents a significant departure from the way this threat was perceived in the past. Indeed the idea that a terrorist can appeal to people's hearts and minds, and not just merely scare the public, is fundamentally inconsistent with traditional definitions of this threat. Until recent times the danger of terrorism was interpreted through its capacity to inflict fear on its target population. It is only in recent times that terrorism is conceptualized as an ideological competitor.

An increasingly important dimension of the war against terrorism is the battle for moral authority. The kind of issues raised by Manningham-Buller indicates that this is also a war for the hearts and minds of people. What is interesting about this battle for ideas is the defensiveness with which officials like Manningham-Buller approach it. It is difficult to avoid the conclusion that the political and cultural elites of Western societies feel less than confident about conducting a successful campaign on the battlefield of ideas. Their apprehension about the powerful attraction of radical ideas often betrays the belief that they cannot convince others of the superiority of their own way of life. A day after Manningham-Buller's statement, it was reported that intelligence officials were concerned about the ability of Islamic hip-hop artists to indoctrinate young people against the West.[39]

With all the talk about young Muslims being 'indoctrinated' through websites, jihadist videos and chat rooms, it is easy to forget that Western societies possess a powerful media network that extends into virtually every part of the world. How can relatively under-resourced, small media outlets out-compete the global media industry? And why is the Western media less than successful in matching terrorist indoctrination with its own view of the world? Apprehension about the influence of Islamic music is underpinned by unease about the ability of pro-Western opinion-makers to match the appeal of the ideas promoted through radical politicized hip-hop. According to Madeleine Gruen, an American intelligence analyst, 'the music is very persuasive because it is giving young people ideas, and those ideas are what might motivate someone to become a jihadi'.[40] Concern with the fact that someone is 'giving young people ideas' betrays a profound sense of defensiveness about the ability of Western culture to influence and inspire its youth. Analysts and opinion-makers are reluctant to acknowledge the obvious problem, which is 'Why are we not giving young people ideas?' Gruen's observation indicates that intelligence analysts are not worried simply about the violence of the jihadists, but also about the appeal of their ideals. This response may constitute a degree of overreaction to the menacing-sounding music that officials do not quite understand, but it also reflects a crisis of confidence about the West's ability to give meaning to its war against terrorism.

Politicians and their officials find it easier to issue statements about the influence that jihadist radicals are able to exert through the internet rather than to dwell on the weakness of their own case. Sometimes Western leaders even contrive to present themselves as the underdogs fighting a technologically superior foe. This was the intent of Blair when he stated, 'and to give credit where it's due, the extremists play our own media with a shrewdness that would be the envy of many a political party'. What really concerned Blair was not the communication skills of the extremists but the defensiveness of his side.[41]

Western analysts are intensely apprehensive about the likely outcome of the battle of ideas with terrorism. American intelligence analysts appear confused and at a loss to explain what they refer to as the 'radicalization process'. One US intelligence survey, published in April 2006, observed that 'the radicalization process is occurring more widely, and more anonymously in the Internet age, raising the likelihood of surprise attacks by unknown groups whose members and supporters may be difficult to pinpoint'. Blaming communication technology for promoting radicalization cannot entirely distract attention from a far more fundamental problem – which is that the US is losing the battle for ideas. As this report concedes, the jihadists have increased their influence and numbers.[42]

If anything, British intelligence analysts are even more defensive than their American counterparts. Sir Ian Blair has drawn attention to the fact that young British Muslims are 'willing to die for an idea' and that 'this is a phenomenon we have not seen en masse, since the Spanish Civil War and the battle against fascism'. Idealism seems to be monopolized by the wrong side of this conflict. Of particular concern for Sir Ian Blair is the fact that the appeal of their 'coherent narrative of oppressions, war and jihad' seems 'very potent':

> One of the truly shocking things – in addition to their intent – ... is the apparent speed with which young, reasonably affluent, some reasonably well-educated British born people were converted from what appeared to be ordinary lives – in a matter of some weeks, and months, not years – to a position where some were allegedly prepared to commit suicide and murder thousands of people at the same time.[43]

It is likely that Blair's shock at the speed of radicalization expresses a belated recognition of a problem that the British Government failed to recognize for a very long time. The response towards the problem of home-grown terrorism has been confused to say the least. Until the summer of 2005, the government tended to act as if this problem did not exist. Less than four months before the July 2005 bombings in London, the Joint Intelligence Committee (JIC), the main body charged with assessing intelligence on security threats, believed that 'suicide attacks' were unlikely in Great Britain and 'would not become the norm in Europe'.[44] Until the July bombings the British security services did not regard the 'home-grown threat' as sufficiently important to integrate into its 'strategic thinking'.[45]

What if they are us?

Apprehension about the problem of the home-grown threat endows the question 'Why do they hate us?' with a new meaning. The very posing of the question by Bush and others conveys a sense of genuine surprise and bewilderment. The question also expresses frustration and distress about the discovery that not everyone loves us. It resembles the kind of gesture that children make when they discover that they are not the centre of everyone's undivided attention. Even in its slightly less infantilized form this query hints at a sense of disappointment about being betrayed by someone close. The implicit premise of this question is that they ought really to like us. This is not a sentiment that one directs at clearly acknowledged enemies. Neither President Roosevelt nor Churchill needed to ask why do the Nazis hate us. Nor was this the type of question that Western leaders directed at the Kremlin. So the anxiety expressed by this question semi-consciously refers to the concern that they might be uncomfortably close to us. Worse still, since the apparent emergence of 'home-grown terrorism', there is great concern that 'they' might be 'us'.

When this question was originally formulated by President Bush, it was based on the premise that the enemy came from somewhere far way. The problem and sources of terrorism were conceptualized as being external to Western societies. Many of the theories about Muslim rage or clash of civilizations have as their focus distant and exotic places such as Afghanistan or Iran. Ironically many of the critics of American and European foreign policy also offer an externalist perspective and argue that what provokes terrorism is the oppression of Palestine and Western domination of the Middle East. Radical critics of the West also locate the problem of terrorism as the consequence of developments in the Middle East.[46] In Britain the Oxford Research Group regularly publishes reports that condemn the war in Iraq for encouraging global terrorism.[47]

Since September 11 it has become increasingly difficult to ignore the fact that the threat of terrorism is not just an external but also a domestic problem. The difficulties that political leaders have in spelling out 'our' way of life acquires momentous significance in relation to the flourishing of anti-Western movements on the domestic front. With the rise of so-called home-grown terrorism, the question 'Why do they hate us?' is linked to queries about why they are repelled by us and why they don't want to be like us. British officials and analysts have been shocked by the discovery that a significant section of its Muslim youth has become sympathetic to a radical Islamic outlook. Press reports frequently draw attention to the way in which young people who apparently lived a life of English-born westernized teenagers can become suddenly radicalized and turn into bitter enemies of their country. Take the following account of the life of Hasib Hussain, one of the suicide bombers responsible for the carnage of the 7 July bombings in London:

> He liked playing cricket and hockey, then one day he came into school and had undergone a complete transformation almost overnight ... He started wearing a topi hat from the mosque, grew a beard and wore robes. Before that he was always in jeans.[48]

Here is a young man who is apparently just like us, but who incomprehensibly has a sudden character transformation and turns against his neighbours and country! Like the perpetrators of the Madrid bombings, he lived and worked among the people he chose to target.

The realization that they are not like us, do not want to be like us and hate us gives this threat an all-too-intimate status. It is not just in Britain that people have discovered that their neighbours were not who they thought they were. Holland, Denmark, Norway, Sweden, Germany, Belgium, Canada and the US are some of the countries who have discovered that some their young people have developed extreme hatred for the Western way of life. 'We were flabbergasted to learn that she had become a fanatic,' noted a teacher of Bouchra El-Hor, a young Dutch Moroccan mother who has been charged in Britain with a terrorist offence. According to her teacher, she was 'a normal Dutch girl'. Reports indicate that she 'looked like an immigrant success story', and 'hung out at the pub with her friends and was known for her fashionable taste in clothes'.[49] Next door in Belgium, people were shocked to discover that Muriel Degauque, a 38-year-old blonde, white Catholic convert to Islam travelled to Iraq to blow herself up in November 2005. Across the Atlantic, American authorities were unpleasantly surprised to learn that a group of six men who pleaded guilty to providing material support to terrorists lived in Upstate New York and 'grew up watching football, played sports, and enjoyed barbecue'.[50]

The discovery of home-grown radicalization implicitly calls into question the conventional portrayal of the war on terror. Not only has the distinction between them and us become more confused, but the conflict also increasingly points to tension within the Western society itself. It is recognized that in recent years 'the majority of terrorist activities inside the West come from independent, homogeneous networks'.[51] It is difficult to avoid the conclusion that, at least for some people living in the West, their society's way of life appears repulsive. This development poses the question of 'Who is next?' The problem posed by the ascendancy of the home-grown radical is that it can be anybody. In Europe security analysts concede that it is proving impossible to make a profile of the terrorist.

Since the arrest of 17 men suspected of attempting to blow up targets in southern Ontario in June 2006, North American officials have also 'discovered' that 'they' may be at home. Canadian officials were disconcerted to learn that all the suspects were born in or were long-time residents of the country. 'Their alleged target was Canada: Canadian institutions, the Canadian economy, the Canadian people,' stated Prime Minister Stephen Harper.[52] This alleged plot also led Washington to acknowledge that it too had concerns about home-grown terrorism. In a major speech, Robert Mueller, Director of the FBI, drew attention to terrorists, who 'for whatever reason' have come 'to view their home country as the enemy'. According to Mueller the radicalization of domestic extremists is an important feature of the 'changing shape of terrorism'.[53]

For the FBI, what seems most disturbing is the feeling that potential terrorist recruits can emerge in just about any part of the US. An FBI press release answers its question '**Where can they be found?**' in the following terms: 'Anywhere – from schools and universities to mosques to prisons to community centers to the 5000+ virtual extremist websites on the Internet'.[54] The implications of this depiction of home-grown terrorism are enormous. A threat that can be found 'anywhere' in the community has indeed acquired a ubiquitous and menacing character. Its very proximity to people's everyday lives serves as a reminder that the enemy is at home. Such intimate enemies are said to represent a threat *sui generis*. One report states that:

> Their deep knowledge of Western cultures and languages, possession of Western passports and relative lack of overt ties to large terrorist organizations make their detection a difficult task for authorities. Their proven determination to strike their own countries, combined with the relatively easy access to explosive substances and weapons, makes them an immediate threat to the security of Western countries.[55]

From this perspective the new threat from within acquires significance precisely because they are from within.

From time to time analysts compare today's home-grown terrorists with those of the past. 'From the Ku Klux Klan to the Weather

Underground, American society has reaped its share of violent dissident groups,' notes one reporter.[56] However, the threat of today's home-grown Islamic radical is not experienced as that posed by a small isolated fringe group. On the contrary, they are perceived as part of a global revolt against the Western way of life. That anti-Western sentiment can serve as a focus for the radicalization of young people living in Europe and America exposes the problem that these societies have in inspiring enthusiasm and loyalty. On the contrary. The emergence of home-grown anti-Western radicalism indicates that, at least for some, rather than possessing any positive meaning, 'our way of life' provokes hatred and disgust.

In a different world, terrorism could be dismissed as an episodic threat posed by a handful of malcontents whose heinous deeds repelled the vast majority of ordinary citizens. When governments sought to crack down on terrorists they could invariably count on public support. This was a threat that could be swiftly criminalized and isolated as an illegitimate threat. Acts of terror directed at members of the political elites were successfully presented by governments as threats to anyone. The battle lines were clear with a small group of extremists on one side and the rest of society on the other.

At a time when home-grown and external threats appear so confusing the elevation of terrorism as the enemy provides little obvious meaning. Increasingly it is recognized that this conflict is not so much about weapons of mass destruction as it is about ideas. At present the predominant tendency is to interpret the problem as that of disgruntled people becoming radicalized and drawn to a movement with mass appeal. One important analyst of this process writes how jihad has 'become a millenarian movement with mass appeal' and about the need to counter the 'terrorist narrative – and draw potential recruits away from the lure of jihad'.[57] However it is unclear just what constitutes the lure of jihad. Young people who are attracted to jihadist videos rarely adopt a new world view. Their response is not all that different to the numerous non-Muslim Westerners who visit nihilistic websites and become fascinated by destructive themes and image. Those who visit jihadist sites opt for a fad rather than a coherent worldview. It is worth noting that some radicals who have been arrested for terrorist activities in Europe do not fit the image of the religious zealot. According to one report on members of the Mujahedon network, a Swedish internet forum, their knowledge of Islam was 'virtually non-extent' and their 'fascination with jihad seems to be dictated by their rebellious nature rather than a deep ideological conviction'.[58] In other words, the dominant influence appears to be estrangement from society rather than the pull of a vibrant and dynamic alternative.

It is not so much the lure of radicalism but the unravelling of meaning that is predominantly responsible for the emergence of a home-grown threat in the West. It appears that at least since the end of the Cold War, Western political ideals have become exhausted and their capacity to endow experience with meaning has become significantly diminished.[59] As Laidi noted, 'to define oneself by contrast with communism no longer has any meaning'.[60] At the same time the West has become uncomfortable about its own tradition and its intellectual, scientific and moral inheritance rarely succeeds in providing a positive sense of meaning. Bin Laden himself attempted to incorporate into his statements many of the doubts that Westerners have about their legacy. In his October 2002 message to the Americans he wrote:

> You are a nation that exploits women like consumer products or advertising tools, calling upon customers to purchase them. You use women to serve passengers, visitors, and strangers to increase your profit margins. You then rant that you support the liberation of women ...
>
> You have destroyed nature with your industrial waste and gases, more than any other nation in history. Despite this, you refuse to sign the Kyoto agreement so that you can secure the profit of your greedy companies and industries.[61]

The ease with which conventional anti-consumerist, environmentalist themes merge with radical jihadist ones is testimony to the confluence of internally driven anti-modernism with externally inspired anti-Western ones. In such circumstances it is not surprising that Western governments find it difficult to give a name to the enemy.

Within the West there are formidable cultural influences that disparage its historical achievements and belief in progress and enlightenment. Some commentators take the view that the West faces a moral crisis and finds it difficult to believe in itself. The authors of *Suicide of the West* believe that 'most Westerners no longer believe in the ideas that have made the West so successful'.[62] Others argue that even the police force and intelligence-gathering agencies are influenced by a mood of 'Western self-loathing' which undermines their operational judgement.[63] Those who look and find a home on a jihadist website may well represent but a variant of such a response to the crisis of belief afflicting the West.

One reason why the war on terror has failed to consolidate a sense of solidarity against the enemy is because of the crisis of meaning afflicting the West. Uncontained by a robust system of meaning, the threats have been far more effective in producing fears than in encouraging the emergence of new solidarities. Sadly, shared meaning for most people is confined to fear of being a target rather than being inspired to stand up for a way of life.

Fear without meaning

Social responses to threats are experienced and mediated through taken-for-granted meanings about the nature of social reality and in particular of personhood. One of the most insightful sociologists of the twentieth century, C. Wright Mills, has argued that people's consciousness of being threatened is mediated through their system of values. Mills claimed that whether or not people feel well or insecure is influenced by their relationship with the prevailing sense of meaning. So, 'When people cherish some set of values and do not feel any threat to them, they experience *well-being*'. In contrast, 'When they cherish values but *do* feel them to be threatened, they experience a crisis'. 'And if all their values seem involved they feel the total threat of panic,' adds Mills. Mills also projected a scenario that captures an important dimension of the construction of social anxiety. 'Suppose, finally they are unaware of any cherished values, but still are very much aware of a threat,' he states before concluding, 'that is the experience of *uneasiness*, of anxiety, which, if it is total enough, becomes a deadly unspecified malaise'.[64]

Following Mills's line of approach it becomes evident that it is not simply the threat to our security, but our ability to make sense of it that influences the way we fear. That is why the historically significant fears that define an era – fear of mass unemployment, fear of Communism, of nuclear disaster – do not constitute merely a response to a problem. They also represent a test of the prevailing system of meaning. 'It is when the traditional defenses in a given society appear incapable of either subduing or containing the perceived danger (e.g. the struggle with Communism) that social anxiety results, for the threat is perceived as involving existence itself, or the values identified with existence,' observed a study at the height of the Cold War.[65] This insight is confirmed by research into the human response to disaster. This research indicates that violent disruptions – such as a war, an act of terror or an earthquake – do not always provoke a uniform response. As Enrico Quarantelli, one the leading figures in disaster research, states, there is a degree of autonomy in the reactions of people to such disasters. More importantly, the response of the public to an emergency or a disaster is not a direct consequence of the scale of destruction and physical disruption. The way that humans respond to a disaster is only in part influenced by the external agent that caused it. Experience suggests that culture plays an important role in shaping the response. In particular the meaning attributed to a violent and destructive incident has a strong influence over the way its impact is experienced.[66]

Nor is anxiety at the level of society a direct response to a perceived threat. Its power is inversely proportional to the authority of the prevailing system of meaning – 'the system of rules, principles, and the assumptions which are taken for granted'.[67] One of the most interesting attempts to conceptualize fear through its relationship to the system of meaning is by Parkin. Parkin's historical account points to a shift in attitude from a concept of fear that 'encompassed that of respect' to what he calls 'raw fear'. The former is described as an 'institutionally controlled fear', whereas 'raw fear' has more of a free-floating and unpredictable character. 'Respectful' and 'raw' fear express very different relations to human experience. Parkin claims that respectful fear presupposes a 'predictable response to behaviour'. It is a form of 'knowable fear'. It is knowable because it is embedded in informal taken-for-granted and culturally sanctioned formal relations. In contrast, 'raw fear' has as its premise 'an unpredictable aspect sustained by the victim'.[68] This is a fear that is neither rooted in folk culture nor guided by a generally accepted narrative of meaning. It is the lack of clarity and consensus about how to interpret threat that endows fear with an unpredictable and diffuse character.

The attempt to conceptualize fear through focusing on an emotional response to a perceived threat fails to capture the meaning of the act. The tendency to objectify fear such as that of terror as a response to stimuli can only capture one dimension of the construction of fear. Raw fear is bound up with circumstances where cultural authority is weak, diffuse or contested. In such conditions 'not knowing' in the Rumsfeldian sense becomes the norm. 'It seems suddenly as if nobody really believes in what he still takes for granted,' wrote Riezler in his discussion of the collective insecurity of the 1940s.[69] How society does the work of meaning influences what it means by fear. Studies of the human response to disaster indicate that people's response to violent and catastrophic events is processed through the prevailing system of meaning. In an important early study, Carr argued that the crucial variable in explaining how a community responds to a violent disruption to their lives is culture. 'How a community reacts to disaster is probably determined by its culture, its morale, its leadership, and by the speed, scope, complexity and violence of the catastrophe itself,' concluded Carr.[70] Carr clearly recognized that the character of the disaster and the scale of destruction inflicted on people played a crucial role in the shaping of the public's response to it. But he insisted that this response was not a direct reaction to the impact, but was mediated through the system of meaning, norms, institutions and leadership that prevailed in the community.

The difficulty that society has in making sense of uncertainty is what gives contemporary fear its raw character. Uncertainty does not merely refer to a mood or emotional climate. It also refers to a tendency to disagree about what constitutes a threat and what should be done about it. The distinction that Parkin made between the predictability of respectful fear and the uncontrolled character of raw fear can be understood as an expression of the growing tendency to contest the meaning of a threat. Arguments over the side effects of vaccinations, medicine and GM food express a contestation of authority. Increasingly the questions of what we should fear and who to blame have become subjects of acrimonious debate. In the relative absence of consensus, blame itself is in search for targets. The candidates are not simply the usual suspects – witches, Jews, communists. As Hewitt stated, 'Many people are no longer content to accept the inevitability of adverse effects' and 'each event requires an explanation, and often the search for explanation is linked to a search for the locus of responsibility – someone to blame'.[71] Hence the influence of 9/11 conspiracy theories. Questions like 'Who is really behind the terrorists?' resonate with contemporary times. Lack of consensus over the meaning of misfortune bequeaths fearing a private, individuated and even arbitrary character. Disagreement about the meaning of misfortune is not new. As Russell Dynes points out, the debate surrounding the meaning of the 1755 Lisbon earthquake led to a confrontation between rival views of the world.[72] But past debates about the causes of disasters involved a clash of competing systems of meaning. Today, the protagonists in such a debate lack such moral and intellectual support and engage in the controversy as isolated individuals. Instead of a consensus forged around a society's fear, the way we respond to threat tends often to isolate us. 'Cancer and crime, pain and pollution: these fears isolate us,' notes a historian of fear.[73]

The dynamic of individuation has encouraged fear to be experienced in a fragmented and atomized form. That is why the fear of terrorism is not always experienced as a form of collective insecurity along the lines of previous generations. This development is well captured by Ellin, who argues that fear has 'come home' and become privatized.[74] The real significance of this development is the highly personalized even customized way that fear is experienced. Or as Bauman argues 'with fears privatized ... there is no hope left that human reason, and its earthly agents, will make the race a guided tour, certain to end up in a secure and agreeable shelter.'[75] The privatization of fear encourages an inward orientation towards the self. People interviewed about the risks they faced tended to represent 'crisis, fears and anxieties as self-produced and individual problems, the products of "personal biography"'.[76]

We fear alone because of the difficulties that we have in constructing a moral consensus about the threats facing our communities. We all attempt to make sense of these threats but the fragmentation of moral consensus has forced individuals to look for their own system of meaning. The weakening of shared values fragments the quest for meaning. In turn the fragmentation of the search for meaning privatizes it and lends it an individualized character. A quest that is so private often looks for personal solutions and meanings. That is why psychology and therapeutics have emerged as a dominant paradigm through which meaning is bestowed on our experience. Therapeutics is oriented to the experience of atomized individuals and tries to give meaning to the experience of the isolated individual.[77] The more so with terrorism, whose impact is in any case pre-dominantly psychological. One consequence of the representation of the impact of 9/11 through the medium of psychology is to one-sidedly exaggerate the vulnerability of the public. It is the emergence of the condition of vulnerability as the default response to terrorism that constitutes the subject of the next chapter.

Notes

1. Johnson (2002) p. 213.

2. Moore (2003) p. 217.

3. Beck (2003) p. 255; and Beck (2002) p. 39.

4. Omand (2005) p. 110.

5. Transcript of Osama bin Laden interview by Peter Arnett, 20 March 1997, www.anusha.com/osamaint.htm.

6. House of Commons (2006).

7. Simon (1995) p. 78.

8. Omand (2005) p. 210.

9. The Commission on the Intelligence Capabilities of the United States Regarding Weapons of Mass Destruction, Report to the President of the United States, 31 March 2005, Washington DC.

10. See, for example, Fareed Zakaria, 'The Politics of Rage: Why Do They Hate Us?' *Newsweek*, 15 October 2001.

11. Carr (1932) p. 211.

12. The influence of the Blitz spirit on people coping with adversity is explored in Furedi (2007a).

13. Laidi (1998) p. 1.

14. Ibid., p. 1.

15. David Bell, 'Was 9/11 really that bad?', *Los Angeles Times*, 28 January 2007.

16. Mueller (2006a).

17. Johnson (2002) p. 215.

18. Laidi (1998) p. 16.

19. Laqueur (1996) p. 24.

20. Abshire (2002) pp. 3 and 7.

21. Wisniewski (2004).

22. Betts (1980–81) p. 551.

23. Fritz (1996) p. 17.

24. See Jones, Woolven, Durodié and Wessely (2006).

25. See 'A third of US public believe 9/11 conspiracy theory', *Scripps Howard News Service*, 2 August 2006.

26. *USA Today*, 2 June 2006, 'Troops will get "values training"'.

27. Leonard, Small and Rose (2005) p. 11.

28. See 'Poll shows Muslims in Britain are most anti-Western in Europe', *Guardian*, 23 June 2006.

29. See speech by British Foreign Minister Lord Triesman, 'Britain's New Approach to Public Diplomacy; Promoting a Vision', FCO, 7 June 2006.

30. Cited in Joseph S. Nye, 'The Decline of America's Soft Power', *Foreign Affairs*, May/June 2004, Vol. 83, issue 3, p. 17.

31. *The President's National Strategy for Combating Terrorism*, Office of the Press Secretary, 5 September 2006.

32. 'President says Terrorists won't change American Way of Life', 23 October 2001, www.state.gov/s/ct/rls/rm/2001/5559.htm.

33. Blair (2006) p. 16.

34. See Furedi (2004) Chapter 2.

35. Sir Ian Blair, Commissioner of Police of the Metropolis, 'Speech for Urban Age Summit', Berlin, 11 November 2006.

36. Omand (2005) p. 109.

37. Richard Norton-Taylor, 'MI5: 30 plots being planned in UK', *Guardian*, 10 November 2006.

38. Omand (2005) p. 109.

39. *The Times*, 11 November 2006.

40. Sean O'Neill, 'Islamic hip-hop artists are accused of indoctrinating the young against the West', *The Times*, 11 November 2006.

41. Blair (2006) p. 16.

42. See 'Declassified Key Judgments of the National Intelligence Estimate "Trends in Global Terrorism: Implications for the United States"', dated April 2006.

43. Sir Ian Blair, Commissioner of Police of the Metropolis, 'Speech for Urban Age Summit', Berlin, 11 November 2006.

44. Cited in *Report into the London Terrorist Attacks on 7 July 2005*, Cm 6785, May 2006, pp. 26–9.

45. Ibid.

46. See for example Gary Younge, 'We must be honest about our past to be truly hopeful about our future', *Guardian*, April 16 2007.

47. See 'Iraq policy "spawned new terror"', *BBC Politics*, 11 April 2007.

48. 'Suicide bomber profile: the teenager', *Mail on Sunday*, 13 July 2005.

49. See Craig Whitlock, 'Terrorists proving Harder to Profile', *The Washington Post*, 12 March 2007.

50. See Patrik Jonsson, 'New profile of the home-grown terrorist emerges', *The Christian Science Monitor*, 26 June 2006.

51. See Lorenzo Vidino, 'The Danger of Homegrown Terrorism to Scandinavia', *Terrorism Monitor*, Vol. 4, issue 20, 19 October 2006.

52. 'Indepth: Toronto Bomb Plot', *CBC News Online*, 4 August 2006.

53. 'Remarks Prepared for Delivery by Director Robert S. Mueller', III FBI, The City Club of Cleveland, Cleveland Ohio, 23 June 2006, FBI Press Release.

54. FBI, Press Room, 'Protecting America from Terrorist Attack, Director Addresses the Threat of Homegrown Terrorism', 23 June 2006, www.fbi.gov/page2/june06/homegrownterrorism062306.htm.

55. Lorenzo Vidino, 'The Danger of Homegrown Terrorism to Scandinavia', *Terrorism Monitor*, Vol. 4, issue 20, 19 October 2006, p. 5.

56. See Patrik Jonsson, 'New profile of the home-grown terrorist emerges', *The Christian Science Monitor*, 26 June 2006.

57. Jessica Stern, 'Jihad – a global fad', *The Boston Globe*, 1 August 2006.

58. Lorenzo Vidino, 'The Danger of Homegrown Terrorism to Scandinavia', *Terrorism Monitor*, Vol. 4, issue 20, 19 October 2006, p. 6.

59. This problem is discussed in Furedi (2005).

60. Laidi (1998) p. 172.

61. 'To the Americans', 6 October 2002, Lawrence (2005) p. 168.

62. Koch and Smith (2006) p. 2.

63. Neumann and Smith (2005) p. 100.

64. Mills (1959) p. 11.

65. Lincoln (1960) p. 282.

66. Quarantelli (1978).

67. Riezler (1944) p. 494.

68. Parkin (1986) pp.158 and 159.

69. Riezler (1944) p. 497.

70. Carr (1932) pp. 211–12.

71. Hewitt (1983) p. v.

72. Dynes (2000).

73. Bourke (2005) p. 293.

74. Ellin (1999) p. 149.

75. Bauman (1992) p. xviii.

76. Tulloch and Lupton (2003) p. 38.

77. See Furedi (2004) Chapter 4.

CHAPTER 5

Enduring Vulnerability

The terrorist threat to America takes many forms, has many places to hide, and is often invisible. Yet the need for improved homeland security is not tied solely to today's terrorist threat. It is tied to our enduring vulnerability.

(Tom Ridge, 17 July 2002)[1]

In this important statement the former Homeland Security Secretary, Tom Ridge clarified the relationship between the specific threat of terrorism and a more general condition that afflicts the United States, which is that of **enduring vulnerability**. Far from posing the only danger to people's security, terrorism represents only one threat among many. Although it exists as a distinct and specific threat, it is also 'tied' to the general condition of vulnerability. It renders the experience of vulnerability more alarming and in turn the general state of precariousness encourages the intensity with which terrorism is experienced. This interaction is elaborated by a CNN correspondent in the following terms:

Three years ago, New York City went black, along with dozens of other cities in the eastern United States and Canada. A massive power failure sent millions of people pouring into the streets trying to figure out how to stay at work, head home, or do much of anything with no electricity. And immediately, fears arose that the crippling blackout might be the work of terrorists. It was not, of course, but three years later many of the major systems we rely on for everyday life remain vulnerable. Protecting our electrical supplies, computer networks, transportation systems, our economy, food, and water, remains an almost overwhelming challenge for security analysts.[2]

Since 'everyday life' is vulnerable according to this interpretation of American reality, Homeland Security must encompass every aspect of life. This state of insecurity is a neverending problem which represents an 'almost overwhelming challenge' for society. Worse still, a power failure is not simply a power failure. A derailed train or a plane crash is not merely an accident. Such disasters may be 'the work of terrorists'. The readiness with which the normal problems of life are perceived as probably 'their' work serves to expand the threat they represent.

Tom Ridge uses the term 'enduring vulnerability' in a double sense. It connotes a permanent condition of insecurity – something of a way of life. It also hints at a subjective state of how people feel about themselves. Ridge writes of 'our' enduring vulnerability. It is not simply a condition of life. It is also the way in which people are expected to experience the world – vulnerability is constitutive of identity. In the post-9/11 world vulnerability has acquired an idiomatic character that pertains to individuals as much to entire communities. Bush did not have to elaborate on his words when he noted that on 'September the 11th, 2001, America felt its vulnerability'.[3] His audience would understand that insecurity, apprehension and fear represented permanent and important dimensions of the nation's psyche. The formulation 'America the Vulnerable' consciously represents vulnerability as not simply a condition to be endured, but a defining feature of American identity. In this vein *The 2002 National Security Strategy of the USA* insisted that the 'characteristics we most cherish – our freedom, our cities, our systems of movement, and modern life – are vulnerable to terrorism'. It also warned that 'this vulnerability will persist long after we bring to justice those responsible for the September 11 attacks' since 'this is a new condition of life'.[4]

The premise of this diagnosis is that vulnerability to terrorism now constitutes a new condition of life. This premise which underpins the official thinking that informs the response to the events unleashed in September 2001 represents a foundational perspective on twenty-first-century life. The prognosis that it will continue 'long after we bring to justice those responsible for the September 11 attacks' has something of a prophetic quality about it. It is a statement that declares 'this is it' or 'this is the future'. This is also a condition that exists independent of any specific terrorist threat. 'Stop pretending that disasters are extremely rare and unforeseeable,' stated the voiceover in a recent CNN documentary programme. One television journalist declared that 'over the past hour we have been exploring America, the vulnerable' and then explained that the programme is about 'how gaps in our security have made us weak, puts us in the crosshairs of hidden terrorists and nature's fury'.[5] In this scenario the meaning of America the Vulnerable embraces not just the hidden terrorist, but also nature's fury.

The idiom of vulnerability does not only define the condition of a nation, it also expresses a statement about the state of mind of the individual. It signifies a sense of powerlessness with which people and their community confront adversity. This idiom conveys the idea that people are badly affected by what they endure. In the aftermath of 9/11 Bush declared that 'we are a generous people, a thoughtful people who hurt'.[6] In line with prevailing cultural norms, hurting refers not to physical but to emotional pain. The rhetoric of hurt communicated by Bush points to the significance of a therapeutic vocabulary through which this catastrophe is interpreted. The message conveyed through these words makes no attempt to stir a people's sense of sacrifice or heroism. At best it seeks to assure that the people will be able to cope with their pain. Instead of a traditional wartime call to arms, Bush offers a diagnosis. It indicates that when Bush and his colleagues attempt to endow the post-9/11 events with meaning they turn to a psychological or therapeutic interpretation of the experience of adversity.

Bush's representation of the problems is fully in line with prevailing cultural norms about how people are expected to respond to acts of terror. The diagnosis that vulnerability to terrorism now constitutes a condition of life is not simply an idea. It is a powerful theme that is constantly circulated through popular culture in the West. Official accounts about society's vulnerability to terrorism are not simply about the physical damage that acts of violence can inflict but about the human response to such acts. Since the impact and influence of terrorism is so significantly defined by the response to it, it is important to try to understand why officialdom tends to display a mood of vulnerability.

The ascendancy of the idiom of vulnerability
The characterization of vulnerability as a condition of life predates official concern with new terrorism. The association of vulnerability with a condition of life emerged in the 1970s and was principally promoted by writers devoted to raising public concern about environmental issues. The concept was central to an emerging outlook that regarded social problems from an ecological perspective. From this perspective the vulnerability of the environment represented a global problem of permanent crisis. It claimed that 'disasters occur

because a community is vulnerable to the vagaries of the environment'.[7] From this standpoint a pre-existing state of vulnerability was conceptualized as the point of departure for catastrophes to come. The claim that 'societies and communities are always vulnerable', was inspired by an ecological critique that pre-supposed vulnerability as an expression of the fragile state of the global ecology. Vulnerability-framed analysis of the environment depicts disasters as a normal feature of societies that are unable to deal with the hazards they confront. From this perspective the cause of misfortune is not a singular catastrophic event. It is a long-standing and durable regime of vulnerability that constitutes the pre-history of a disaster and of catastrophes to come. Indeed the very condition of vulnerability constitutes an invitation to misfortune. This fatalistic orientation towards the future suggests that vulnerability transcends any given social arrangement. It is an orientation that applies to anxieties towards new technology and the environment as much as terrorism.

Since the late 1970s, the concept of vulnerability has effortlessly migrated from ecology to the social sciences, particularly psychology. Indeed the term is often perceived by psychology as its very own invention. 'Vulnerability was originally conceived as a purely psychological concept that depended upon individual resources and personality traits,' notes mistakenly an influential handbook on mental health.[8] Quite swiftly a concept oriented towards the psychological analysis of personality traits was transformed into one that was also applied to groups. The rhetoric of vulnerability has acquired an important role in the psychologically oriented vocabulary that plays such an important role in contemporary culture.[9] The projection of a scenario where individuals and their communities exist in a permanent state of vulnerability towards nature has been reframed through a therapeutic narrative to suggest that people's mental health is perpetually at risk from the uncertainties they face. The term 'vulnerability' is increasingly used to highlight the claim that people and communities lack the emotional and psychological resources necessary to engage with the challenges of everyday life. When confronted with a terrorist attack on their communities, people are expected to react as trauma victims instead of as concerned citizens.[10]

Today's unprecedented cultural sensitivity to the vulnerability of people to emotional injury is underwritten by a distinct outlook about the workings of human subjectivity and personhood. Prevailing attitudes about the state of people's emotions can be understood through the concept of ethnopsychology. 'Every culture contains a set of ideas and beliefs about the nature of human beings, what motivates them to act, the way they perceive the world, how their minds work, and the emotions that are natural to them', writes Hewitt.[11] Ideas about emotion, individual behaviour and vulnerability are underpinned by the particular account that a culture offers about personhood and the human potential. As Derek Summerfield asserts, such accounts embody questions as 'how much or what kind of adversity a person can face and still be "normal"; what is a reasonable risk; when fatalism is appropriate and when a sense of grievance is, what is acceptable behaviour at a time of crisis including how distress should be expressed, how help should be sought, and whether restitution should be made'.[12]

The twenty-first-century version of personhood transmits the view that queries people's emotional capacity to deal with individual and social crisis. The transformation of distress into a condition of emotional injury has as its premise the belief that people are likely to be damaged by unpleasant encounters and the setbacks thrown up by everyday life. Trauma has become an all-purpose term to describe the individual's state of mind in the aftermath of an adverse experience. The portrayal of psychological damage as a long-term affliction flows from a lack of belief in the capacity of people to cope with the experience of misfortune. Distress is not something to be lived, but a condition that requires treatment. That is why the discussion on how communities deal with an act of terror invariably focuses on mental health impacts. In previous times deliberations about the likely impact of a war were interpreted through a broader concern with public morale. The concern was with how to stiffen the resolve of the civilian population rather than with the mental health issues of individuals.

An analysis of UK- and US-based newspapers through the database *LexisNexis* and the index of *The Times* and *The New York Times* indicates that the presentation of vulnerability as an enduring condition is a relatively recent development. It has been mainly since the 1990s that groups that are presumed to deserve economic, social or moral support have tended to be described as 'vulnerable' or 'the vulnerable' or 'the most vulnerable'. Government publications on health, education, crime and welfare continually refer to the targets of their policy as 'vulnerable children', 'vulnerable adults' or just as 'the vulnerable'. Such official reports echo the media narrative of vulnerability which conveys a diffuse sense of powerlessness through this term.

The past three decades has seen a steady expansion of people and groups who are defined as or who present themselves as vulnerable. In the 1960s and 1970s the term was mainly but very selectively applied to children and the elderly. In the 1980s, ethnic minorities, the homeless, single parents, the mentally ill, people in care and the unemployed were added to this list. A search of UK newspapers indicates that since the 1990s, vulnerability has encompassed the experience of a new range of emotional distress of 'depressed men', 'stressed employees' and 'career women'. In more recent times, young Muslim men, university students, teenagers under pressure to be thin and people addicted to internet pornography are only a small sample of the ever-growing constituencies who have been characterized as vulnerable.[13] A similar pattern is evident in the US. By the 1990s the term 'vulnerable' was commonly used to refer to virtually every group facing a difficult predicament. One *New York Times* headline, 'We're All Vulnerable Now', illustrates this sensibility.[14]

Yet it is worth noting that until the mid-1980s the term 'vulnerability' was used selectively and in relation to a discrete set of circumstances. It was never used to signify a condition of life. It rarely referred to an entire social group in the 1950s and 1960s. In rare instances, it was used in relation to children and the elderly, who were confronted with a specific predicament. According to an early account published in 1964, vulnerable groups are said to be 'similar' to the social workers' concept of 'needy groups'.[15] The earliest reference to a vulnerable group uncovered through *LexisNexis* was in June 1969 in connection with the appointment of a Presidential Consultant charged with organizing a Conference on Food and Nutrition by the Nixon White House. At a press briefing Nixon stated that this conference would seek to develop new survey methods to keep track of malnutrition levels and improve the nutrition of the nation's 'most vulnerable groups'.[16] In this instance, vulnerability to malnutrition was the subject of concern.

During the 1950s and 1960s the term 'vulnerable group' described people facing a clearly defined problem. In one instance, large families were represented as a vulnerable group because of the nutritional problems they faced.[17] Those deemed to be in a vulnerable group were individuals who faced a specific, often temporary predicament. So, during a strike of electrical engineers in 1973, people living in homes that relied on electricity were described as constituting 'the most vulnerable group'.[18] It is worth noting that today a report on the loss of electricity would describe the elderly, children and a variety of other groups as vulnerable. In 2005 when electricity and gas suppliers threatened to cut off supplies of customers who have not paid their bills, 'more support and advice to customers in financial difficulties, particularly those in vulnerable groups' was demanded. In this context the vulnerable groups referred to the elderly, the unemployed and single parents.[19] In contrast to the 1970s people facing an electricity cut today are represented as vulnerable even prior to a disruptive event.

Until the 1980s those who were depicted as members of a vulnerable group were seen to suffer from a specific impediment. The elderly were represented as vulnerable because they were isolated from the members of their community. In one article those who were housebound were described as vulnerable because they ate less food than other elderly people. Single mothers were portrayed as a vulnerable group because of the predicament they faced due to a shortage of housing. Ethnic minorities were depicted as vulnerable due to the discrimination they faced from others.[20] In contemporary times it is no longer necessary to specify in what way a group is vulnerable. The symbolic currency of vulnerability is so powerful that its meaning can be taken for granted. No longer are people simply vulnerable to just one or two problems. Today the elderly are vulnerable as such and constitute a group whose very existence is defined by its vulnerability. This expansive sense of vulnerability is expressed through statements such as:

> *Vulnerable groups are not just unemployed spongers. The elderly and disabled would also fall into that category.*[21]

> *Fear of crime deters vulnerable groups such as the elderly, women and children from using the streets, leaving them open to those bent on less innocent activities.*[22]

> *Dangerous pursuit of beauty: the media's notion that thinliness is next to godliness plays havoc with vulnerable young minds.*[23]

In these cases the condition of vulnerability constitutes a presupposition of people's existence.

Since the early 1990s in the US too, 'vulnerable' is increasingly used as an intrinsic quality of an individual or group rather than referring to an episode in their lives. Rather than being vulnerable to something, groups are described as 'the vulnerable'. An article entitled 'Protecting the Vulnerable' refers to a report about mentally ill people being vulnerable to attack. A discussion of the problem of access to health provision is titled, 'What Will Protect Us from Managed Care? Targeting the Vulnerable'. In 2005 a *New York Times* article about disaster victims was headlined, 'The Vulnerable Become More Vulnerable', and 'Concern for the most vulnerable' refers to a state prosecutor's preoccupation with crime victims.[24]

In everyday vernacular, the term 'vulnerable' now signifies an essential feature or identity of the group under discussion. In certain circumstances it is no longer even necessary to mention any specific group, since we can take for granted that we know who we are talking about. The statement, 'This innovative project will address the specific health needs of a wide variety of vulnerable groups' speaks for itself, as does the claim that there are 'vulnerable groups of people at both ends of the age spectrum'.[25] These are people who clearly cannot manage on their own. They are certainly unlikely to be able to deal with a major disruption to their lives such as a violent act of terror.

Once vulnerability assumes the characteristic of a group it ceases simply to express an individual's relation to experience. It becomes a condition that exists independent of any specific event and becomes an intrinsic dimension of a way of life. That is why the designation 'America the Vulnerable' is so readily accepted by the public as an apt description of their society.

Vulnerability-led response to risk

The tendency to approach the threat of terrorism from the standpoint of vulnerability encourages an attitude of pessimism, dread and foreboding towards this risk. Instead of asking the question 'What do we know?', we prefer to speculate and ask the 'What if?' question. And once this mode of questioning becomes the norm then literally every dimension of life can be transformed into a vulnerable target for terrorists. The vulnerability-led response to risk, which is based on possibilistic thinking continually encourages feverish speculation. That is why there is so much mental energy devoted to the exploration of speculative risk. 'Corporations must re-examine their definition of risk and take seriously the possibility of scenarios that only science fiction writers could have imagined possible one year ago,' argued an economist five months after 9/11.[26]

An understandable preoccupation with the question of where a terrorist is likely to strike next has imperceptibly meshed with a search for science fiction-like scenarios. The fear that no area of social life is immune from the terrorist threat has encouraged officials and experts to perceive everything as a potential target. The reigning paradigm of vulnerability has fostered a climate where terrorism is regarded as what

Tony Blair described as an 'existential threat'. Dick Cheney too, spoke of an 'existential conflict', while Condoleezza Rice has warned of an 'existential threat' and back in 2005 the then Senate majority leader, Bill Frist described bio-terrorism as 'the greatest existential threat we have in the world'.[27] Anxiety about the risk posed by terrorism is shaped by the assessment that these individuals are capable of doing anything. As the experience of the past decade indicates, terrorist actors – for example, suicide bombers – have few inhibitions about causing mass casualties. But just because these actors are deemed to be ready to do anything does not mean that their capabilities are unlimited. While their determination is not in doubt, they are far from omnipotent. This point is frequently overlooked in the vulnerability-led response to risk. Its emphasis on enduring vulnerability endows terrorism with potentially unlimited powers.

Perceptions of vulnerability are that it has a free-floating character that attaches itself to a wide variety of phenomena. This is a concept without boundaries. The past and the present are seamlessly connected through a chain of events whose cumulative outcome is enduring vulnerability. The strong claims made on behalf of the salience of the vulnerability concept give it an almost indefinable metaphysical quality. Take the following explanation of the concept in a recent discussion of the impact of Hurricane Katrina.

> Socially created vulnerabilities are largely ignored in the hazards and disaster literature because they are so hard to measure and quantify. Social vulnerability is partially a product of social inequalities – those social factors and forces that create a susceptibility to various groups to harm and in turn affect their ability to respond and bounce back (resilience) after the disaster. But it is much more than that. Social vulnerability involves the basic provision of health care, the livability of places, overall indicators of quality of life, and accessibility to lifelines (goods, services, emergency response personnel), capital and political representation.[28]

The qualification 'it is much more than that' is a testimony to the expansive ambition contained in what works more as a cultural metaphor than a precise concept. Writing of the 'mental images that the concept of vulnerability evokes', De Chesnay points to its free-floating transcendental quality:

> For some, the concept might be associated with people of color or those who are socially marginalized. For others, it might evoke images of those

who are poor, those who are frail, or those who are without a voice. Vulnerability is equally at home with those who rely on others to speak for them, as it is with those who are homeless or disenfranchised. Vulnerability might extend to those who experience violence as part and parcel of human existence or those who go to bed hungry every night.[29]

And to underline the free-floating character of the concept, De Chesnay adds, if we look at the 'private face of vulnerability, we might be surprised to see our own face'.[30]

As a condition of life, vulnerability is unbounded and often becomes the dominant influence in threat assessment. This is why a vulnerability-led response is likely to result in the amplification of the terrorist threat. As Lawrence Freedman hints, it is not the terrorist but the sense of vulnerability that in the end influences how society perceives and engages with this threat.[31] The very feeling of vulnerability which exists independently of any violent act contains the potential for amplifying a sense of terror. Ultimately a vulnerability-led response represents a statement about how society feels about itself rather than a strategic analysis of terrorism. As the consciousness of vulnerability dominates the imagination, threat assessment often acquires the form of worst-case thinking. Instead of asking the question of 'What do we know?', opinion-formers prefer to speculate and ask the 'What if?' question. As Jenkins argues, 'in present attempts to anticipate and prepare for what terrorists might do next, virtually no scenario is dismissed'.[32] Traditional threat analysis 'assessed an enemy's intentions and capabilities,' notes Jenkins, whereas today's 'vulnerability-based analysis identifies a weakness and hypothesizes a terrorist and a worst-case scenario'.[33] One of the principal problems with this approach is that the worst-case scenarios have a habit of migrating from the realm of fantasy to the domain of policy deliberation. They then often assume the status of a new cultural norm. 'Often, such a scenario is reified and becomes a threat: it is successively considered possible, probable, inevitable,' warns Jenkins. As a result, the threat of terrorism may become inflated as the intentions of terrorist groups become confused with our fears. As Jenkins concludes, the 'terrorists' actual capabilities, ambitions blur with our own speculation and fears to create what the terrorists want: an atmosphere of alarm'.[34] In other words, we end up terrorizing ourselves.

Vulnerability analysis is based on a highly pessimistic, disoriented and risk-averse view of the world. From the previous discussion it should be evident that a vulnerability-led response is not simply a form of analysis. It is a response that is informed by a powerful cultural script that regards vulnerability as an enduring feature of life. This script's pessimism is particularly directed at the human potential for recovery and resilience and the capacity to engage with risks.

The sense of vulnerability towards risk in general creates a climate where any perceived threat can be seen as a potential weapon that terrorists may deploy. Consequently, the line that divides ordinary threats from terrorist ones can often become blurred. 'In present attempts to anticipate and prepare for what terrorists might do next, virtually no scenario is dismissed,' argues Jenkins.[35] Take the perception of the threat posed by the outbreak of foot and mouth disease in Britain. In September 2001, Sir William Stewart, a former government chief scientific adviser, warned that the difficulty that the government had in dealing with the foot and mouth outbreak indicated just how vulnerable Britain was to any future threat from biological warfare.[36] The ease with which Sir William made the conceptual jump from the crisis of British farming to the spectre of biological warfare demonstrates how the contemporary sense of vulnerability helps transform difficult problems into a potential source of asymmetric threat. And this scenario was dreamt up a few days **before** 9/11!

Within a few weeks, Stewart's speculation about the risk of a foot and mouth terrorist had become reified. Concern about this threat was echoed in a report published by the Select Committee on Defence. The report stated that the 'recent foot and mouth epidemic has demonstrated' that 'controlling the spread of some viruses is very difficult', which 'may suggest that the threat of biological attack is more serious'.[37] Numerous other commentators and officials have echoed the view that foot and mouth disease should be interpreted as a potential terrorist threat.

The prevailing sense of vulnerability towards the unexpected not only leads to the proliferation of alleged threats but also continually expands the range of potential terrorist targets. From this perspective every hazard has the potential for becoming a weapon in the terrorist arsenal. And every public space contains a potential terrorist target:

> *Analysts and the public seriously consider the possibility that terrorists may send waves of suicide bombers to America's shopping malls; wipe out Boston's waterfront with a hijacked liquid-natural-gas carrier; topple the George Washington Bridge in New York City; crash planes into the Houses of Parliament in London, the Capitol in Washington, or*

a nuclear reactor; spray anthrax over a city; sink tankers to block narrow straits; release hoof-and-mouth disease; sabotage the banking system; spread smallpox; or destroy Manhattan with a nuclear bomb.[38]

Every new terrorist threat scenario expands the number of new targets. Consequently, previously untroubled aspects of life are constantly turned into new targets.

The vulnerability-led approach to threat assessment necessarily involves an element of second-guessing. However, the prevailing climate of risk aversion leads to the continuous identification of areas of potential vulnerability before they become targets. So, for example, sections of American agribusiness have become preoccupied with the danger of 'agro-terrorism'. Such concerns are motivated by the perception that US agriculture may be vulnerable to acts of biological warfare. 'Given the tremendous economic, political, and strategic value of US agricultural resources, the Washington policy community has been slow to realize their vulnerability to attack,' warns Jonathan Ban of The Chemical and Biological Arms Control Institute.[39] This concern was echoed by the European Commission after 9/11. Its health commissioner at the time, David Byrne, warned that the UK's foot and mouth epidemic showed 'just how vulnerable the industry was to the biological terror threat'.[40] Of course it did no such thing. Nothing was 'shown' – the threat of biological terror was merely another fantasy scenario dreamt up through vulnerability-led thinking.

The contemporary sense of vulnerability dictates that virtually every sector of civilian life can become a target of asymmetric threat. That is why the American President's Commission on Critical Infrastructure Protection identified so many potential targets. These are:

o The transportation infrastructure
o The oil and gas production and storage infrastructure
o The water supply infrastructure
o The emergency services infrastructure
o The banking and finance infrastructure
o The electrical power infrastructure
o The information and communication infrastructure
o The government infrastructure
o The defence infrastructure
o The population.

The proliferation of potential targets is the inexorable consequence of vulnerability-led analysis. Vulnerability analysis assumes that human life is continually under threat from harms that are both known and unknown. This is an analysis that looks for the worst in all dimensions of life. Its focuses are all 'the forms of physical, social, political, economic, cultural and psychological harms to which individuals and modern societies are susceptible'.[41]

One consequence of the vulnerability-led response to terrorism is a compulsive desire to second guess future targets. This leads to the continuous identification of new areas of potential vulnerability before they become targets. To take the example of the US chemical industry, it is claimed that 'an attack on one of the many toxic-chemical plants in the United States could endanger more than a million people'. One critic argues that 'environmentalists, security experts and even the Army surgeon general have been raising the alarm about this threat since September 11, 2001, but Congress has yet to do anything about it'.[42] Such criticisms represent an implicit demand for greater vigilance for new targets. An ever-expanding list of potential terrorist targets suggests that the prevailing form of threat assessment frequently ventures into the realm of fantasy. The Department of Homeland Security's database includes 'targets' such as Old Macdonald's Petting Zoo in Woodville, Alabama, the Mule Day Parade in Columbia, Tennessee, the Sweetwater Flea Market, the Amish Popcorn Factory and the Apple and Pork festival in Clinton, Illinois.[43] By the end of 2004, Homeland Security's target list had expanded to 80,000.[44]

With so much of everyday life transformed into a potential target, vulnerability is increasingly experienced as a defining condition of existence. Official warnings regarding new sources of vulnerability can often contribute to the intensification of public anxieties. For example, press reports about the possibility of terrorists using crop-dusters to conduct biological or chemical warfare had the effect of reinforcing public fears during the immediate post-9/11 period. 'Practically everyone has been scared stiff,' noted a reporter in *The Washington Post*. Some analysts recognize that an orientation towards vulnerability may inadvertently help those looking for targets to attack. 'Parading our worst fears could encourage the terrorists' desire to acquire unconventional means of attack,' writes Sir David Omand, the British Government's former Security and Intelligence Coordinator. Nevertheless, he adds that 'the tragic scenes in New Orleans in the aftermath of Hurricane Katrina were a terrifying reminder of the vulnerability to massive disruption of those who live in modern cosmopolitan cities, and of the fragility of the complex systems that support food, water and sewage distribution, medical services, telecommunications and power'.[45]

Often it is difficult to avoid the conclusion that the condition of vulnerability is used as a metaphysical diagnosis for the human condition by individuals who suffer from a powerful dose of cultural pessimism towards the process of change. According to the vulnerability paradigm people can do very little to rid themselves of this condition. There are no technological or scientific solutions to this problem. On the contrary, in line with ecological thinking, the condition of vulnerability is itself the product of technological development. It is frequently asserted that it is technological advance that renders societies intensely vulnerable. The question 'What conditions foster extreme vulnerability?' is answered by one leading risk expert with, 'Large densely populated cities, jumbo jetliners, skyscraper buildings, modern communications, media, computers'.[46] This point is also reiterated by a British analyst who associates the prevailing 'sense of vulnerability' with the 'information revolution' where governments find themselves 'ever more inter-connected' with changes that 'reverberate unpredictably – and often chaotically throughout society'.[47] From the perspective of this security analyst, change itself is directly responsible for bestowing a sense of vulnerability on society.

This profound consciousness of vulnerability itself represents an invitation to be terrorized. Opponents of the West understand that they can make an impact on their target public with a relatively minimal investment of resources. It may even encourage them to shift their target from the military to the civilian one. As Thomas observes, 'foreign societies may believe it is easier to attack the Western psyche or will to fight than to meet it on the battlefield in a contest between technologies'.[48] As we noted before, an intense sense of vulnerability empowers hostile groups to achieve objectives through essentially psychological means. That is why, regardless of the scale of physical destruction, they can expect to make an impact through sowing fear in their target society. Official preoccupation with the public's vulnerability to terrorist threats may inadvertently stimulate and encourage attacks against the civilian population.

Under the guise of constructing threat assessments many parties are constructing their own agendas. In the US the terror target list is driven by local special interest groups who are interested in attracting funding via the various subsidies available through the Department of Homeland Security. As a result the federal target list is the outcome of the rivalries between competing groups of claim-makers rather than a rigorous process of threat assessment. That is why, in January 2006, the state of Indiana with 8,591 potential terrorist targets had 50 per cent more listed than New York (5,687) and more than twice as many as in California. What this imaginary list of targets claimed to show was that Indiana is the most target-rich place in the universe.[49]

Historical detour

The belief that vulnerability constitutes a defining feature of life and that it fundamentally shapes the public's response to violent disruptions gained ascendancy in the 1990s. This cultural narrative of vulnerability stands in sharp contrast to the way that people in previous decades were encouraged to perceive their engagement with adversity. Throughout most of the past century the ideals of 'strength through adversity' and the 'Blitz spirit' were integral of a cultural script that transmitted the expectation that people would respond with fortitude to violent threats. This script celebrated the capacity of British people to cope when their lives were badly disrupted by German bombing. In the post-war period, the narrative of the Blitz, promoting the ideal that the 'British can take it' continued to influence people's outlooks. The public's identification with the legacy of the Second World War ensured that the ideals of resilience, resourcefulness and adaptability continued to be influential well into the 1980s.[50]

Today's representation of vulnerability as an enduring feature of existence is alien to the cultural norms associated with the Blitz spirit, which celebrated the ideal of a hardy people fighting back. Britain's wartime Prime Minister Winston Churchill expressed this sentiment in the aftermath of his army's retreat at Dunkirk when he stated that 'I have nothing to offer but blood, toil, tears and sweat'. Churchill's declaration demanded that the British people fight, regardless of how they felt. This is a very different approach to the vulnerability-led response of Bush to 9/11, which simply sought to provide assurance that the American people would be able to cope with their hurt.

Communities were not diagnosed as suffering from the condition of vulnerability until the 1980s. Before this time, research into disaster response suggested that communities were surprisingly good at coping with even the most tragic disruption to their lives. Experiences such as the civilian response to the horrors of the Spanish Civil War, the bombing of Britain, the allied bombing of Germany and the dropping of atomic weapons on Hiroshima and Nagasaki, as well as to a variety of natural disasters in the 1950s and 1960s indicate that communities were able to develop resilience and therefore minimize the destructive consequences of these incidents on their morale. In a review of these experiences, Charles Fritz, a pioneer researcher into the human impact of disasters, argued that most 'disasters produce a great increase in social solidarity', which tends to reduce the incidence of most forms of personal and social pathology.[51]

Experience suggests that the impact on the national psyche of sudden military attacks, such as the bombing of Pearl Harbor, the Blitz, IRA attacks in London and suicide bombers in Jerusalem is mediated through cultural and political influences and institutions. Such violence need not simply traumatize its targets. It can provoke a determination to fight or stimulate the construction of a community around a common cause. It is worth recalling that at the outbreak of the Second World War it was commonly expected that one of the outcomes of the conflict would be an increase in the number of psychiatric patients.[52] And although arrangements were made to receive this expected flood, there was no increase in numbers. Studies have reported a similar pattern from experiences as varied as the conflict in Northern Ireland and the Spanish Civil War. As Bracken argues, 'There is good evidence that wartime suffering and trauma is not inevitably associated with increased morbidity.' In these instances, an increased sense of solidarity and community provided people with a sense of meaning through which they could make sense of the experience of adversity.[53]

Sociological and community studies indicate that, throughout history, threats to human survival have played an important role in the construction of communities. The sociologist James Coleman argued that 'it may seem paradoxical that problems create community organization, but such is nevertheless the case.' He added that 'each problem successfully met leaves its residue of sentiments and organizations' and that 'without them, future problems could not be solved'.[54] Even in today's highly individuated globalized society, calamities have a unique capacity to encourage acts of solidarity and altruism. In his pioneering study, *Communities in Disaster*, Allen Barton pointed to the difficulty in arousing altruistic behaviour in a modern societies 'which prescribe few obligations and little emotional attachment among community members in general'. Nevertheless, 'most studies of sudden natural disasters report great emotional solidarity and mutual helpfulness in the disaster-stricken population'.[55] Others too point out that, contrary to expectations, disaster situations contain potential for the emergence of social solidarity and community purpose. Quarantelli and Dynes drew attention to research carried out on the impact of the Xenia and Topeka tornados, which indicated that in 'some cases disasters have been beneficial to the victims involved'. It appears that victim families were 'better off with respect to family solidarity and relationships than matched nonvictim families in the same community with which they were compared'.[56]

As Dynes remarks, the destruction of physical capital need not lead to the loss of social capital. On the contrary, 'social capital is the only form of capital which is renewed and enhanced quickly in emergency situations'.[57] From this analysis it follows that an act of terror which destroys physical capital does not necessarily diminish social capital. On the contrary, in such an emergency there is a potential for social capital to increase significantly.

The shift from the narrative of the Blitz to that of vulnerability has important implications in the way that the legacy of a disaster – the period of readjustment and reorganization – is conceptualized. In the 1950s, it was assumed that the communities that bore the brunt of the floods would soon return to normalcy. Today, it is frequently asserted that there is considerable potential for long-term emotional damage to the individual. Whereas in the 1950s the dominant cultural narrative communicated a sense of a quick return to normalcy, in recent times the impact of an act of violent disruption is perceived as indeterminate. More importantly its effect on the individual is frequently represented as for a very long time, if not for life. 'The myth that things go back to normal within a few weeks is especially pernicious,' argues Noji.[58] The disorganization of the identity of the individual, which is a key feature of the narrative of vulnerability, directly influences the way that terrorism is perceived. In contrast to previous experience the emphasis is not on returning to normal life but on providing support for people to cope with the new life ahead of them.

Cultivating a response of powerlessness to an act of terror

Through the paradigm of vulnerability, the sense of powerlessness is cultivated as part of the normal state of being. The positing of people as victims of circumstance reflects Western cultural sensibilities towards the supposed unprecedented uncertainties confronting twenty-first-century society. In this era of uncertainties, Western culture nevertheless succeeds in communicating a sense of certainty about the enduring quality of vulnerability. It is remarkable just how prevalent the idea of human powerlessness has become. The emphasis placed on human vulnerability in worst-case scenarios dooms people to the role of helpless victims of circumstance. The deflation in the status of human agency coincides with the inflation of threats such as that of terrorism. In this scenario, the counterposition of the helpless self to the overwhelming force of the external world helps validate the proposition that people lack the power to contain the challenge of terror. As Linenthal recorded in his survey that the Oklahoma bombing was internalized by people, the 'traumatic vision' of the event strongly influenced the public's reaction. This 'traumatic vision' revealed a self that was 'intrinsically weak, passive and seemingly helpless amid the onslaughts of traumatic events,' notes Linenthal.[59]

The vulnerability-led response to terrorism transforms the trauma and sense of helplessness recounted by Linenthal into an objective mental health condition. However, as we noted in the previous chapter, a community's sense of helplessness can more usefully be understood as the sentiment of disorientation caused by the difficulty of giving meaning to adverse experience. As Bracken suggests, 'vulnerability with regard to meaningfulness may not simply be the result of trauma but might, in some way, be a predisposing factor for the development of problems after such events'.[60] There is considerable evidence to suggest that communities who possess a robust system of meaning are able to deal remarkably well with disasters and violent conflict. 'Social disintegration increases traumatic stress, while a strong sense of community, like political commitment, enhances the resilience of individuals in the face of danger,' writes Vanessa Pupavac. Pupavac drew on research carried out in different parts of the world to argue that people's response to violent episodes can be influenced by community strength, moral and ideological commitments'.[61]

The vulnerability and impotence of the individual stands in sharp contrast to the formidable powers that are attributed to the everyday challenges that people face. As we note in the next chapter, the transformation of vulnerability into a condition diminishes the capacity to deal with violent threats.

The relationship between vulnerability and the wider global threats to human existence is most clearly represented through the concept of being 'at risk'. The conceptualization of being 'at risk' is a relatively recent innovation that is bound up with the crisis thinking of the 1980s. The concept of **being at risk** encapsulates an outlook which is dramatically different from the classical notion of **taking a risk**. The formulation, to take a risk, contains the assumption that individuals can both exercise choice and choose to explore and experiment. Taking a risk has as its premise active subjects whose actions have the potential to realize positive outcomes and to alter their circumstance. In contrast, the concept of being at risk reverses the previous relationship between human beings and experience. To be at risk assigns to the person a passive and dependent role. To be at risk is no longer about what you do – it is about who you are. It is an acknowledgement of powerlessness – at least in relation to that risk. Increasingly, someone defined as being at risk is seen to exist in a permanent condition of vulnerability.

It is not only individuals who are said to be at risk. Communities and entire nations are depicted as living in this condition. For example the report *The National Security Strategy of the United States of America* declares that 'we are today a nation at risk to a new and changing threat'.[62] That the White House prefers to portray the United States as 'at risk' rather than as a risk-taker is symptomatic of a climate of risk aversion that dominates proceedings in Western capitals. As we argue in the next chapter, the main beneficiaries of risk aversion are those drawn towards terrorism.

Notes

1. Written Statement of Governor Tom Ridge, On the Department of Homeland Security Senate Committee on Agriculture, Nutrition and Forestry, 17 July 2002, agriculture.senate.gov/Hearings/Hearings_2002/July_17__2002/71702rid.htm.

2. Posted by Tom Foreman, CNN correspondent, 14 August 2006, Anderson Cooper 360 Blog, www.cnn.com/CNN/Programs/anderson.cooper.360/blog/2006/08/america-vulnerable.html.

3. Speech made at Cincinnati Museum Center, 6 October 2002, www.whitehouse.gov/news/releases/2002/10/20021007-8.html.

4. www.whitehouse.gov/nsc/nssall.html, 2002.

5. CNN 'Planet in Peril: Inside Brazil; extreme Preemie: Beating the Odds', 20 February 2007.

6. www.whitehouse.gov/news/release, 30 October 2001.

7. Westgate and O'Keefe (1976) p. 61.

8. Scheid and Horwitz (1999) p. 152.

9. Furedi (2004).

10. Ibid., p. 16.

11. Hewitt (1998) p. 35.

12. Summerfield (2001) p. 322.

13. 'Cruel pursuit of stick women', *Observer*, 9 November 2003.

14. 'Is Big Brother Watching? Why Would He Bother? We're All Vulnerable', *The New York Times*, 12 January 1998.

15. Wilkins (2001) p. 202.

16. *The New York Times*, 12 June 1969.

17. 'A Disquieting Trend', *The Times*, 3 September 1956.

18. 'How to Stop Worrying and Live With Power Cuts', *The Times*, 1 November 1973.

19. 'Utilities: National Firms Warned on Cut-Offs', *Guardian*, 1 November 2005.

20. 'Mothers on their own', *The Times*, 22 November 1968; 'How to Stop Worrying and Live With Power Cuts', *The Times*, 1 November 1973; 'Saving The Housebound', *The Times*, 16 January 1973; 'Minorities the Most Vulnerable and the Most Difficult to Help', *The Times*, 21 May 1974.

21. 'Should Digital TV be Given Out Free? Express Debate', *Sunday Express*, 23 October 2005.

22. 'Letter; A Seminar on Fighting Crime', *Guardian*, 2 July 1997.

23. 'Dangerous pursuit of beauty: the media's notion that thinness is next to godliness plays havoc with vulnerable young minds', *Observer*, 9 November 2003.

24. 'Protecting the Vulnerable', *The New York Times*, 24 June 2004; 'What Will Protect Us From Managed Care? Vulnerable Targeted', *The New York Times*, 3 August 1993; 'The Vulnerable Become More Vulnerable', *The New York Times*, 2 January 2005; 'Concern For The Most Vulnerable', *The New York Times*, 2 May 1998.

25. 'Lottery Gets Health Drive Up-and-Running', *Aberdeen Press and Journal*, 7 November 2001; 'Linked futures; Grandparents: There are vulnerable groups at both ends of the age spectrum', *Guardian*, 12 August 1998.

26. Cited in Furedi (2002) p. 13.

27. Jan Freeman, 'Existentially speaking', *The Boston Globe*, 4 February 2007.

28. Cutter (2005) p. 2.

29. De Chesnay (2005) p. xix.

30. Ibid., p. xix.

31. See Freedman (2003) p. 10, www.terrorismresearch.net/finalreports/Freedman/LF%20article.pdf.

32. Jenkins, M. J. (2006) 'The New Age of Terrorism', in Kamien, D. (2006), p. 119.

33. Ibid., p. 120.

34. Ibid.

35. Ibid., p. 119.

36. *BBC Online*, 2 September 2001.

37. Select Committee on Defence, 2001, para. 68.

38. Jenkins (2006) p. 119.

39. Ban, J., 'Agricultural Biological Warfare', www.cbaci.org (website of the Chemical and Biological Arms Control Unit), June 2000.

40. 'Agriculture "vulnerable to bio-terrorism" warns EU commission' *Epolitix*, 23 October 2001.

41. Slovic (2002) p. 425.

42. Amanda Griscom Little, 'Chemical Engineering', www.salon.com, accessed 17 July 2006.

43. See Eric Lipton, 'Come One, Come All, Join the Terror Target List', *The New York Times*, 12 July 2006.

44. Mueller (2006b) p. 144.

45. Omand (2005) p. 111.

46. Slovic (2002) p. 425.

47. Edwards (2006) p. 5.

48. Thomas (2001) p. 23.

49. Eric Lipton, 'Come One, Come All, Join the Terror Target List', *The New York Times*, 12 July 2006.

50. Furedi (2007b).

51. Fritz (1996) p. 10.

52. See Jones, Woolven, Durodié and Wessely (2006).

53. Bracken (2002) pp. 67–73.

54. Coleman (1976) p. 567.

55. Barton (1969) p. 206.

56. Quarantelli and Dynes (1977) pp. 35–6.

57. Dynes (2003) p. 15.

58. Noji (2005) p. 3.

59. Linenthal (2001) p. 92.

60. Bracken (2002) p. 81.

61. Pupavac (2002) p. 10.

62. *The National Security Strategy of the United States of America*, September 2002, p. 15.

CHAPTER 6

Perceptions of Terror and a Clash of Cultural Attitudes towards Risk

From the previous chapter, it should be evident that the sense of vulnerability that prevails in Western societies is not the product of terrorism. The mood of powerlessness and anxiety towards uncertainty pre-existed 9/11. As we shall see, the condition of vulnerability is crucial for making sense of the problem under discussion because it frames the response to terrorism. The sensibility of vulnerability and the problem of meaning which underpins it influence both the current perception and the response to terrorism. Many of the beliefs that shape the current response to terrorism – the idea that humanity faces unprecedented threats, that we inhabit a new era of terror, that we are confronted by a new species of terrorist threat, that what we must really fear is the unknown – are the product of a cultural imagination that is dominated by a sense of vulnerability. This chapter argues that it is these cultural attitudes rather than any novel objective or physical threat that inform perceptions of terrorism in contemporary times. This chapter also contends that Western cultural attitudes encourage the consciousness of terror and inadvertently offer an invitation to be terrorized.

Fear promotion

Experience shows that a community does not need real live terrorists to feel terrorized. During the 1980s, surveys indicated that despite suffering virtually no casualties a large majority of Americans regarded terrorism as their number one concern.[1] Frequently, unexplained phenomena and even hoaxes can have the effect of terrorizing the public and disrupting the routine of everyday life. An unattended bag in a lounge can close down an airport. The discovery of white powder in an envelope often leads to mayhem and to the temporary shutting down of businesses. A disposition to feel alarmed by the unexpected is widespread and represents an important resource to anyone who wants to scare the public. For Osama bin Laden such an alarmist sensibility represents a vital resource that can be mobilized to support his project. As he sarcastically noted in a video broadcast in 2004, it is 'easy for us to provoke and bait' Americans. He stated that 'all that we have to do is to send two mujahidin' to 'raise a piece of cloth on which is written Al-Qaeda in order to make the generals race there to cause America to suffer human, economic, and political losses'.[2]

Osama bin Laden possesses an understanding of the rules of fear that prevail in Western societies. His statements are attuned to the anxieties that are constantly conveyed through popular culture and the media. Along with spokesmen from other jihadist groups, they seek to transmit an image of themselves as the personification of unrestrained violence. Videos celebrating the beheading of hostages, carefully orchestrated invasions of theatres and schools are designed to convey the message that 'we will stop at nothing'.

Osama bin Laden's project of preying on the alarmist imagination prevailing in Western culture parallels the activities of commercially motivated Western fear entrepreneurs, who use fear to promote their products and brands. Who needs alarmist Al-Qaeda videos, when the fear market can flourish through the activities of Western interest groups, entrepreneurs and advocacy organizations? Since September 2001, claim-makers have sought to use the public's fear of terrorism to promote their own interests. Politicians, businesses, advocacy organizations and special interest groups have sought to further their narrow self-serving agendas by manipulating public anxiety about terror. All seem to take the view that they are more likely to gain a hearing for their case if they pursue their arguments or claims through the prism of security. Businesses have systematically used concern with homeland security to win public subsidies and handouts. And, paradoxically, the critics of big business use similar tactics – many environmentalist activists have started linking their traditional alarmist campaigns to the public's fear of terror attacks.

So after 9/11, the Worldwatch Institute issued a statement entitled 'The Bio-terror in Your Burger', which argued that although past attempts to clean up America's food chain had 'failed to inspire politicians', a patriotic demand for homeland security could 'finally lead to meaningful action'. The author noted that 'if we are lucky, today's rallying cries for homeland security will finally lead to meaningful actions to secure our food supplies from the threats of both accidental and terrorist epidemics'.[3] So while Osama bin Laden advises sending two mujahidin to 'raise a piece of cloth on which is written Al-Qaeda', the Worldwatch Institute advocates waving the flag of bio-terror to scare the public to achieve 'meaningful action'.

The threat of terrorism has been appropriated to promote a bewildering variety of causes. The Detroit Project, a campaign started by liberal commentator Arianna Huffington and Americans for Fuel-Efficient Cars, links its campaign against sports utility vehicles (SUVs) with the war on terrorism, arguing that Americans need to 'free ourselves from the nations and terrorists holding us hostage through our addiction to oil'. Some environmentalists argue that their programme offers the most effective counter-terrorist strategy of all. In an article for the online journal *OnEarth*, David Corn, the Washington-based editor of America's left-leaning weekly *The Nation*, claimed that 'technologies long challenged by environmental advocates are potential sources of immense danger in an era of terrorism'. 'Environmentalism will have to be an essential component of counter-terrorism,' he added.[4]

There is very little to distinguish the substance of the claims made by competing groups of fear entrepreneurs. Environmentalist advocacy groups are quite happy to harness the security concerns of the Pentagon to advance their cause. So Greenpeace International embraces a report written for the Pentagon which predicts that 'future wars will be fought over the issue of survival rather than religion, ideology or national honour'.[5] Competing claims about what constitutes the greatest threat to global security represent an exercise in what sociologist characterize as **domain expansion**. 'Once a problem gains widespread recognition and acceptance, there is a tendency to piggyback new claims onto the old name, to expand the problem's domain,' writes the sociologist Joel Best.[6] In other words, once the problem of terrorism and security are perceived as legitimate issues requiring serious attention, fear entrepreneurs can appropriate these issues to serve their own interests. Packaging problems as global threats leads to the ever-expanding definition of the problem of terrorism. 'The initial claims become a foot in the door, an opening wedge for further advocacy,' adds Best. So anxieties about international terrorism are not simply mobilized to promote the 'war against terrorism'. They are also activated to endorse claims about problems that have little to do with terrorists. When a report concludes that the spread of HIV is 'as big of a threat as terrorism', it draws on the powerful mood of vulnerability constructed in the post-9/11 era.[7] In the same way, fear entrepreneurs can present their objective of poverty-reduction as indispensable for curbing international terrorism.[8]

The Worldwatch Institute self-consciously expands Washington's anti-terrorist agenda to encompass its own objectives. In its report, *Climate Change Poses Greater Security Threat than Terrorism*, it argues that 'the parallels with terrorism are compelling'. It adds: 'As with terrorism, we know that changes will occur, but not when or where they will strike'.[9] The well-known Homeland Security sound bite, 'The question is not if but when ...', is adapted and recycled as a statement about the imminent threat posed by climate change. Almost seamlessly the metaphorical parallels are turned into linkages. Drawing parallels with terrorism is a rhetorical strategy favoured by fear entrepreneurs. This approach is adopted by the author of a report on the influenza pandemic, published by the Australian Homeland Security Research Centre. The report states that 'pandemics are like terrorism – both are probable but no one knows when, or what their consequences will be'.[10] Accordingly, uncertainty about the future is recast as an immediate security problem.

Through the rhetorical expansion of the meaning of security, terrorism has acquired the status of a benchmark with which other threats are compared. In effect, terrorism serves as an idiom for transmitting anxiety about other issues. So last November, the then UK Health Minister, Rosie Winterton informed an international meeting of her counterparts that 'recent events have shown that terrorist attacks and natural disasters can happen anywhere and at any time, and that all our citizens are potentially at risk'.[11] The ease with which Winterton made the conceptual jump from the spectre of terrorism to the threat of natural disasters demonstrates the working of the contemporary imagination. The public's concern about terrorism has become a resource that can be mobilized for giving other threats greater definition.

Expanding the number of potential casualties is a key dimension of the strategy of domain expansion. 'Climate change already claims more lives than does terrorism according to the World Health Organization', argues the Worldwatch Institute. The figure of 160,000 deaths per year is produced to underline the incredible dimension of this threat. As against such large numbers of casualties, the threat posed by terrorism appears to be almost benign.

To take one example of the way that advocacy groups attempt to piggyback their claims on the terrorism agenda, since the 1970s advocates of population control have been on the defensive.[12] The traditional

Malthusian argument that food production could not keep up with population growth has been discredited through the experience of the past century and a half. As a result, the Malthusian movement has sought to find new arguments to justify its objective of population control. In recent years it has sought to gain support for its objectives by claiming that population growth constitutes the root cause of global insecurity and terrorism. The Malthusian fantasy about a Population Bomb has been recycled in a new form into the Human Bomb. According to this simplistic Malthusian scenario, overpopulation creates a lot of poor, unemployed, discontented men. Many of them turn into troublemakers, some of them become canon fodder for terrorist networks and they end up on the wrong side of the war on terror.

In the 1970s, Paul Ehrlich, author of *The Population Bomb*, argued that population growth in the South inexorably led to the triumph of Communism. Today he has recycled this simplistic diagnosis to account for the rise of international terrorism. He argues that demographic factors are 'likely contributors' to terrorism. Why? Because the 'vast majority of terrorists are young males' and there are 'huge numbers of boys under 15' who live in Muslim nations.[13] The idea that a large number of young males equals a potential terrorist threat is systematically promoted by supporters of population control. 'It is impossible to ignore the link between rapid population growth and terrorism,' claims the director of the Population Coalition.[14] In reality, the link is based on the logic of the simpleton, which is that population growth and terrorism happen to coincide, so therefore they must be linked. According to this logic anything that coincides with current demographic patterns – Hurricane Katrina, the boom in the price of property in London, the popularity of iPods – is linked to population growth.

Prominent Malthusian organizations such as the Worldwatch Institute and The Population Institute have sought to repose population control as an effective counter-terrorist measure. Take the Population Institute's study, *Breeding Insecurity: Global Security Implications of Rapid Population Growth.*[15] It argues that 'rapid population growth in developing countries creates national security problems, including civil unrest and terrorism'. The report cites a study by another Malthusian advocacy group, Population Action International, which claims that 'youth bulges create instability and increase the likelihood for terrorism and civil unrest by as much as 50 percent'.[16] Now 50 per cent sounds like a big number! But this is a made-up figure, which is the figment of an imagination fixed on constructing a relationship between demographic growth and terrorism. The obvious conclusion to be drawn from the figure of 50 per cent is that the threat of terrorism can be halved with the implementation of a vigorous programme of population control. The solution for tackling the problem of terrorism is to stop them breeding. As the report concludes, 'While family planning programs will not create a more secure world on their own, they will go a long way toward reducing pressures on societies that lead to instability, unrest, and terrorism'.[17]

As the sociologist, David Altheide remarked, the fear market has 'spawned an extensive cottage industry' that promotes new fears and an 'army of social scientists and other intellectuals – or "issue fans" – serve as claims makers, marketing their target issues and agendas in various forums, such as self-help books, courses, research funds, and expertise'.[18] The trend outlined by Altheide constitutes a crucial dimension of claims-making. The promotion of fear represents a claim on moral authority and on resources.

In the private sector, numerous industries have become devoted to promoting their business through the fear market. In some cases, entrepreneurs seek to scare the public into purchasing their products. Appeals to personal security constitute the point of departure for the marketing strategy of the insurance, personal security and health industries. As Haggerty states, 'personal security has become commodified'. He notes that fear is 'frequently used to sell security products' and adds, '[it] help[s] to channel and focus diffuse and amorphous anxieties about crime and other forms of social breakdown into distinct and personalised fears about someone entering your bedroom window, stealing your car, or attacking you on your evening jog'.[19] Fear is used by the IT industry and its army of consultants to sell goods and services.

The cumulative effect of the promotion of insecurity and anxiety on the fear market is to strengthen society's sense of powerlessness. The manipulation of the public's anxiety towards terrorism serves to continually remind people of the immediacy of this threat.

But does all this fear-mongering mean that the public is really scared? Is the fear of terrorism more severe than anxieties about physical security in the past? It is impossible to satisfactorily answer these questions, since we have no way of measuring the intensity of the emotion of fear today and compare it to the past. Moreover, an increase in the quantity of fear is difficult to measure, since its very meaning is itself subject to continuous alteration. The sense of powerlessness associated with the condition of vulnerability does not mean that the public is more scared that in previous times. The sensibility of powerlessness is important because it influences how people fear. It serves to frame the manner in which a community interprets the threats it faces. Typically the consciousness of vulnerability encourages people to believe that they are more or less unable to do very much about the threats out there. Such an outlook fosters a mood of fatalism and passivity and not necessarily paralysing fear.

The current mood of fatalism towards future threats does not inexorably lead to the constant augmentation of the fear of terrorism. Fatalism also breeds suspicion and mistrust towards the world in general. That is one reason why the authority of governments is continually under challenge and why the official version of events regarding the war on terrorism faces widespread public scepticism. On both sides of the Atlantic a significant section of the public mistrusts official pronouncements on security issues. Cynicism regarding the motives of politicians and their officials is widespread. In August 2006, a YouGov survey found that 35 per cent of the people questioned took the view that British politicians 'generally exaggerate the terrorist threat'. According to one BBC journalist, the public is afflicted with 'terror fatigue'.[20] Mistrust of official statements and suspicion towards politicians' motives indicate that people are not overwhelmed by a fear of terrorism. The public's response contains elements of anxiety and confusion which interact with mistrust to produce an uneasy sense of foreboding.

However, while it is difficult to measure the public's fear of terrorism, it is possible to assess its impact on public life. At the very least it is evident that the prominent role assumed by the narrative of the terrorist threat indicates that it serves as a frame through which society interprets its experiences. Iconic landmarks, national symbols or tall buildings are frequently perceived as not just impressive but as potential targets of terror.

Contemporary terrorism has acquired an unprecedented historical significance because it personifies the threatening dimension of the condition of society's uncertainty. 'Terrorists are not the cause of uncertainty, nor of the condition of fear it generates, but living in fear, and working with it, they become its agents,' observes Chris Sparks.[21]

Precautionary culture

By all objective accounts it is difficult to explain why Western societies should feel so overwhelmed by the condition of vulnerability. Compared with the past, people living in Western societies have less familiarity with physical pain, suffering, debilitating disease, poverty and death than previously. Western societies enjoy what is by historical standards a high level of stability and relative prosperity. Critics of the vulnerability thesis note that:

> By any historical measure, Americans are particularly safe. And we live in an especially safe neighborhood. The sorts of security threats that plagued nations since their invention, indeed that necessitated their creation – invasion and civil war – are unthinkable here.[22]

And yet despite an unprecedented level of stability and prosperity contemporary culture continually communicates the idea that humanity is confronted by powerful destructive forces that threaten our everyday existence. Despite a 'century of extraordinary successes in public health: we complain of more symptoms, spend more days in bed and rate our health as worse than we did 40 years or even 80 years ago'.[23]

Of course the perception of safety is an existential rather than an objective fact. Social scientists know that whether people feel safe or insecure is to a considerable extent a matter of subjective judgement. Surveys show that young men are far less likely to be worried about crime than elderly women. Yet crime statistics indicate that elderly women suffer far lower levels of victimization than young men. Societies' sense of safety is also not directly an outcome of the statistical incidence of physical threats. It is widely known that people in prosperous societies living in relatively privileged circumstances can feel unsafe and insecure. Individuals who are freed from the grinding routine of day-to-day survival can shift their concern from being worried about hunger and chronic disease to a preoccupation with their emotional wellbeing.

In contemporary society, we can never feel safe or healthy enough. With every advance in medical science, communities demand an even higher standard of health. It is widely recognized that contemporary society regards safety as an end in itself and tends to look upon failures in safety regimes as unacceptable. Twenty-first-century obsession with safety has become so pervasive that in the UK some officials have warned that 'enough is enough – it is time to turn the tide'. One report has called for a campaign to emphasize the 'importance of resilience, self-reliance, freedom, innovation and a spirit of adventure in today's society'.[24] However, such pleas are overwhelmed by powerful cultural forces that insist that people can never be safe enough. Consequently safety and the attitude of caution are now treated as inherently positive values across the entire political spectrum. According to this ethos of safety, even the term 'accident' is now regarded as inconsistent with contemporary Western values. Public health officials often claim that most injuries suffered by people are preventable and that to attribute such an event to an accident is irresponsible. The American emergency medicine establishment has been in the forefront of the campaign to expunge the word 'accident' from its vocabulary.

Safety consciousness is not simply the direct consequence of the growth of prosperity. Society's obsession with safety has also gained momentum through the growth of scepticism towards innovation, change and experimentation. Throughout modern times people looked to medicine, science and technology to make their lives safer. They still do of course. But there is now a powerful mood of suspicion towards innovation and change. The very term 'human intervention' has acquired negative connotations. Terms like 'human impact', 'human intervention' and 'ecological footprint' convey a negative sense of folly and destruction. Human intervention has always been associated with the belief that its positive consequences outweighed its downside. This modernist orientation has given way to a more pessimistic account, where human intervention is associated with loss as much as gain, and increasingly the former is seen to outweigh the latter. Rather than serving as a solution to our problems, new technology is often indicted for its potential for increasing the power of human destructiveness. Former American Vice President Al Gore expressed this concern when he warned that the 'power of technologies now at our disposal vastly magnifies the impact each individual can have on the natural world'.[25]

Western societies have become so obsessed with safety that virtually every human experience comes with a health warning. It is not simply children's playgrounds and schools that have become dominated by the ethos of safety for its own sake. Even organizations such as the police and the army have become subject to the dictates of health and safety. Cultural attitudes towards risk and safety are not confined to the civilian population. They have enveloped the institutions of the police and the military. As a result both of these institutions are becoming increasingly risk averse. One British journalist has noted that the police rarely venture out, and even when they are confronted with a serious situation they rarely take risks. In one case, armed police stood for 15 days besieging a London home, only venturing in after the hostage had escaped by his own efforts and the lone gunman perished in the fire which he started.[26] The ethos of safety has also become institutionalized within the military. Army commanders have to draw up risk assessments for every dimension of their soldiers' training. Some have given up testing soldiers to the limit lest they inadvertently contravene health and safety rules.[27] General Sir Michael Rose, former head of the SAS, has spoken out about the destructive consequences of risk aversion and the ethos of safety for the morale of the military. He has denounced the 'moral cowardice' that has encouraged what he describes as the 'most catastrophic collapse' of 'military ethos in recent history'.[28] If anything, the decline of the warrior ethos is far more comprehensive within the US military. One analyst believes that risk aversion has undermined the effectiveness of the US military. 'As emphasis on risk avoidance filters down the chain of command, junior commanders and their soldiers become aware that low-risk behavior is expected and act accordingly,' he notes.[29]

Unlike some institutions in society, the military cannot survive without taking risks. However, the military values associated with the warrior ethos face a challenge from potent cultural influences that negate risk-taking behaviour. Despite the many Hollywood action-packed movies that celebrate heroism and bravery, there is little cultural valuation for risk-taking military behaviour. The military are not immune to the influence of precautionary culture. Prevailing norms towards health and safety decry risk-taking behaviour. A culture that shows a low threshold towards losses in everyday life is unlikely to possess the capacity to celebrate risk-taking behaviour within military institutions. That is also one reason why the status and the authority of the military have declined. The elites of society have distanced themselves from military values and the military, and their participation in this institution has significantly diminished. Even the mainstream of society has become estranged from military values. As two radical critics remark, 'the representative image of the US soldier is no longer that of a John Wayne, and more important, the profiles of US soldiers do not resemble the profiles of the US citizenry'.[30] In Britain too, fighting a war is increasingly outsourced to private contractors, foreign mercenaries and the most economically disadvantaged section of society.

One of the most striking manifestation of society's estrangement from military and warrior values is the ascendancy of a powerful mood of casualty aversion. The military are continually concerned about the ability of the public to tolerate casualties. Casualty aversion appears to have influenced the 1989 decision of the US Department of Defense to prohibit media coverage of deceased military personnel returning from Dover Air Force Base.[31] One critic of what he calls America's 'elite casualty phobia' has noted that in many recent military engagements – Bosnia and Kosovo – 'US ground forces were deliberately withheld from participation', and that in Afghanistan local ground forces were often used to hold down casualties.[32]

The significance attached to safety and loss avoidance not only undermines the capacity of Western societies to deal with violent opponents, but also makes them uniquely vulnerable to the risk of terrorism. Preoccupation with safety and the constant acknowledgement of vulnerability acts as an invitation to terrorism. As Homer-Dixon observed, 'Our increased vulnerability makes us more risk-averse, while terrorists have become more powerful and more tolerant of risk'. He added that, as a result, 'terrorists have significant leverage to hurt us'.[33] These different cultural attitudes have important implications for the way that the so-called war on terror is played out globally. It appears that Western concerns towards avoiding losses encourage the response of terror.

The powerful sense of vulnerability and insecurity that prevails in the Western world is frequently blamed on a rapidly changing globalized world that produces unprecedented levels of uncertainty. Virtually every official document and expert statement on the problem of terrorism repeats a version of this mantra. 'It has become something of a cliché that the beginning of the twenty-first century is marked by increasing complexity and uncertainty, on a national, regional and international scale,' begins a report arguing a case for a new national security strategy for the UK.[34] Yet the cliché of unprecedented levels of uncertainty is rarely contested. However, ideas about certainty and uncertainty are not founded on objective facts but are shaped by cultural attitudes towards the future. Humanity actually knows quite a lot about the world. There are some threats that lurk in the background and occasionally catch us unawares, but most of the time, at least by the standards of historical experience, we live in a relatively stable world. What makes us feel uncertain are not the uncontrollable forces unleashed by globalization, but our lack of clarity about our place in the world. Concerns about risk and safety express the difficulties that Western culture has in making sense of its experience. The response of precaution is an attempt to deal with this problem.

Clash of cultural attitudes

The significance that Western culture attaches to health and safety stands in sharp contrast to the values upheld by their opponents. This clash of cultural attitudes was clearly spelled out in an allegedly Al-

Qaeda-produced tape released on 14 March 2004 after the Madrid bombing massacre that led to the loss of almost 200 lives. In this message an individual who described himself as Al-Qaeda's military commander in Europe declared, 'You love life and we love death'. The same theme has been repeated time and again in numerous Islamist communiqués. For example, Ismail Haniya, a Hamas leader, informed an American journalist in 2003 that his people were prepared to die, whereas 'the Jews love life more than any other people, and they prefer not to die'.[35] Back in October 2001, Suleiman Abu Ghaith, an alleged spokesman for Osama bin Laden, told a news conference that there were 'thousands of young men' eager for martyrdom, who 'loved death as you love life'.[36] In these statements Islamist leaders seek to draw attention to the claim that their side believes in something worth dying for whereas their opponents do not. More importantly, the message conveyed through these statements attempted to highlight the different cultural attitude towards risk and loss of the two sides. The point of these statements is to alarm a risk-averse culture. This public embrace of death is designed to intimidate opponents through reminding them that 'through sacrificing our lives we are prepared to take an incalculably greater risk than you can possibly imagine'. Such statements also attempt to convey the message that 'unlike you, we have nothing to lose in this conflict'.

Either consciously or unconsciously, Islamist communiqués target the sense of vulnerability that afflicts their opponents. It is the expansive mood of vulnerability and risk aversion of Western society that invites its cultural opposite – a self-conscious flaunting of indifference to risk-taking and dying. The almost casual and theatrical manner with which death appears to be embraced is incomprehensible to a culture where the smallest health problem is treated as a major personal crisis. For a risk-averse, self-consciously vulnerable culture the suicide bomber personifies invulnerability. The willingness of some individuals to adopt a 100 per cent risk perspective provokes incomprehension and confusion among many commentators. Consequently, such individuals are often described as desperate, irrational, but nevertheless powerful actors, whose motives are said to be beyond comprehension. In awe of these super-terrorists the German sociologist Ulrich Beck exclaims that 'the police are incapable of eliminating a cell of perpetrators who obviously fear nothing'.[37]

Individuals and groups who 'obviously fear nothing' are indeed formidable foes. Such super-warriors who are indifferent to death or pain enjoy a moral advantage over ordinary mortal souls for whom life is very important. Beck gives voice to a widely shared view that believes that the 'suicide mass murderers' have 'revealed the vulnerability of Western civilization'.[38] But why should small groups of suicide bombers constitute an existential threat to Western civilization? It surely cannot be their physical power? Even with the assistance of anxious Western fantasies about enemies who 'obviously fear nothing', it is difficult to imagine how relatively small groups of zealots can threaten an entire way of life. Compared to the powerful foes of the Cold War, the threat posed by the fanatical suicide bomber pales into insignificance. If these relatively small groups of suicidal bombers are able to reveal the 'vulnerability' of the West, it is mainly because it takes very little to reveal this condition. On the contrary, Western culture is all too ready to attest to its weakness. And the constantly repeated expressions of concern about fanatics who fear nothing merely creates an incentive for militants to step up and adopt the role of zealous warriors who will stop at nothing to achieve their objective.

It seems that suicide bombing – which many in the West find incomprehensible – is motivated by the rational calculation that such tactics are likely to weaken the morale of the target population. As Sprinzak argues, 'the perception that terrorists are undeterrable fanatics who are willing to kill millions indiscriminately just to sow fear and chaos belies the reality that they are cold, rational killers who employ violence to achieve specific political objectives'.[39] Labelling terrorists as zealots and fanatics can lead to an underestimation or at least a misunderstanding of the problem. The main threat posed by these individuals is shaped by the response to it. One factor that endows this threat with force is the different cultural assumptions about risk taking. To put it simply, **Western assumptions towards risk are influenced by a one-dimensional concern with loss, whereas those involved in terrorist action regard risk from the perspective of gain**.

Differential cultural attitudes towards risk taking are particularly striking in relation to what kind of loss a society is prepared to countenance. Typically, affluent societies have more to lose than their poorer counterparts. Consequently attitudes towards loss of life and injury vary from culture to culture. The disposition of Anglo-American culture is relatively loss-averse, while its opponents have little to forfeit by taking risks. As Gerald Wilde, a risk psychology expert stated, 'the September 11th terrorists were willing to sacrifice their lives' while 'comfortable middle class North Americans demand a high level of perceived safety and security'.[40] This differential outlook on the risk of death empowers those who are prepared to die. 'The power of terrorist action grows' through 'deeds and the willingness of the perpetrators to extinguish themselves,' notes Beck.[41]

The conventional explanation for the linkage between the growth of the power of terrorism and the willingness to die is that it is very difficult to stop or to defend oneself against someone who does not care about staying alive. A 'human bomb' may indeed be difficult to stop but what makes this phenomenon so disturbing is that puts in relief our own precarious existence. Their power increases in relation to our sense of powerlessness. In the act of defying what Western society fears most − death − the power of the human bomb grows way beyond its physical impact. The Western cultural imagination is concerned with the symbolic force of the act. It overlooks the fact that the attempt to gain power through death can have few durable consequences on the land of the living.

That different attitudes towards risk-taking and life are expressed through the disparities in cultural attitudes towards casualties is evident even in the sphere of military affairs. America's abhorrence of casualties has encouraged some military strategists to rely on technology during the conduct of conflicts. The so-called Revolution in Military Affairs (RMA) doctrine adopted by the US military can be seen as an attempt to avoid having to commit troops to a protracted and bloody encounter. 'Do US policy-makers now envisage their forces remaining dislocated from the potential bloody battlefield?' asks Quille in his exploration of the implication of RMA for the UK.[42] There is little doubt that some politicians and planners are captivated by the RMA because it promises a form of low-casualty warfare. According to Record the first Gulf War was the 'first war in which casualty minimization became from the start an independent operational objective'. Record describes this concern not so much as casualty aversion, but 'casualty phobia'.[43] Some military analysts believe that the 'fear of even the smallest number of casualties limits' the options available to the US.[44]

One analyst has noted that many 'statesmen and generals believe, with absolute and unquestioning conviction, that the United States can no longer use force successfully unless American military casualties are virtually nil'.[45] Yet the very attempt to deploy technology and avoid casualties provides asymmetric actors with an incentive to exploit Western aversion to loss. As O'Hanlon indicates, opponents of the US are 'particularly likely to exploit the US military's dependence on large bases, ships, and other vulnerable assets ... as well as Americans' aversion to suffering casualties'.[46] A military policy underwritten by the assumption of loss aversion has the potential for empowering actors who are prepared to accept higher levels of casualties. This point has been emphasized by Mueller in relation to the conduct of US foreign policy: 'The belief that the United States will avoid risking the lives of its troops, and will capitulate if they are killed in quantity, encourages America's enemies by offering an apparent means to defeat the numerically and technologically superior superpower'.[47] This observation appears to have been internalized by Chinese military strategists. Reports indicate that one of the key US vulnerabilities identified by Chinese strategists is the 'intense US aversion to taking casualties during military missions', as indicated by the abrupt withdrawal of US forces from Somalia in 1993 after casualties began to rise.[48]

It was not only the Chinese who ascribed such significance to the US's unhappy adventure in Somalia. It appears that Osama bin Laden interpreted America's panic-like withdrawal from Somalia as evidence that Washington lacked the will for a bloody military encounter. He informed a British reporter in 1997 that he expected America to put up less resistance than the Soviet Union did in Afghanistan. He noted that 'some of our mujahideen who fought in Afghanistan also participated in operations against the Americans in Somalia – and they were surprised at the collapse of American morale'. And he added that 'this convinced us that the Americans are a paper tiger'.[49]

Osama bin Laden has used the fiasco in Mogadishu to score a propaganda point against his opponent. He boasted:

> Your most disgraceful case was in Somalia, where after vigorous propaganda about the power of the USA and its post Cold War leadership of the new world order you moved tens of thousands of international force, including twenty eight thousand American soldiers into Somalia, However, when tens of your soldiers were killed in minor battles and one American pilot was dragged in the streets of Mogadishu you left the area carrying disappointment, humiliation, defeat and your dead with you. Clinton appeared in front of the whole world threatening and promising revenge, but these threats were merely a preparation for withdrawal. You have been disgraced by Allah and you withdrew; the extent of your impotence and weaknesses became very clear.[50]

The very attempt to institutionalize a risk-averse security policy actually encourages acts of high-profile public terror. Hardt and Negri, two radical critics of American foreign policy, point out that suicide bombing represents an effective counter to the risk-averse RMA. They add that 'at a more abstract and symbolic level, the ideology of an RMA is also contradicted by the growing phenomenon of suicide bombings'.[51]

There is little doubt that casualty phobia has become a factor in the war on terrorism. 'Indeed, casualty phobia has been seen as America's Achilles' heel, the strategic premise behind the Al-Qaeda attacks,' argue the authors of a study of public opinion about war.[52] Although the strength and prevalence of the force of casualty aversion is a subject of debate, there is little doubt that its reality constitutes the premise for the behaviour of violent groups who aim to terrorize the Western public.[53] This point was clearly understood by President Bush, when he told a journalist in December 2001 that 'I do believe there is an image of America out there that we are so materialistic ... almost hedonistic ... that when struck, we wouldn't fight back'. Bush added that 'it was clear that bin Laden felt emboldened and didn't feel threatened by the United States'.[54]

Cultural values regarding loss avoidance are conceptually related to attitudes towards risk-taking and risk perceptions. Al-Qaeda activists appear to take incalculably greater risks than their opponents do. This tendency assumes its most intense form in the case of suicide bombing. The willingness of suicide bombers to take very high risks is itself experienced as a threat. Cordesman warns that 'terrorist movements may be willing to take catastrophic risks', as 'may leaders' who 'see martyrdom as a valid alternative to victory'.[55] From their perspective the West's casualty phobia provides an incentive to intensify action. Politicians and military planners are conscious of the potential negative consequences of the difference in cultural attitudes towards losses. Back in June 2005, President Bush showed that he had internalized these concerns when he told soldiers at Fort Bragg, North Carolina that 'the terrorists believe that free societies are essentially corrupt and decadent, and with a few blows they can force us to retreat'.[56]

Attitudes towards risk-taking are fluid and reflect changing cultural values.[57] Until recently, Anglo-American cultural norms accepted that there were 'good' as well as 'bad' risks and that it was unreasonable to expect absolute safety. In recent decades, this neutral quality of risk has given way to one which is by definition a problem, and it is no longer conceptualized as the weighing up of positive and negative outcomes. In line with the imperative of possibilistic thinking, the weighing up of positive and negative outcomes, which was traditionally involved in the conceptualization of risks, has been replaced by one where only danger enters into the equation. Macintosh and Hills have developed these points in relation to the threat of mass-casualty terrorism. They suggest that a one-sided emphasis on policies which are 'intended to avoid or mitigate risk' by policy-makers may encourage a form of defeatism against opponents who are 'perhaps better attuned to asymmetric risk'.[58]

Differential cultural attitudes towards risk-taking have a crucial bearing on the impact of the threat of violence. It is not simply the case that potential terrorists regard risk-taking from the vantage point of an opportunity; the very risk-averse culture of their target society may encourage them to exploit this difference in attitudes. At the same time, the prevailing risk-averse culture weakens the effectiveness of those officials assigned to deal with this threat. Officials concerned with reassuring a risk-conscious public may well become distracted from the task of preparing society to deal with violent threats. In some cases, official reassurance can actually amplify the public's sense of insecurity and, in others, government warning can actually serve to intensify public fears. This was one of the unintended outcomes of the vague warnings issued by the American Government in October 2001.[59]

Returning to the problem of meaning

From the available evidence, it appears that the purchase of a terrorist threat is often psychological and that its power is significantly enhanced by the fears generated by a risk-averse culture. It is the capacity of such threats to engage with the central cultural characteristics of Western society – risk aversion and sense of vulnerability – that gives them a power disproportionate to the damage inflicted.

An exaggerated representation of the power and risk of terrorism inadvertently empowers those who want to intimidate the public. Three years before 9/11, in his important contribution, 'The Great Super-terrorism Scare', Ehud Sprinzak warned that the 'unprecedented fear of mass destruction terrorism' that spread amongst Western elites could have destabilizing consequences. He wrote that 'Not only are many of the countermeasures likely to be ineffective, but the level of rhetoric and funding devoted to fighting super-terrorism may actually advance a potential super-terrorist's broader goals: sapping the resources of the state and creating a climate of panic and fear that can amplify the impact of any terrorist act'.[60] The phenomenal level of resources devoted to the war on terror confirms Sprinzak's warning. In the US, literally billions of dollars are spent on airport security alone while trillions of dollars have been diverted to finance the wars in Iraq and Afghanistan.[61] Such levels of spending and attitudes towards risk-taking may limit the choices open to policy-makers. In contrast, small radical Islamic groups prepared to take risks are able to experiment and innovate and enjoy a competitive advantage over their opponents. As Sprinzak observed, the people responsible for 9/11 are 'innovators' and 'developers' who 'incessantly look for original ways to surprise and devastate the enemy'.[62]

An inflated sense of vulnerability itself represents an encouragement to terrorists, who understand that they can make an impact on their target public with a relatively minimal investment of resources. That is why they have an incentive to shift their target from the military to civilians. As Thomas observes, 'Foreign societies may believe it is easier to attack the Western psyche or will to fight than to meet it on the battlefield in a contest between technologies'.[63] The intense sense of vulnerability of the target community empowers violent risk takers to achieve objectives through essentially psychological means. That is why regardless of the scale of physical destruction, they can expect to make an impact through sowing fear in their target society. Official preoccupation with the public's vulnerability to asymmetric threats may inadvertently stimulate and encourage attacks against the civilian population and symbolic targets.

It is widely recognized by analysts and experts that the impact of terrorism depends on the response to it. Back in the 1970s, Fromkin argued that 'terrorism wins only if you respond to it in the way that the terrorists want you to; which means that its fate is in your hands and not in theirs'. He also claimed that 'if you choose not to respond at all, or else to respond in a way different from that which they desire, they will fail to achieve their objectives'.[64] Indeed this insight has become a truism that is constantly repeated in books and reports on this subject. However, instead of acting on this insight, Western societies respond to this problem in ways that actually inflate the problem of terror and empower those who wish to inflict it. Instead of posing the question of what can be done, policy-makers constantly ask, 'What if ...?'

Cultural attitudes such as risk and loss aversion and the consciousness of vulnerability are frequently represented as predictable responses to the confusing uncertainties of global society. But such attitudes are not an inevitable response to the threat of physical violence. When people know what they are fighting for they are often capable of acts of bravery and risk-taking behaviour. As we noted in our discussion on the global battle of ideas, Western governments and political elites have become rather inept at communicating ideals that can inspire the public to adopt a robust risk-taking orientation towards security matters. In the very attempt to mobilize the public against terrorism, governments reveal that they have real difficulties in motivating citizens to stand firm and fight. In a penetrating analysis of elite communications in the aftermath of 9/11, David Altheide noted that official propaganda promoted acts of individual consumption and financial giving as the patriotic duty of the American people. The message of 'Keeping America Rolling' served as the focus for the elite's propaganda efforts. Altheide observed:

> Unlike reactions to previous 'external attacks' (e.g. Pearl Harbor) that stressed conservation, personal, sacrifice, and commitment, a prevailing theme of consumption as character and financial contributions as commitment and support pervaded mass-media messages surrounding the 9/11 attacks. These messages made giving and buying commensurate with patriotism and national unity.[65]

This message of 'buying' your way out of a crisis is unlikely to foster a sense of purpose and resolve. It also served as testimony to the low expectation that the US Government had of its people. Historically, threats to a nation are usually countered with fighting talk, appeal to sacrifice and heroism around a cause worth defending. The displacement of the ideal of sacrifice by that of consumption signifies the passive role assigned to people in this conflict. One American journalist recalled that 'we were being asked to bounce back in the name of commerce'. With a hint of irony he added that 'somehow running out and buying stuff or suffering through TV's increasingly excessive commercials would serve as a rebuke to Osama bin Laden and all those who had helped perpetrate the atrocities'.[66]

When the US Government did not appeal to the public to adopt the role of busy consumers it sought to treat people as vulnerable victims. The media in particular represented the 9/11 attacks as proof that 'all Americans were vulnerable'. Altheide concludes that 'the collective identity of victims of terrorist attacks was promoted by news reports stressing communal suffering as well as opportunities to participate in helping survivors and defeating terrorism'.[67] Whatever the impact of these messages they were unlikely to help the public make sense of the circumstances it faced. Public commentators and the media have continually reinforced this sense of meaninglessness through a language that insists that terrorists are senseless, irrational and beyond comprehension and that their motives and targets are unknown. Is it any surprise that a lack of clarity about the enemy, reinforced by an absence of inspiration about what to fight for, contributes to a mood of confusion? It may well be that the differential attitude to death discussed previously could reflect the feeling that there is no obvious cause worth dying for.

In a society that finds it difficult to celebrate causes that are worth fighting for, there is little room for heroism or military virtues. Individual interest and safety trumps other concerns. That is why contemporary culture continually invites soldiers, policemen and other emergency professionals to think of themselves as emotionally vulnerable individuals. For today's cultural elite, heroism has become a distinctly unfashionable, even offensive trait. They can just about put up with a deeply flawed and vulnerable hero but find the strident, self-sufficient and self-confident variety to be somewhat anachronistic. One symbol of the end-of-the-century anti-hero is Captain O'Grady, the American pilot shot down during the war in Bosnia in June 1995. After he was shot down, O'Grady managed to bail out of his aircraft and hid to evade Serb troops on the ground. 'Can I have a tissue please?' he asked, as he cried during a press conference celebrating his rescue. 'Everyone is saying, "You're a hero, you're a hero," but all I was, was a scared little bunny rabbit trying to survive,' he informed the media. Although other pilots were scathing about O'Grady's failure to follow basic procedure, the media celebrated this tearful military hero.[68] O'Grady neatly fitted the role because he personified the mood of vulnerability of his era. Whereas, in the past, heroes were celebrated for saving other people, O'Grady needed only to save himself.

Compared to the cringing scenes of 15 captured British sailors behaving on television as if they were confused children, even O'Grady's request for a tissue appeared heroic. Captured by the Iranians in March 2007, the sailors behaved like naive tourists who had walked into a Hollywood docudrama set by mistake. Arthur Batchelor, one of the captured sailors who revealed how he was tormented by Iranians who had called him Mr Bean, succeeded in portraying himself as a frightened schoolboy paralysed by the normal name-calling of his peers. Is it any surprise that after this public relations fiasco General Rose declared that the British Navy is no longer fit for modern warfare? Rose declared that 'there has to be a psychological preparation, developing of values which allow people in the end to make the ultimate sacrifice willingly.'[69] Yet these are the values that run against the grain of contemporary Western culture.

Bereft of clarity of purpose and meaning, some communities appear to lack the cultural resources to deal effectively with the threat of violence. The response to the Madrid bombings in March 2004 indicates how a handful of terrorists can exert a disproportionate impact on the life of the nation. Within days, 8 million Spaniards took to the streets to demonstrate against terrorism. But instead of serving as a gesture of defiance, these events demonstrated people's feelings of powerlessness. The main effect of these marches was to vote out of government the Popular Party and replace it with the Socialists who promised to withdraw Spanish troops from Iraq. Many voters hoped that in response to a change of government and withdrawal from Iraq the terrorists would spare Spain from further atrocities. Whatever one thinks of the war in Iraq, the election sent out the signal that acts of terror work and can force a nation to repudiate its government and security policy. If that is how a mature Western society reacts to a single atrocity, how would it respond to a more determined and powerful enemy? It does not require a significant leap of the imagination to understand that a society like Israel could not survive for long if it responded like the Spanish every time a bomb went off in Tel Aviv.

In an interesting aside, the British journalist Brendan O'Neill has pointed to the comparison that some commentators drew between the Madrid atrocity and the horrific bombing of the Basque town of Guernica by Hitler's Luftwaffe during the Spanish Civil War in 1937. O'Neill questions this comparison, noting that the planting of bombs on a train by a handful of individuals should not be compared to the saturation bombing of Guernica – an event that destroyed 70 per cent of the town and killed 1,500 people.[70] However despite the difference in the scale of destruction, an important lesson can be gained through this comparison. Guernica turned into a symbol of defiance and gave meaning to those committed to the struggle against fascism, while the bombing of Madrid tended to remind people of their powerlessness with the effect of demoralizing people. 'The fallout from Madrid powerfully demonstrates that terrorism's impact is determined less by what the terrorists do, than by how governments and the public respond to it,' argues O'Neill. He believes that 'how we experience terrorism depends on how we feel about ourselves, our way of life, our society and our values.'[71] Having examined what our response to terrorism says about ourselves, we shall soon explore what our response should be.

Notes

1. Zulaika (2003) p. 191.

2. Full text of Osama Bin Laden's remarks on videotape (29 October 2004), www.cesnur.org/2004/osama_video.htm.

3. Brian Halweil, 'The Bio-terror in Your Burger', 6 November 2001, www.worldwatch.org/node/1710.

4. Cited in B. Johnson (2005) 'The Next Asian Plague', *FrontPage Magazine*, 14 January 2005.

5. See 'World Bank, Pentagon: global warming red alert; Weather of mass destruction bigger threat than terrorism', 22 February 2004, www.greenpeace.org/international/news/world-bank-pentagon-warn-cli.

6. Best, J. (1999) *Random Violence; How We Talk About New Crimes and New Victims*, Berkeley: University of California Press, p. 168.

7. 'UNAIDS Executive Director compares Aids pandemic to threat of terrorism, says EU "has failed" to deal with diseases', *The Body*, 20 April 2004.

8. Abbott, C., Rogers, P. and Sloboda, J. (2006) *Global Responses To Global Threats; Sustainable Security for the 21st Century*, Oxford Research Group, p. 18.

9. See Sawin, J. L. 'Global Security Brief no. 3 Climate Change Poses Greater Security Threat Than Terrorism', 1 April 2005, Worldwatch Institute.

10. Athol Yates (2005) *Business Survival and the Influenza Pandemic*, Australian Homeland Security Research Centre, p. 4.

11. 'International Health Ministers Agree Action on Pandemic Flu', *Medical News Today*, 19 November 2005, www.medicalnewstoday.com.

12. See Furedi, F. (1997) *Population & Development*, Cambridge: Polity Press.

13. See 'Paul Ehrlich Comments', News Release, Stanford University, 15 November 2002.

14. 'From Director', Press Release, Population Coalition, October 2001.

15. Weiland (2005).

16. Ibid., p. 6.

17. Ibid., p. 16.

18. Altheide (2002) pp. 3–4.

19. Haggerty (2003) pp. 194 and 205.

20. Cited in Edwards (2006) p. 18.

21. Sparks (2003) p. 204.

22. Friedman and Sapolsky (2006) p. 4.

23. Wessely (2005) p. 464.

24. Better Regulation Commission (2006) pp. 3 and 4.

25. Al Gore, 'The time to act is now – the climate crisis and the need for leadership', www.mi2g.net, 5 March 2006.

26. Mick Hume, 'A police state, without any police', *The Times*, 25 February 2004.

27. See the *Daily Telegraph*, 23 February 2004.

28. 'J'Accuse! Top General lambasts "moral cowardice" of government and military chiefs', *Daily Mail*, 12 April 2007.

29. Lacquement (2004) p. 46.

30. Hardt and Negri (2005) p. 47.

31. Lacquement (2004) p. 41.

32. Record (2002) p. 1.

33. Homer-Dixon (2002) p. 12.

34. Edwards (2006) p. 5.

35. Cited in 'You love life, we love death', *Asian Times*, 23 March 2004.

36. Cited in Eric Ormsby, 'The Echo Effect', *The Wall Street Journal*, 19 October 2001.

37. Beck (2003) p. 255

38. Ibid., p. 262.

39. Sprinzak (2000) p. 18.

40. Cited in Dan Keegan, 'September 11th; an earthquake in risk perception', *Drivers.Com*, 17 October 2001.

41. Beck (2003) p. 260.

42. Quille (1998) p. 72.

43. Record (2002) pp. 1 and 5.

44. Major Donald Vandergriff, 'truth@readiness.mil', *Proceedings Magazine*, June 1999.

45. Mueller (2000) p. 12.

46. O'Hanlon (2000) p. 3.

47. Mueller (2000) p. 12.

48. D. Wood, 'China Explores Ways to Defeat Superior US Forces', *San Francisco Chronicle*, 20 April 2001.

49. Cited in Record (2002) p. 7.

50. Osama bin Laden, 'Declaration of War against the Americans Occupying the Land of the Two Holy Places', 23 August 1996, available at www.comw. org/pda/fulltext/960823binladen.html.

51. Hardt and Negri (2005) p. 45.

52. Cited in Keith Lawrence, 'Reviving Draft Would Sway Public Opinion About War', 9 January 2003, *Duke University, News and Communications*, www.dukenews.duke.edu/2003/01/drafttip0109._print.ht

53. Lacquement (2004), along with others, claims that it is not the American public but its elites who are casualty-averse.

54. Cited in Record (2002) p. 7.

55. Cordesman (2000) p. 1.

56. www.whitehouse.gov/news/releases/2005/06/20050628-7.html.

57. See Furedi (2006).

58. Macintosh and Hills (2000) pp. 53 and 57

59. C. Meade, 'Don't Scare the Public with Vague Warnings', *Los Angeles Times*, 24 October 2001.

60. Sprinzak (1998) p. 27.

61. Mueller (2006a) p. 31.

62. Sprinzak (2001) p. 43.

63. Thomas (2001) p. 25.

64. Fromkin (1975) p. 697.

65. Altheide (2006) p. 88.

66. *Washington Post* journalist Tom Shales is cited in Altheide (2006) p. 96.

67. Altheide (2006) pp. 97 and 111.

68. See Lena Williams, 'What It Takes to make a Hero', *The New York Times*, 18 June 1995.

69. J'Accuse! Top General lambasts "moral cowardice" of government and military chiefs', *Daily Mail*, 12 April 2007.

70. Brendan O'Neill, 'Creating the Enemy, how a risk-averse West has inflamed the terrorism it fears', www.spiked-online.com, 18 July 2005.

71. Ibid.

CHAPTER 7

So What Is the Problem of Terrorism?

More so than with most controversial subjects, it is difficult to know what to believe about the danger of terrorism. Governments are frequently and quite legitimately accused of playing the terrorist card. Sometimes governments are castigated for falsely blaming an individual or group to create a pretext for acts of repression. Too often a terrorist attack appears as the predictable prelude for the withdrawal of civil rights. In turn, critics of government policies are castigated for either being complacent or in denial about the threat posed by terrorism. They are accused of the 'denial' of a lethal adversary that has 'for too long impeded its effective prosecution'.[1] In this chapter we explore the arguments put forward by the protagonists in this debate and offer an alternative explanation of why terrorism appears as such a major global problem.

Playing the terrorist card

The official version of the terrorist threat that is communicated through government press releases and statements is widely contested by a significant constituency of critics. Questions are constantly raised by opposition politicians, journalists and commentators. Some of these critics go so far as to claim that the terrorist threat is a myth, invented by a small political cabal in Washington to mobilize support for President Bush and/or legitimize the expansionist foreign policy objectives of the United States.

There are numerous variations of the terrorist card argument. Some concede that there is a threat, but contend that it has been 'exploited' or 'manipulated' by a Bush or a Blair. Others reject the very idea of a terrorist threat and argue that virtually the entire sequence of events from 9/11 onwards are acts of official deception designed to fool the public and gain their acquiescence for a host of militaristic and repressive measures. In its most simplistic form this argument portrays President Bush as a latter-day Hitler practising the 'big lie':

> *In George Bush's America psychological warfare aimed directly at the American public is designed to manufacture the political platform to launch a perpetual state of war that will produce a totalitarian regime headed by a Commander-in-Chief who is nothing more than a military dictator.*[2]

The writer of this analysis believes that the motive for launching a 'perpetual state of war' is 'xenophobia; the demonization of immigrants; fears of foreign cultures'. In its most extravagant form, the thesis that governments have invented the threat of terrorism is transmitted through conspiracy theories that hint at government involvement in 9/11 or claim that there was an official cover-up.[3]

Most proponents of the playing-the-terrorist-card thesis eschew conspiracy theories. The burden of their argument is that governments inflate and exaggerate the threat of terrorism to strengthen their authority and to gain political advantage over their opponents. 'Not for the first time, the Government twisted a particular event for propagandistic scaremongering about the repressive measures supposedly needed to combat the undoubted threat from terrorism,' argues one UK newspaper editorial.[4] Such criticisms have become widespread in the media and in academic commentaries. In recent years the manipulation of the issue of terrorism is frequently described as the 'politics of fear'. So a group of British academics urged 'the government to abandon talk of a "War on Terror"', since this 'terminology is misleading and disproportionate and leaves the Prime Minister open to the charge that he is exploiting a politics of fear'.[5]

The term 'politics of fear' is widely used and has acquired the status of an everyday idiom. Its frequent usage indicates that beliefs about the official manipulation of the terrorism issue are widely held and extensively circulated through popular culture and the media.[6] For some observers, the very fact that Bush won the November 2004 election is itself testimony to the formidable power of the politics of fear: 'It is increasingly apparent that the climate of fear promoted by the Bush Administration in the wake of a series of national traumas is having a wide effect,' warned the editor of the online publication *AlterNet*.[7] Since that time similar accusations are constantly levelled at the Bush Administration: 'President George W. Bush, Vice President Cheney and the entire Republican election theme are scrambling to make their so-called war on terror the focus for the next seven weeks,' sneered one critic before warning of the 'scare tactics used by the White House'.[8] Similar charges were levelled at the Blair Government during the 2005 General Election campaign.[9]

Since 9/11, the number of prominent opinion-makers who believe that the Bush Administration has self-consciously promoted the politics of fear through the war on terror has grown. Such a view conveyed by Zbigniew Brzezinski, former national security adviser to President Carter, is paradigmatic of the politics of fear thesis. Brzezinski has denounced the Bush Administration for creating a 'culture of fear' in America through the elevation of the war on terror into what he characterizes as a 'national mantra'. He claims that the very 'vagueness of the phrase' war on terror was 'deliberatively (or instinctively) calculated by its sponsors' to spread fear. 'Fear obscures reason, intensifies emotions and makes it easier for demagogic politicians to mobilize the public on behalf of the policies they want to pursue,' argued Brzezinski.[10]

Those who uphold the thesis of the manipulative promotion of the politics of fear don't have to search hard to find illustrations of their argument. They can point to self-serving, highly charged statements made by politicians who appear to seek to gain electoral advantage through exaggerating the threat of terrorism. In an incisive contribution to this discussion, the political scientist Ian Lustick highlights the example of the Republican pollster and strategist Frank Luntz, whose tactics aimed to exploit the legacy of 9/11 in order to assist the Bush–Cheney 2004 election campaign. Luntz's memorandum, *Communicating the Principles of Prevention and Protection in the War on Terror*, outlined a strategy that relied on continuously appealing to the memory of 9/11 to ensure that this event dominated the debate. He recommended that 'no speech about homeland security or Iraq should begin without a reference to 9/11'.[11] Subsequent experience indicates that this strategy was followed to the letter as the Republicans embraced the symbolism of 9/11 in their campaign.

There is considerable evidence that the politicization of security issues was frequently pursued by governments and transmitted through official communication. Supporters of the politics of fear thesis frequently draw attention to the alarmist security culture underpinning official policy. Governments have repeatedly issued unspecific terrorist warnings and threat alerts. They do this even though they understand that such knee-jerk reactions may help those who want to terrorize society.[12] That is why even former Homeland Security Head Tom Ridge resented the pressure he experienced from Washington to elevate threat levels to orange, or 'high' risk of terrorist attack. After he resigned from his post, Ridge remarked that there was only flimsy evidence to justify raising threat levels and that his agency was often the 'least inclined to raise it'.[13] In the UK there are numerous examples of 'crying wolf' threat alerts. In April 2005, the Home Office was forced to apologize to ten men who were placed under anti-terrorist control orders after the highly publicized ricin factory plot in 2002 proved to be the product of the crying-wolf syndrome. There was no ricin, but there were castor oil beans and a so-called cook book and lots of imaginative thinking.[14]

Before we evaluate the current role of the politics of fear, it is important to note that there is nothing unique about the exaggeration of threat or its manipulation in a conflict situation. The war of words that surround a conflict or a counter-terrorist campaign are always subordinate to the imperative of propaganda. Threats are invariably portrayed in a form that is likely to mobilize public support and to legitimate official policy. So it is not particularly surprising that the post-9/11 environment continued with this tradition. If anything, what is unusual is the speed and force with which scepticism concerning the official version of events has been raised. As a result, counter-terrorism policies are frequently questioned in the media and elsewhere. For example, the raising of a threat alert in Britain is often immediately followed by criticism from the media which queries the official version of events.

So to what extent is the problem of terrorism an outcome of mendacious propaganda and the politics of fear? Answering this question is far from straightforward. Politicians who exaggerate a threat are not always acting entirely dishonestly. Nor are they necessarily inventing or exploiting the threat. In fact there is little that is unique or distinct about the alarmist communications that warn the public about an impending danger. The amplification of threat alerts and alarmist (mis)communications are a part of the normal routine of official communication strategy. Governments feel that they are entitled to adopt such a strategy because it promotes the public's 'awareness'. Indeed the effectiveness of such fear alerts is under regular discussion by its practitioners. Campaigns on public health issues, climate change, drugs or children's welfare self-consciously inflate the dimension of the threat. In these instances, exaggeration and manipulation are often acts that aim to gain support for policies that their authors actually believe in. Indeed it is precisely the conviction that this is an issue that is far too important to leave to chance that motivates officials to assume that they are entitled to espouse the use of deception. It is worth noting that many critics of Bush's alarmist inflation of the threat of terrorism also use similar tactics. During the 2004 election campaign, Democrats were not averse to spreading scare stories about an impending flu epidemic and attacked Bush for not taking this threat seriously. So, in so far as the politics of fear represents a significant influence on people's behaviour, it is not confined to the issue of terrorism.

That politicians play the terrorism card to gain electoral advantage is also not particularly surprising. But what does that mean? Take the case of US Senator Joe Lieberman, for example. In 2006 he lost the Democratic primary election in Connecticut because of his pro-war stance, and decided to run for re-election as an independent candidate. In the aftermath of the arrest of 24 people in Britain for terrorist offences in August 2006, Lieberman issued the following statement:

> I am worried that too many people, both in politics and out, don't appreciate the seriousness of the threat to American security and the evil of the enemy that faces us – more evil or as evil as Nazism and probably more dangerous than the Soviet Communists we fought during the long Cold War.[15]

This statement represents an extreme variant of threat inflation. Lieberman can also be accused of attempting to exploit the issue through implying that, unlike himself, his opponent did not take this threat seriously. However, the fact that Lieberman self-servingly 'used' this issue does not mean that he does not believe that it is a real problem. That Lieberman adopted a politically illiterate rhetoric about the evils of Nazism is symptomatic of the decline of standards of public discourse. He can be accused of poor judgement, but not necessarily of dishonesty. Sadly he probably meant every word of his hysterical statement.

From our analysis we would draw the conclusion that the numerous manifestations of the politics of fear are not so much an outcome of the dishonest behaviour of an individual politician, but the consequences of the workings of the contemporary cultural imagination. Take the electoral strategy proposed in Frank Luntz's memorandum discussed above: the fundamental premise of his approach was to 'continually draw attention to the point that 9/11 changed everything'.[16] This advice was followed to the letter by the Republicans. But Vice President

Cheney was not trying to deceive the world when he remarked that '9/11 changed everything' and that it changed 'our recognition of our vulnerabilities'.[17] On the contrary, the conviction that 9/11 has changed everything, and that we therefore now live in a very different world, strongly resonates with the temper of our time. The belief that humanity faces an intensely uncertain future that bears little relationship to the past is not confined to a small group of malevolent political manipulators. Change and uncertainty have acquired negative connotations in the contemporary imagination. Such sentiments are expressed through the idea that the rapid pace of change has created a dangerous world where the future is uniquely unforeseeable and threatening. This outlook has been internalized by a significant section of opinion-makers, from left-wing and liberal academics to environmentalists and producers of popular culture. Such sentiments fuel a palpable sense of dread towards the unknown and acquire a coherent expression through the ascendancy of possibilistic thinking.

There is little doubt that from time to time governments have played the terrorist card. Governments have frequently been economical with the truth and selective in their presentation of the issues. Through politicizing and dramatizing security, their action has encouraged the flourishing of the fear market. It has also fostered an illiberal and repressive official attitude towards civil liberties. Post-9/11 repressive legislation is inconsistent with democratic norms and deserves to be condemned. However, we believe that the main driver of the politics of fear is not some hidden Machiavellian agenda, but the imperative of Western precautionary culture. In particular the prevailing mood of vulnerability encourages fear to flourish. And these are fears which afflict the political elites no less than the public: probably even more.

From the previous discussion, it should be evident that the representation of terrorism as an existential threat has little factual basis in reality. But following the Rumsfeldian logic adopted in all examples of worst-case thinking – about the dire consequences of global warming, the global transmission of avian flu, collision with a near-earth object – threat assessments are rarely driven by hard evidence. Rumsfeld's premise that the 'absence of evidence is not an evidence of absence' serves as a warrant for rupturing the relationship between evidence and policy. The tendency to transform threat assessments into forms of risk communication has been questioned by one of the UK's leading academic experts on the subject. Professor Lawrence Freedman believes that the wider imperatives of risk communication lead to 'further distortions' of the original assessment.[18] In line with the mood of our times, the claims made about the threat posed by terrorism have an anticipatory and speculative character. But they are no more anticipatory or speculative than policies pursued in the domain of child protection, the environment or public health. The adoption of the kind of worst-case thinking that shapes official versions of the terrorist threat informs policy-making in general. So the problem is the politicization of fear in general, rather than its manifestation through the issue of terrorism.[19]

One final point: Whatever one says about governments playing the terrorist card, the tactic has not proved to be particularly effective for consolidating public support for the government. From time to time raising the alarm has scared people and served to distract them from more pressing concerns. Opinion surveys indicate that there are high levels of anxiety about terrorism, but this anxiety has not been translated into the growth of national unity and enthusiasm for the war on terror. Contrary to expectations, the legitimacy and authority of governments has not been enhanced through this war. As Brzezinski noted,

> *America today is not the self-confident and determined nation that responded to Pearl Harbor ... nor is it the calm America that waged the Cold War with quiet persistence despite the knowledge that a real war could be initiated abruptly within minutes and prompt the death of 100 million Americans within just a few hours. We are now divided, uncertain and potentially very susceptible to panic in the event of another terrorist act in the United States itself.[20]*

As the war on terror progressed, governments on both sides of the Atlantic have experienced an erosion of support. Arguably it has discredited the Bush Administration and undermined the Blair regime. A significant section of the public in the US and the UK have become deeply suspicious of official statements about terrorism. A UK newspaper headline, which accuses the government of 'The Cynical Manipulation of Fear And Security' and warns of the 'cynicism it generates among the public', illustrates the deep divisions in society.[21] In a survey carried out in the UK in March 2007, more than half of the respondents stated that they would distrust the government if it stated that military action was needed to protect Britain from another country.[22] There is little evidence to substantiate the claim that the politics of fear has succeeded in promoting a mood of unity in face of an external enemy. Those who played the terrorist card certainly lack a winning hand.

Disproportionate response to the physical threat posed by terrorism

The war on terrorism has also been queried by a group of academics and analysts who, while accepting the reality of this threat, believe that the response to it has been wildly disproportionate to the danger it represents. Unlike critics who regard the official policy simply as a cynical attempt to scare people into acquiescence, the focus of this group is its disproportionate and out-of-control character. They believe that not only is this policy very costly in economic and non-economic terms, it can actually do far more damage than that caused by the terrorists.

Through attempting to provide a cost-benefit analysis of anti-terrorist policies, Clark Chapman concluded that the 'disproportionate reaction to 9/11 was as damaging as the direct destruction of lives and property'. He argued that 'the economic and emotional damage unleashed by 9/11, which touched the lives of all Americans, resulted mostly from our reactions to 9/11 and the anthrax scare, rather than from objective damage'.[23] Chapman's arguments have been convincingly elaborated by John Mueller, who in his book *Overblown* focuses on what he perceives as a colossal overreaction to 9/11. He writes that 'international terrorism generally kills a few hundred people a year worldwide – not much more, usually than the number who drown yearly in the bathtubs in the United States'. According to Mueller, since 2001, 'fewer people have been killed in America by international terrorism than have drowned in toilets or have died from bee stings'. As evidence of the unfortunate consequences of this overreaction, Mueller points to the fact that 'considerably more than 3,000 Americans have died since 9/11 because, out of fear, they drove cars rather than flew airplanes, or because they were swept into wars made politically possible by the terrorists events'.[24] For Mueller, the response to the threat represents a greater problem than acts of terrorism.

The main strength of Mueller's contribution is his attempt to place the threat of terrorism into a wider historical perspective. He puts up a convincing case that shows that the destructive potential of terrorism is far more modest than the way it is presented in accounts of new terrorism. He believes that it is the response to terrorism that is causing the real damage to the US. The huge economic costs of fighting the war on terror can be quantified, but it is difficult to put a price tag on the cost of losing civil liberties and of reorganizing life around the expectation of a terrorist attack. Mueller fears that the US Government is actually playing into the terrorists' hands. It is difficult to disagree with his conclusion that 'thus far, at least, international terrorism is a rather rare and, appropriately considered, not generally a terribly destructive phenomenon'. On the other hand, the responses to it have been 'misguided, foolish, overwrought, and economically costly, and sometimes they have been unnecessarily destructive'.[25]

Mueller's warnings are also reinforced by the persuasive analysis contained in Ian Lustick's *Trapped in the War on Terror*. Lustick is scathing about the 'immense costs of the war on Terror' and its damage on society. As far as he is concerned, the real problems facing the US are 'self-inflicted'. He writes:

> The war on Terror itself, not Al-Qaeda or its clones, has become the primary threat to the wellbeing of Americans in the first decade of the twenty-first century. My fundamental conclusion is that the war on Terror is vastly out of proportion to the actual problems we face from terrorists and terrorist groups.[26]

Lustick provides compelling evidence to show the limited threat that terrorism represents within the US. He notes that, despite the massive expansion of surveillance, the introduction of new security measures and investigations, hardly any terrorist activity has been detected. Despite an expenditure of phenomenal resources on security, since 9/11 the authorities in the US have convicted virtually no one of posing a serious terrorist threat.[27]

The disconnection between reality and the war on terror is also the focus of a series of articles by the UK-based analyst Bill Durodié. Like Lustick, Durodié believes that the official reaction to terrorism is disconnected from its reality. He is scathing of the attempt to represent this problem as an existential threat and argues that through presenting this risk in such an exaggerated manner the government is inadvertently helping the terrorists.[28] He notes that 'constant warnings readily lead to a self-fulfilling demand for the authorities to do something – distracting them and us from real risks and diverting social resources accordingly'.[29] One of the most dramatic consequences of the imperative of 'doing something' has been the displacement of probabilistic-led risk management by possibilistic-oriented policies. Ron Suskind has drawn attention to what he calls, in the title of his book, *The One Percent Doctrine*.[30] The title refers to an event in November 2001 where top American officials were discussing how to respond to the risk of another low-probability but high-impact event like 9/11. At this discussion, Vice President Cheney came up with the one per cent doctrine. He argued that if there was a one percent risk of a threat it had to be treated as if its likelihood was absolutely certain. Through converting a potential danger into one that had to be treated as an actual danger, Cheney provided the argument for the institutionalization of threat amplification.

In one sense, what these critics are saying about the disconnection between the perception and the reality of the risk of terrorism can be applied to other controversies, and are typical of a broader pattern of risk aversion. Indeed, Durodié acknowledges this point. In a series of articles, he has drawn attention to the promotion of similar appeals to fear in communications about the environment, new technology and health.[31] It is now widely recognized that what we truly dread is often not a serious threat to our lives. This pattern is strikingly evident in relation to periodic panics about child abductions, crime, pollution and food scares. As in the case of the war on terrorism, society's response to these problems is frequently very costly and often makes the situation worse. There is however one important difference between the workings of the one per cent doctrine in relation to the war on terror and similar panic-like reactions to other threats. The response to the fear of terror has had a directly tangible and costly impact on the way we lead our lives. It has also directly and indirectly contributed to the rise of conflict and global insecurity. It has unleashed a military conflict which increasingly appears to have a life of its own. With so much at stake it is important to try to account for officialdom's disproportionate, and in many ways self-defeating, reaction to the risk of terrorism.

Authority without meaning and the crisis of elite authority

Critics of the war on terror who rightly insist that this threat is overblown have made a valuable contribution to clarifying the disjuncture between the true dimension of this threat and its inflated representation. However, there is still one very important question that needs to be considered, which is how do we account for the constant exaggeration of this threat? One contributing factor has been noted previously. This is influence of the culture of precaution that continually seeks to transform the risks facing society into threats that call into question human survival. Another crucial factor that needs to be considered is the behaviour of officialdom and the political elites. It is simplistic to assume that official policy is merely the outcome of a dishonest and cynical stratagem. Our analysis suggests that the political elites are genuinely concerned, possibly even more so than the public, about the threat of terrorism.

Fear of terrorism appears to be more pronounced among the political elites than the rest of society. This response goes against the grain of the general pattern that prevails today. Most of the time governments attempt to manage risks through messages that seek to reassure the public that the situation is under control. Consequently governments are often accused of covering up major risks to the public. Advocacy organizations regularly demand that officials acknowledge a hidden danger and take action to deal with this or that threat to people's wellbeing. But when it comes to terrorism governments appear far more concerned than the public! Indeed governments who are denounced for playing the terrorist card, exaggerating this threat or intentionally creating fear, are seldom accused of playing the fear card in relation to climate change, or AIDS or child obesity or pollution. Instead they are castigated for their do-nothing complacency. But when it comes to the fear of terrorism it appears to have a more powerful resonance amongst the political elites than the rest of society.

The response of Western governments to terrorism is not only disproportionate to the threat, it is also at variance with the precedent of the past. Throughout the twentieth century governments attempted to treat terrorism as a policing matter. British authorities took the view that the 'principle of minimum force' was the most effective way of dealing with this problem.[32] The aim of this perspective was also to criminalize terrorist activities. The policy of criminalization self-consciously attempted to discredit the political claims made by opponents. As one leading expert on terrorism observed, 'In separating terrorist tactics from their political context, the intent clearly was to criminalize a certain mode of political expression'.[33] One of the key objectives of criminalization is to facilitate the project of moral condemnation. A police action that targets criminals helps governments to occupy the moral high ground. Governments still attempt to morally condemn, hence the use of terms like fanatic, extremist, zealot and evil to describe the enemy. However, by treating the conflict as a military one rather than as a policing matter, they have fundamentally altered the approach. If this is a war on terror, then the policy of criminalization becomes inappropriate and officials will find it difficult to gain the moral authority that is usually bestowed on those fighting criminals. Wars are not fought against criminal gangs or terrorists. Is it any surprise therefore that officials in the UK and the US appear to have such difficulty in defining the adversary? In the very act of raising the stakes and opting for a global war on terror, governments signal their confusion about the constitution of the enemy.

One of the clearest symptoms of the sense of elite disorientation towards this issue is the difficulty it has in trying to reassure the public about its security. Normally governments devote considerable resources to retain public confidence in their capacity to deal with threats to society. Usually they attempt to convey the message that 'we are in control' and that effective measures have been taken to maintain public safety. As a rule governments respond to serious threats by downplaying the dangers they represent and exaggerating their capacity to deal with them. But since 9/11 governments appear to have exhausted their capacity to boost public morale when confronted with a violent foe. As the American commentator James Fallows remarked on the fifth anniversary of 9/11, 'the political market failure is that over the last five years, it has been far more effective for politicians to appeal to sky-falling fears than to try to calm them'.[34] In other words, politicians are much better at raising the alarm than in calming the public's nerves. The implicit official message of 'be afraid' has come to dominate public deliberations on the legacy of 9/11. Through their behaviour politicians have succeeded in raising the emotional temperature rather than lowering it.

It is almost as if the political elite cannot help but continually heighten public anxiety. Mueller noted that whereas the message in the past was 'life as usual', today the opposite story is communicated. He cites one Homeland Security official who instructed people: 'Be scared. Be very, very scared. But go on with your lives'.[35] In May 2002, Rumsfeld declared that it is only a matter of time before terrorists who are determined to destroy America will obtain nuclear, biological or chemical weapons. 'They inevitably will get their hands on them and they will not hesitate to use them,' Rumsfeld informed the Senate Appropriation Subcommittee.[36] In private hearings, one hears top government scientists warn that anyone with a $50 chemistry set could cause mass mayhem. Although such statements are manifestly absurd and underestimate the equipment and expertise required for perpetrating such acts, they reveal important insights about the outlook of officialdom. Such irresponsible speculative statements should be interpreted in a two-fold sense both as a warning to the public and an acknowledgement of official fright. Frequently government communiqués transmit the defeatist message that terrorists can strike any place and at any time. These communications barely conceal a mood of official panic when they warn the public that a 'determined' terrorist 'cannot be stopped' and the question is 'not if, but when' the

next 'big one' will occur. In a speech that Tom Ridge gave to a group
of security analysts and academics in London in November 2002, he
used the word 'vulnerability' ten times. The audience was informed
that 'we must direct our resources towards securing against the greatest
vulnerability ... We must reduce America's vulnerability to terrorism
... We must integrate analysis about evolving terrorist strategies with
an assessment of our vulnerabilities'.[37] Instead of the traditional tone of
triumphalism associated with wartime rhetoric, Ridge and his colleagues
opt for a downbeat tone of insecure defeatism.

Official rhetoric continually betrays a sense of powerlessness towards
the enemy. When FBI Director Robert Mueller warned that 'there
will be another terrorist attack – we will not be able to stop it', other
top officials joined in with their gloomy predictions. 'We don't know
the specifics, the time and the place, but we have great reason to believe
that we could be hit anytime in the next few years,' said Senator Richard
Shelby, the top Republican on the Senate intelligence panel.[38] There
was a time when such pessimistic statements regarding warnings of
unspecific threats were regarded as an act of defeatism. Today officials
appear to believe that through revealing their worst fears they are
performing an act of public duty.

While the Director of the FBI was crystal-ball gazing and predicting
that a suicide bombing in the US was inevitable, his colleagues in the
British Home Office were also doing their bit to raise the temperature.
On the morning of 8 November it issued a statement about a possible
weapons of mass destruction terrorist attack on London. However,
embarrassed by its potential for sowing confusion, the Home Office
withdrew the warning and issued a toned-down version. This
humiliating episode of the hasty withdrawal of a panicky threat alert is
a testimony to a mood of elite disorientation. Officials are not only
exaggerating a threat, but also revealing their own confusion and
anxieties about the future of their society. In this case the Home Office
appeared to get so carried away with its own sense of insecurity that it
simply blurted out in public the anxieties that haunted its own
imagination.

In some instances, the intemperate language used by British officials
to describe problems of security has been misinterpreted as evidence
of aggressive propaganda. In November 2003, the then Home
Secretary David Blunkett was criticized in the media for making over-
the-top statements about a recently arrested terror suspect, Sajid Badat.
He was accused of chasing 'cheap headlines and of prejudicing a fair

trial for the suspect'. Blunkett's statement condemned Badat for posing 'a very real threat to the liberty and life of our country'.[39] The critics were right to draw attention to the fact that these comments could prejudice a trial in the future. However, what Blunkett's comment also exposed was a deep-seated sense of insecurity towards the challenge posed by terrorism. Blunkett's remarkable statement that one man posed a 'very real threat to the liberty and life of Britain' is testimony to the insecurity and defeatism of officialdom. Through attributing such fantastic power to one individual, Blunkett drew attention to his own powerlessness. That Britain's political elite feels threatened by the action of one man is evidence of its own inner sense of malaise.

The political vocabulary of the twenty-first century lacks concepts that can make sense of a situation where relatively small numbers of individuals are attributed with the power to call into question a way of life of a mature Western society. Just listen to President Bush, when in the aftermath of 9/11 he attempted to 'reassure' his audience with the words that 'when the terrorists struck our homeland, they thought we would fold'.[40] Of course, even in their wildest dreams those who planned and carried out the attacks on 9/11 never imagined that the US would 'fold'. This is an idea that appears more plausible to the President of the US than to the enemies of that nation. **Defensive statements such as this indicate that the threat of terrorism is the product of both the disoriented cultural imagination of a defensive Western cultural elite as well as of disgruntled and alienated individuals and groups who feel that they have little to lose**.

One of the recurrent themes of our analysis has been the incoherent and visibly defensive attitude of Western officials and politicians towards the question of security. It genuinely appears to be lost for words and concepts, and continues to find it difficult to give a name to its enemy. More important is its difficulty in knowing what it stands for in the global battle of ideas. Its moral defensiveness has led to a situation where it lacks a vocabulary through which it can give meaning to the challenges it faces. This mood of defensiveness is particularly noticeable in its reaction to the phenomenon of home-grown terrorism. This is clearly a problem that exists within the homeland! The estrangement and radicalization of significant sections of the public calls into question the ability of the political elites to exercise authority.

As noted before, the fact that terrorism is regarded as not merely a physical but also an ideological threat represents an important departure from the way it was conceptualized in the pre-9/11 era. In the late twentieth century the motive of religious fundamentalism was regularly linked to the phenomenon of new terrorism. But these so-called fundamentalist movements were rarely perceived as ideological competitors by Western governments. They certainly were not seen as a potential pole of attraction to people living within Western societies. Not so long ago – the end of the 1980s – saw the rise of the 'end of history' thesis which argued that the end of the Cold War proved the triumph of Western liberalism and the exhaustion of other ideologies. This was the time when the new terrorist became the object of official concern. But at the time anxiety about this new threat was confined to the physical damage and mass casualties that they could cause. Today the problem has been expanded into a threat that threatens a 'way of life'. Concern with the radicalization of dissent and the ideological appeal of anti-Western and more specifically anti-American sentiments indicates why in the official mind the danger of terrorism is experienced as a threat to a way of life. It is perceived as an ideological challenge that has demonstrated its formidable influence through its success in 'radicalizing' a section of the public within the homeland. Indeed this ideology is endowed with supernatural powers of frightening proportions. According to one account, 'The international terrorist ideology now has a life of its own beyond the lives of the men in the cave that spawned it'. This 'ideological virus' mutates as it spreads 'into forms that can infect previously untouched groups'.[41] The belief that this monstrous threat can infect people in any society says a lot about its ideological immunity system.

As noted in Chapter 4, the perception of terrorism as an ideological threat is linked to the apparent decline of the moral authority of the West. Even before 9/11 there was more than a hint of defensiveness about the capacity of Western values to prevail over those of hostile opponents. One conservative American contributor gave voice to this sentiment and concluded that 'protecting Western culture from foreign assault requires domestic revival'. A decade before 9/11 he warned that 'the twenty-first century could once again find Islam at the gates of Vienna, as immigrants or terrorists if not armies'.[42] Today there is little evidence of a domestic revival. Indeed Western governments are sensitive about their very limited capacity for inspiring their own public. The problem of engaging the public and gaining its support is strikingly evident in relation to the post-9/11 political landscape. One report on British public diplomacy claims that it is far more difficult to convince the public to back the official line on the war on terror than it was during the Cold War.[43]

Almost imperceptibly the threat of terrorism has been reinterpreted predominantly as an ideological one. Joseph Nye, a leading American foreign relations expert, places an emphasis on what he calls the *soft power* of terrorist organizations. Soft power, which Nye describes as 'the ability to get what you want through attraction rather than coercion or payments' seems to directly contradict the conventional representation of terrorism with its focus on realizing objectives through inflicting fear.[44] Official concern about the influence of jihadist websites, videos and other forms of communications indicates the seriousness with which the soft power is taken. 'Terrorism depends crucially on soft power for its ultimate victory,' states Nye, who also believes that 'it depends on its ability to attract support from the crowd at least as much as its ability to destroy the enemy's will to fight'.[45]

Nye's shift in focus from mass-casualty and weapons of mass destruction terrorism to the danger of soft power represents an important motif in official thinking. In effect, concern about ideas rather than just physical force shapes elite perceptions of the problems. Terrorism is feared as an ideological competitor for the allegiance of the very same publics that Western governments are attempting to influence. Anxiety about the capacity of terrorist organizations to succeed in the battle of ideas exposes a crisis of confidence that haunts Western political elites. This is why the war on terror is frequently described as a battle to defend a way of life. Tony Blair was not exaggerating when he declared that 'if we want to secure our way of life, there is no alternative but to fight for it'.[46] Feeling less than 100 per cent confident about the support of the home front, Blair and his colleagues are entitled to feel beleaguered. Four years after the invasion of Iraq, with less than a third of the UK population supporting the war, Blair is entitled to be concerned about winning the argument.[47]

The crisis of elite authority directly contributes to the recurring over-estimation of the terrorist threat. The very fact that governments perceive relatively incoherent jihadist opponents as representing a serious ideological challenge to the Western way of life draws attention to their feeble sense of self-belief. Paradoxically, while they continually inflate the physical threat of weapons of mass destruction terrorism, governments are reluctant to fully acknowledge their concern about winning the hearts and minds of sections of their own public. The deliberations about the problem of home-grown terrorism tend to focus on the problem of 'radicalization'. This challenge is interpreted as a consequence of the external influence of global jihadist forces rather than what it may well be – a rejection of the Western way of life. So one American intelligence report indicates that home-grown terrorism in the US and Europe is likely to become a growing problem without posing the question of why young people growing up in these places come to hate their country's way of life.[48]

The tendency to associate the problem of radicalization with the influence of external global forces peddling anti-Western sentiments serves to detract attention from the crisis of elite authority on the home front. It is important to note that the growth of 'anti-US and anti-globalization sentiment' recorded by US intelligence sources are often fuelled by cultural forces closer to home.[49] Anti-Americanism and contempt for aspects of the so-called Western way of life exercise widespread influence in many European countries. These sentiments are most systematically expressed through cultural critiques of consumerism, capitalist selfishness, greed and ambition. Ideas that denounce Western arrogance and its belief in science and progress are actually generated from within the societies of Europe and America. The authors of the book *Suicide of the West* note that the crisis of the West 'is *internally* generated' and it 'lies in Western heads'.[50] As we noted in our discussion of the problem of meaning, the internally generated critique of the West overlaps on many points with those mounted by jihadist movements.

Instead of looking for external influences driving radicalization, Durodié believes that it is more profitable to focus on developments closer to home. 'It may prove more productive to ask why it is that a small element of Asian youth, and quite a few others as well, fail to find any sense of solidarity or purpose within Western society,' states Durodié.[51] Numerous observers have drawn attention to the fact that a significant proportion of the individuals linked to terrorist outrages have grown up in the societies that they have learned to hate and want to destroy. 'Arguably the greatest potential threat in the world today lies with uprooted and egalitarian Muslim young adults in European cities, who provided the manpower for both the 9/11 and Madrid train-bombing attacks,' notes Scot Atran.[52] Yet there is little attempt to discuss why it is that a significant minority of young people have developed such intense hostility towards their own society. The same commentators who exaggerate the threat of WMD terrorism appear to ignore or pay only a fleeting attention to a threat which is far too close to home. This response is entirely understandable, for it is through this threat that the political elites are painfully reminded of the crisis of their authority. The widely observed rule of silence on this subject stands in sharp contrast to the shrill rhetoric surrounding the peril of the new terrorist.

We can now make sense of the prevailing mood of elite alarmism towards the threat of terrorism. Unable to offer a meaningful account of its own way of life, and insecure about its own authority, it cannot help but overreact to the challenge it faces. Through insecure musings about existential threats and a war without an end it expresses its worst fears about the transience of its own authority. Its reaction to the risk of terrorism may be disproportionate and likely to intensify problems. But given its own insecurity it cannot help but respond in such a self-destructive manner. The emotions of fear and anxiety appear to have gained the upper hand and rationality is in retreat. In previous times political elites stressed what they knew rather than advertise their ignorance. With the emergence of the official obsession with unknown unknowns, pessimism and insecurity are legitimized as the sensible orientation towards the future. When unmasked, the problem of terrorism reveals the crisis of confidence of the Western elites.

The erosion of elite self-belief and its inability to give meaning to its activities help explain its systematic overreaction to the threat of terrorism. The absence of purpose and a sense of mission compromises authoritative behaviour and weakens the elite's sense of power which is experienced as the condition of vulnerability. In such circumstances uncertainty acquires an increasingly alarming dimension. It threatens to expose its powerlessness and disorientation. Its overreaction to terrorism can be understood as but a variant of its uninhibited dread of uncertainty. Authority without meaning means that governments lack the moral resources to engage with uncertainty.

We are now in a position to understand why the official imagination regards the future with such a sense of foreboding. As mentioned previously, the institutionalization of threat amplification reflects dominant cultural attitudes towards risk and uncertainty. These attitudes have been internalized by officialdom, who are in any case insecure about their own authority. This insecurity is dramatically highlighted in its dread of the future – and of the unknown. The tendency to expand the territory of the unknown is not simply an acknowledgement of an absence of cultural and intellectual resources with which to engage with uncertainty, it is also an admission of the difficulty of projecting a way of life into the future. Governments appear politically too exhausted to make sense of the road ahead. In such circumstances, governments find it difficult to meaningfully exercise authority. Authority without meaning forces political elites to adopt a defensive orientation towards threats. Its risk-averse and precautionary approach invariably leads it to overreact and adopt disproportionate anti-terrorist policies. It clearly does not trust itself and, as we shall see, it clearly does not trust its own public.

Notes

1. Jones and Smith (2006) p. 1100.

2. See Michael Carmichael, 'Propaganda and the Politics of Perception', 12 March 2007, www.globalresearch.ca/ PrintArticle.php?articleId=5058.

3. See, for example, the arguments in Kevin Ryan, '9/11: Looking for Truth in Credentials: The Peculiar WTC "Experts"', Global Research, 13 March 2007, www.globalresearch.ca.

4. 'The Cynical Manipulation of Fear and Security', Independent, 16 February 2006.

5. Blick, Choudhury and Weir (2007) p. 11.

6. See Furedi (2005).

7. Don Hazen, 'Grappling with the Politics of Fear', AlterNet, 9 March 2005.

8. Robert Dreyfuss, 'There is No War on Terror', www.tompaine.com, 13 September 2006.

9. This point is discussed in Furedi (2005).

10. Zbigniew Brzezinski, 'Terrorized by "War on Terror"', The Washington Post, 25 March 2007.

11. Cited in Lustick (2006) p. 104.

12. For example, Prime Minister Blair has noted that, 'If, on the basis of a general warning, we were to shut down all the places that Al-Qaeda might be considering for attack, we would be doing their job for them.' See 'Blair urges balance in war on terror', BBC Online UK Politics, 11 November 2002.

13. Cited in Mimi Hall, 'Ridge reveals clashes on alerts', USA Today, 5 November 2005.

14. Audrey Gillan, 'Home Office Says Sorry to Suspects in Ricin Blunder', Guardian, 16 April 2005.

15. Cited in Susan Haigh, 'Lieberman says Lamont doesn't understand terrorist danger', Associated Press, 10 August 2006.

16. This point is cited in Lustick (2006).

17. Cited in ibid., p. 104.

18. Freedman (2005) p. 386.

19. This point is developed in Furedi (2005).

20. Zbigniew Brzezinski, 'Terrorized by "War on Terror"', The Washington Post, 25 March 2007.

21. 'The Cynical Manipulation of Fear and Security', Independent, 16 February 2006.

22. 'Third "think Iraq war was right"', BBC News, 20 March 2007.

23. Clarke (2003) pp. 1 and 2.

24. Mueller (2006a) pp. 2, 3 and 13.

25. Ibid., p. 48.

26. Lustick (2006) p. 6.

27. Ibid., p. 45.

28. Bill Durodié, 'We are the enemies within', *Times Higher Education Supplement*, 22 September 2006.

29. Durodié (2005) p. 10.

30. Suskind (2006).

31. See Durodié's articles on www.durodie.net.

32. Mockaitis (1990) p. 27.

33. See Brian Jackson, 'Foreword' in Lesser et al. (1999) p. v.

34. James Fallows, 'What Would Bogey Do?' *Foreign Affairs*, posted 11 September 2006, www.foreignaffairs.org/special/ 0-11_roundtable_fallows_2.

35. Mueller (2005a) p. 12.

36. Cited in *Fox News*, 21 May 2002.

37. Cited in Brendan O'Neill, 'America The Vulnerable', 8 November 2002.

38. Both are cited in 'Officials: Terrorists may target tall apt. bldgs', www.cnn. com, 20 May 2002, http://archives.cnn. com/2002/US/05/20/gen.war.on. terror/.

39. Blunkett is cited by Gaby Hinsliff in the *Observer*, 30 November 2003.

40. Speech 'Economy an Important Part of Homeland Defence', 24 October 2004, www.whitehouse.gov/news/ releases/2001/10/20011024-2.html.

41. Omand (2005) p. 109.

42. W. S. Lind, 'Defending Western Culture', *Foreign Policy*, no. 84, Autumn 1991, pp. 47 and 45.

43. Leonard, Small and Rose (2005) p. 11.

44. Joseph Nye, 'Soft Power and Higher Education', www.educause.edu/ir/ library/pdf/ffpiu043.pdf, p. 34.

45. Ibid., p. 51.

46. Blair (2006).

47. 'Third "think Iraq war was right"', *BBC News*, 20 March 2007. Only 29 per cent of 1,000 people polled by ICM stated that taking action against Iraq was right.

48. See 'Declassified Key Judgments of the National Intelligence Estimate "Trends in Global Terrorism: Implications for the United States"', dated April 2006.

49. Ibid.

50. Koch and Smith (2006) p. 1.

51. Durodié (2005) p. 2.

52. Atran (2006a) p. 291.

CHAPTER 8

Refusing to be Terrorized

Previously we have explored how cultural attitudes towards risk interact with the prevailing consciousness of vulnerability to produce an inflated perception of hazards. This sentiment dominates the imagination of the elites, whose own loss of confidence disposes them to approach the threat of terrorism in a defensive manner. An elite that does not quite trust itself and believe in its authority finds it difficult to have confidence in the public. Unfortunately government policies are based on the premise that the public lacks the resilience to deal with acts of terror and cannot be relied on to hold steadfast in the face of violent attacks. Government policies are typically vulnerability-led and provide few opportunities for the public to exercise its initiative. The aim of this chapter is to argue that threats to public security are best contained through a resilience-led response.

Refusing to be terrorized
Acts of terrorism can kill and maim innocent civilians. Now and again such acts can cause catastrophic acts of devastation. They can cause pain and suffering and intimidate sections of the public. However, terrorism cannot seriously threaten the integrity of society nor undermine the way of life of a nation. Acts of terrorism succeed in so far as the target society responds in the way the perpetrators of these deeds intended. 'If you choose not to respond at all, or else to respond in a way different from that which they desire, they will fail to achieve their objectives,' noted Fromkin over two decades ago. Fromkin argued that the ultimate weakness of terrorism as a strategy 'was that its outcome depended so much on how a society responded to intimidation'. If people did not play the role of intimidated targets than terrorism would be defeated. 'You can always refuse to do what they want you to do,' he argued.[1]

Of course, refusing to be terrorized is easier said than done. After 9/11 and a sequence of high-casualty terrorist incidents it may seem callous to expect people to remain calm and collected. Yet such a response is the most effective way of countering and minimizing this threat. We can encourage such a response by constantly questioning the belief that we live in an 'age of terror'. It is up to us to delineate the defining characteristic of our era. Ours is not an 'age of terror' any more than it is the 'age of the internet' or the 'age of environmental consciousness' or the 'age of fear'. We can refuse to be terrorized.

It is true that the relatively few acts of high-casualty terrorism in our societies have had a powerful impact on society's consciousness. But it is important to recall that acts of terror – as opposed to acts of war such as in Iraq – have caused relatively insignificant damage. The vast majority of people in the West have had no direct experience of this threat. Nor is there any reason to suppose that this will change in the foreseeable future. That is why policies that attempt to counter this threat need to communicate to people the limited nature of this particular risk. The very refusal to allow terrorism to take over people's lives needs to inform the response to it. The message that is all too often communicated by official sources, that terrorists can strike any place and any time, is not only fundamentally wrong, it also plays into the hands of those threatening to inflict violence. It is far more accurate to argue that while acts of terror cannot always be prevented, the chances of you being hurt by them are minimal. As Chapman argued, 'by minimizing our negative reactions, we might contribute to undermining terrorists' goals as effectively as by waging war on them or by mounting homeland defenses'.[2] We agree with Smil who believes that 'good arguments can be made for seeing terrorist actions as shocking (also painful and costly) but manageable risk among other risks' and to point out the general tendency to exaggerate the likelihood of new, infrequent, but spectacular, threats.[3]

Self-inflicted terror through the workings of the fear market is responsible for extensive emotional, cultural and economic damage to society. Who needs terrorists to scare us, when officials and fear entrepreneurs constantly warn us to beware of our own shadows? We live in a world where literally every human experience comes with a health warning. We keep children under house arrest because we fear for them when they go outdoors. The elderly voluntarily opt for evacuating public spaces in the evening. Risk aversion has become institutionalized and distracts society from coming to terms with its future. We waste resources on a multi-billion-dollar security industry that only makes us feel even more insecure.

Worst-case thinking is not only self-defeating, it also exacts a very high economic and emotional price from society. The possibilistic perspective that dictates the perception that anything that can possibly go wrong will go wrong inexorably tends towards promoting an ethos of helplessness. This perspective contains a logic of turning virtually everything in life into a target. The belief that worst-case thinking upholds the value of caution and responsibility is in practice contradicted through fostering a climate of anxiety and panic. It continually encourages the rhetoric 'that something must be done' – a demand that invariably leads to hasty makeshift and costly initiatives. The focus on worst-case scenarios detracts from learning to discriminate between risks and threats. It encourages a scatter-gun approach towards confronting problems and can lead to wasting considerable resources on the wrong problems. This point was forcefully argued by Parachini, who claimed that 'the inordinate focus of our antiterrorism policy on vulnerabilities and worst-case planning may skew precious federal resources to less critical aspects of the terrorism problem'.[4]

Possibilistic or 'What if?' thinking leads to a fatalistic assessment of threats. Just because not all acts of terror can be prevented, it does not mean that they can occur anywhere at any time. Arguments that ascribe such omnipotence to terrorism are not only inaccurate, they also boost fears that are not warranted by the facts. Such claims help create the impression that terrorists, especially the suicide bomber, cannot be stopped, which contributes towards the consolidation of a mood of vulnerability and powerlessness. There has never been a time in history when it was possible to prevent every act of human destruction. Today is no exception. But just because society is vulnerable to acts of destruction does not mean that it is powerless to deal with the danger it faces. Open societies are vulnerable to specific discrete acts of terrorism. But their defining feature is not their vulnerability – certainly not in the sense that they can be overwhelmed by terrorism. Evidence shows that in the aftermath of a violent mass-casualty attack people pull together and stand firm. Bombs may frighten individuals but not to the point where they abandon all hope or flee in panic.

Probably the greatest danger with the way that current policies tend to respond to terrorism is the way they contribute to the normalization of vulnerability as the natural condition of life. In Chapter 5 we discussed the regrettable tendency to depict vulnerability as a condition to be endured. The tendency to define human experience through the prism of vulnerability exaggerates and draws attention to society's defensiveness and anxieties. **Such a defensive and fearful reaction represents an open invitation to be terrorized**. Even before 9/11, analysts concerned with this defensive orientation warned that 'frequent discussion about our vulnerabilities draws attention to them.'[5] They could point to the hundreds of anthrax hoaxes that had the predictable impact of disrupting a community's economic and social life. Instead of transforming vulnerability into a condition that dominates the public imagination, policy needs to focus on providing a positive and 'can do' alternative. 'It could be as important to combat our emotional vulnerability to terrorism as to attack Al-Qaeda,' states Chapman.[6]

Of course, the prevailing vulnerability-led response resonates with the contemporary cultural imagination. As I have written elsewhere, society expects people to feel vulnerable and continually transmits signals that affirm the feelings of helplessness and anxiety. Through the influence of therapy culture, people are discouraged from coping without professional support and help-seeking has turned into a virtue.[7] The current obsession with vulnerability is so powerful that even our scientific and technological achievements are often interpreted as a problem rather than as tools that can be used for positive ends. In our darker moments technological advance is feared because it can enhance the power of terrorism rather than help contain this threat. Yet the problem is not technology, but the anxious fantasies that lurk in the imagination. It is important to insist that it need not be so. The human imagination also possesses a formidable capacity to engage and learn from the risks it faces. Throughout history humanity has learnt from its setbacks and losses and has developed ways of systematically identifying, evaluating, selecting and implementing the options for reducing risk. This also has meant being clear about the uncertainties and living with them, rather than panicking that action ought to be taken when in fact action exacerbates the problem. It also means trusting the resilience of the public and relying on its spirit of solidarity and initiative.

Learning from the experience so far

The belief that vulnerability defines the human condition exercises a powerful influence on the thinking of officials and opinion-formers in the media. From this perspective the public is perceived as a passive powerless mass of frightened individuals whose instincts cannot be trusted during a time of crisis. The days when a nation's people were seen as a source of strength have given way to a vision that perceives the home front as society's Achilles' heel. Decision-makers often work on the assumption that the target population will behave according to a script written for a disaster movie. They assume that there is a high probability that people will panic and engage in acts of antisocial and selfish behaviour. 'The perception of the public as inherently prone to panic in the face of scenarios such as chemical, biological, radiological (CBR), or mass casualty conventional terrorist attack is pervasive,' notes a study on this subject.[8] This thesis is widely shared by academic specialists in the field of security studies. As Walter Laqueur, one of the best-known experts on terrorism wrote, a single WMD attack 'could unleash far greater panic than anything the world has yet experienced'.[9] Statements issued by prominent officials often betray a note of anxiety and pessimism about the likely response of the public. General Richard Myers, former Chairman of the Joint Chiefs of Staff typified this reaction when he suggested that if terrorists succeeded in launching an attack that led to the death of 10,000 Americans, they could succeed in doing away 'with our way of life'.[10] References to doing away with a way of life convey an implicit hint about a society that lacks sturdy coping mechanisms and is therefore uncertain about its future. Fortunately such a defeatist assessment of the public's likely response to terrorism also goes against the evidence provided by the experience of history.

Since the destruction of the World Trade Center on 11 September 2001, there has been a renewed interest in the field of disaster research. Concerns about the likely response of communities to a major terrorist incident have led to questions being posed about what we know about public reactions to incidents of disaster.[11] Research into disaster has sought to explore the behavioural response of individuals and communities to the experience of large-scale disruption and destruction. As a result, the findings of this research may help provide insights into the dynamic of public response to large-scale destruction and acts of terror as well as offer ideas for lines of further inquiry. According to one American sociologist involved in the field of disaster research, the 'disaster research literature provides the best model for predicting the likely behavioural scenarios in terrorism involving WMD'.[12] Kathleen Tierney, a leading specialist in this field, concurs. She believes that 'based on both collective behaviour theories and empirical evidence, there appears to be no *a priori* reason to assume that patterns of collective behaviour before and during terrorist incidents will differ markedly from those observed in other types of crisis events.'[13] There is little doubt that learning from the historical experience of how communities cope with disasters can provide useful insights into the problems posed by the threat of terrorist incidents. And the disaster research literature represents an important resource for conceptualizing many of the issues faced by people in the period post-9/11.

Since its inception, the study of disasters has been driven by the wider concern of understanding the likely response of the public to war and violent conflict. In the United States, researchers have been engaged in exploring the public's response to disasters since the 1940s. 'Funded initially by the military in order to learn how the civilian population might respond to a nuclear attack, researchers studied the immediate aftermath of natural and technological disasters as a proxy for a wartime scenario,' notes Webb.[14] The US Government was particularly interested in developing a model for making sense of the civilian population's likely response to possible air raids. Disasters were regarded as a laboratory through which researchers could gain insights into basic human responses to violent disruptions to their lives.

According to the war-oriented legacy of disaster research, 'bombs fitted easily with the notion of an external agent, while people harmed by floods, hurricanes or earthquakes bore an extraordinary resemblance to victims of air raids'.[15] Some of the insights developed from this work can be harnessed to the project of developing a sociological analysis of the likely character of the domestic response to terrorism. One note of caution is in order. Violent disruptions – such as a war, an act of terror or an earthquake – do not always provoke a uniform response. As Quarantelli noted, there is a degree of autonomy in the reactions of people to such disasters.[16] More importantly, the response of the public to an emergency or a disaster is not a direct consequence of the scale of destruction and physical disruption. For example, today a relatively small number of casualties can help stimulate an all-pervasive sense of dread. The way that humans respond to a disaster is only in part influenced by the external agent that caused it. Experience suggests that culture plays an important role in shaping the response. In particular the meaning attributed to a violent and destructive incident has a strong influence over the way its impact is experienced.

Throughout history, people's explanations of what caused a disaster, what would be its likely impact on their lives and what meaning they should attach to it have gone through important modifications. As Carr argued, a disaster is defined by human beings and not by nature. Writing in the 1930s, he noted that 'not every windstorm, earth-tremor, or rush of water is a catastrophe'. If there are no serious injuries of deaths and other serious losses, Carr argued that 'there is no disaster'.[17] Carr's association of disaster with an event associated with the destruction of human lives and economic loss is very much shaped by the modernist imagination of his times. Michael Kempe argues that in the Middle Age, 'solar eclipses and comets were seen as catastrophes, because they were interpreted as signs of divine anger against human sins, as were earthquakes and volcanic eruptions'.[18] It was not so much the intensity of human suffering, but the powerful signals sent by a major act of physical disruption that shaped the perception of a catastrophe.

As in the case of terrorism, the damage caused by a disaster constitutes only half the experience. A far more interesting part of the story is how human communities respond to the disaster episode. At a time when society is concerned about terrorist violence, weapons of mass destruction, global warming and a range of potential technological disasters, it is useful to remind ourselves how communities in the past managed to deal with comparable episodes. The evidence of history shows that disasters can inflict a terrible scale of destruction on people. No one was left alive when the eruption of Mount Vesuvius in AD 79 buried Pompeii. Smallpox – the 'white man's disease' – wiped out the Mandans and other tribes of Native Americans in the nineteenth century. Everyone in St Pierre was killed when Mount Pelée erupted on Martinique in 1902. Yet such catastrophes notwithstanding, most of the time human communities have proved to be rather good at surviving some of the most destructive episodes of history. From the Great Fire of London to the destruction of Hiroshima, experience shows that communities often possess a remarkable capacity to rebuild their lives.

Most accounts of disasters in the nineteenth and twentieth centuries emphasized the impressive degree of social solidarity with which the communities responded to these tragedies. It is worth noting that, from the outset, attempts to conceptualize the nature of the human response to disaster appeared to go against the grain of commonsense-driven caricatures. Many early observers were impressed by the relative absence of panic and the flourishing of acts of solidarity in disaster situations. Freud regarded disasters as occasions when social solidarity emerges and a spirit of altruism influences human behaviour. 'One of the gratifying and exalting impressions which mankind can offer is when, in the face of an elemental crisis, it forgets the discordances of its civilization and all its internal difficulties and animosities, and recalls the great common task of preserving itself against the superior power of nature,' observes

Freud.[19] Post-Second World War researchers tended to concur with this assessment, and their approach directly challenged what they described as 'disaster mythology'. According to Webb, this mythology includes the assumptions that when disaster strikes, people panic and that their communities experience increased level of antisocial behaviour. Other assumptions held by disaster mythology are 'that looting is widespread after disasters; that victims experience shock and become dependent on outside response organizations; that evacuation orders will result in a mass exodus; that public shelters will quickly fill up with dazed and confused survivors; that price gouging will be widespread; and that martial law should be declared to impose order on the disorganized scene'.[20]

The good news is that, contrary to the anticipation of disorganization, disaster research indicates that the immediate response period to natural and technological disasters is socially organized and communities experience an increase in socially responsible behaviours. Enrico Quarantelli, the dominant figure associated with the new field of disaster research, observed in his 1954 review of data gathered by the Disaster Team of the National Opinion Research Center that the 'frequency of panic has been over exaggerated' and that it is a 'relatively uncommon phenomenon'.[21] Quarantelli's findings are consistent with those of a large number of empirical studies carried out in disaster situations during the Second World War. The bombing of Hamburg in July 1943 is instructive in this respect. The bombing killed between 30,000 and 45,000 people and left over 900,000 homeless. In this one incident in Hamburg there were almost as many casualties as those suffered by Britain as a result of German air raids. Yet there was no panic and in a remarkably short period of time the city had managed to resurrect itself. Within five months the city was back to 80 per cent of industrial production. After the dropping of the atomic bomb, the response of the people of Hiroshima was also astonishingly resilient. Although 75,000 people died, out of a population of 245,000, within a few days essential services were restored and after a week economic life was back in full swing. Studies carried out in London during the Blitz also showed that public morale remained relatively high and the local communities showed remarkable resilience in the face of adversity.[22]

Recent reviews of the experience of human response to terrorism and violence bear out the insights provided by disaster researchers. According to one analysis of the evidence from the 1995 sarin attack in Tokyo, 'from 9/11, from the 2001 anthrax attacks, and from the 7

July 2005 London bombings' it appears that 'panic does not typically break out following a CBR terrorist strike or a mass casualty attack'. The authors conclude that 'society is reasonably resilient'.[23] A similar conclusion is also drawn by a recently published survey of the available evidence. It stated that 'far from being the typical reaction to a disaster, panic is actually rare'.[24] Interviews carried out with survivors in disaster situations also confirm the absence of mass panic and the relative absence of selfish behaviour. Accounts provided to researchers by survivors and witnesses to the 7 July London bombings indicate that, although people talked of 'panic', there was no mass panic. The researchers observed:

> Far from the classic stereotype of mass panic in disasters, we found next to no evidence for this concept in people's reactions to the July 7th bombings, despite the word 'panic' being used quite liberally in both press and eye-witness accounts.[25]

In line with experience in comparable situations, the survivors reported that cooperation and helping were common and that selfish behaviour was rare.

One reason that people respond to terrorist attacks through acts of solidarity rather than panic is that their shared experience helps create a strong sense of affinity. The emergence of a shared identity through a common fate appears to have played an important role in people's responses to 7/7. 'Through its effect on creating a common identity, this shared fate appears to be the main cause of the mutual concern, helping and co-ordination of the day,' contend the authors of a study on this subject.[26] The experience of 7/7 draws attention to the significance of social capital. Contrary to expectations, disaster situations contain potential for the emergence of social solidarity and community purpose. As noted before, social capital can actually increase in adverse circumstances. Often in such circumstances the sudden disruption of normality calls into question prevailing norms and attitudes. In such times communities are forced to rethink the purpose of life and 'create new beliefs about what is problematic, new sources of identity and emotional cohesion, and new directions for knowledge'. Indeed it is precisely in such times of upheaval that people gain a capacity for seeing the 'collective bonds of social life'.[27]

Disasters also provide an opportunity for a community to come to know itself and discover not only its weaknesses but also its strengths. Experience indicates that this process is invariably realized through the emerging informal organization that comes into being in the aftermath of a disaster. That is why the public should be given an opportunity to work out its response to an emergency. As Dynes explains, 'emergencies do not reduce the capacities of individuals or social structures to cope, but only present them new or unexpected problems to solve'.[28]

Role of the public

To a considerable extent the impact of terror is shaped by the response of a community to it. That is why government officials and emergency planners – on both sides of the Atlantic – are attempting to promote the public's resilience.[29] However, the term 'resilience' remains a relatively underdeveloped one. It is frequently used in a metaphor-like manner to describe factors that can protect individuals or communities from the consequences of adversity. Resilience appears to be a concept in search of meaning. The lack of clarity about the meaning of the term in official documents is not surprising, since officials do not seem to have much faith in the ability of the public to act with resilience. Our analysis of the available official documentation leads us to conclude that experts do not think that resilience can flourish by itself. As noted in Chapter 1, resilience is perceived as a second-order concept that must defer to vulnerability. Frequently vulnerability is conceptualized as the dominant norm whose effects may be modified by resilience. Resilience is seen as a protective factor that limits the negative impact of adversity on the individual. Waller sees it as 'operating as buffers between individuals and the risk factors impinging on their well-being'.[30] According to the taken-for-granted model used by emergency and counter-terrorist planners, the condition of vulnerability is logically prior to the working of resilience. This point is rarely made explicit, but in most of the discussion around the threat of terrorism, vulnerability is perceived as the natural condition of human existence and resilience is presented as a potential counter-trend against it.

Yet there is a significant body of evidence that suggests that oppressive conditions do not always turn people into feeble passive wrecks. Indeed in some cases individuals who are challenged by adversity emerge stronger, with capacities that they may not have developed otherwise. Numerous researchers have noted that in many cases survivors of difficult and traumatic circumstances have developed a positive sense of themselves through having learned how to cope with adversity.[31] The feeling of being bound to others sharing the same adverse fate is still regarded as a source of strength by many survivors of the Blitz and other violent episodes during the Second World War.

The question at issue is not whether one chooses vulnerability or resilience as the norm or defining condition of individuals and their community. Rather the problem is the representation of resilience merely as an antidote to a prior problem. Downsizing the status of resilience to a secondary role also indicates that far from being natural it is a reaction that needs to be stimulated from the outside. If resilience is perceived as a kind of cultural pain-relief to a community suffering from an illness, it will lack any organic relationship to society. This orientation inevitably turns resilience into a secondary and relatively minor dimension of a community's response. Yet as the experience of the 7 July bombings indicates, for example, people have 'natural coping mechanisms' and resilience can thrive during and even in the aftermath of a terrorist incident.[32]

The tendency for policy-makers and experts to both internalize and recycle the paradigm of vulnerability is also regrettable because it uncritically serves to reinforce the passive side of public life. Disasters are of course terrible tragedies that can have devastating consequences for individuals and the community alike. But disasters also provide an opportunity for a community to come to know itself and discover not only its weaknesses but also its strengths. Experience indicates that this process is invariably realized through the emerging informal organizations that come into being in the aftermath of a disaster. As Kendra and Wachtendorf's study of resilience in the aftermath of 9/11 argues, 'creative thinking, flexibility and the ability to improvise in newly emergent situations is vital'.[33] These responses are often a product of informal solutions arrived at under the pressure of unexpected events. It is a process through which individuals, local institutions and communities learn to develop their resilience. Unfortunately, the tendency to professionalize disaster response may deprive a community of an opportunity to develop its resilience and inadvertently reinforce a sense of passivity and helplessness.

Invariably the professional agenda disregards the potential that communities possess for dealing with calamity. Such a perspective frequently exaggerates the dimension of the hazard and can inadvertently undermine people's confidence. As Tierney argues:

> *Frames and constructions (and here I include both cultural beliefs and crisis management plans and policies) that emphasize the dread and uncontrollable nature of terrorist acts and weapons of mass destruction and that characterize the public as unreasonably fearful, helpless, and*

> *unable to cope with such attacks could well help to produce the very*
> *kinds of behaviours crisis managers seek to avoid. Conversely, approaches*
> *that highlight and seek to reinforce the public's resilience in the face of*
> *threats of all kinds will reduce the potential for maladaptive forms of*
> *collective behavior.*[34]

My own research into the experience of the recent floods and rural crisis in Britain confirms this conclusion.[35] Too often a vulnerability-led response to a disaster cultivates a consciousness of powerlessness and demoralization.

In the post-9/11 environment, an intellectual reorientation towards the conceptualization of potential sources of community resilience is crucial. As Pupavac notes, 'salutogenic studies, which explore people's resilience are relatively rare in trauma literature and have been overlooked in disaster planning in recent decades'.[36] This point is echoed by Joseph, Williams and Yule, who state that 'at present disaster research is constrained by its focus on maladaptive responses'.[37] The relative absence of interest in what some psychologists call community 'hardiness' is understandable in light of the powerful cultural forces that promote the emotional sensibility of vulnerability.[38] Yet community resilience has proven to be a vital resource when people are confronted with adversity.

In recent years, even the concept of resilience has been professionalized and turned into a tool for management. The process of developing resilience is often uprooted from its social context and community setting. There is a discernible impulse towards depicting resilience as something that professionals transmit to people rather than what communities develop in response to the challenges they face. According to two American mental health professionals, Han and Sugrue, 'to develop community capacity, we need to focus on teaching community and family resilience'. They cite a mental health provider from New York, who remarks:

> *Resilience is a critical coping skill that we need to teach families and*
> *kids and parents. We need to teach them how to convert negative to*
> *positive thinking, how to mobilize into action when you are overwhelmed*
> *with anxiety, how to build community. Resilience can be taught.*[39]

An agenda devoted towards teaching people how to be 'resilient' and how to build communities has in fact already presumed that not only can ordinary folk not cope on their own, but that they are going to be the problem rather than the solution in a crisis situation. Of course, teaching people coping skills has little to with resilience; it is what you do to manage the incompetent and powerless.

The belief that professional intervention is the precondition for resilience often informs the technocratic approach. 'I work primarily with cancer patients and I have learned that you facilitate resilience by breaking a massive problem down into smaller parts, by teaching people where to go for some solutions that help get them information, and by promoting support teams when they may see themselves as isolated and alone,' writes one New York mental health professional.[40] Through assigning professionals the primary role for developing resilience, there is a danger of overlooking the potential of informal networks in communities for generating a resilient response.

One of the principal problems with the technical conceptualization of resilience is that it leaves the prior premise of a universal state of vulnerability untouched. Resilience is used in a way that presupposes the primacy of vulnerability. It is the exception, the modifying factor, rather than the defining state. It is frequently presented as a protective factor that 'can outweigh the negative impact' of risk factors.[41] However, the experience of resilience is not one that can be reduced to a factor isolated from the rest of life. It is inextricably intertwined with the everyday life of a community. Underpinned by a sense of individual coherence gained through being embedded in a wider system of social interaction it is not an individual attribute, but part of a wider legacy of community life. It can be encouraged, cultivated or disrupted, but certainly not taught or imparted by well-intentioned professionals.

A technocratic orientation towards the issue of resilience is unlikely to engage the creative and problem-solving capacities of communities who are faced with a violent and destructive threat to their life. Such policies are also likely to institutionalize a top-down professional approach that will leave little room for local initiative. A highly centralized professional response cannot deal with every contingency. In the end encouraging people to take responsibility for their wellbeing is essential for an effective response to an emergency situation. In reality, resilience cannot be taught. It is not a state that exists prior to an event. The ability to bounce back from a disruption and cope with dramatically desperate events can not be learned through training. Resilience emerges through circumstances that are unexpected and therefore new. It develops through improvisation and adaptation to 'rapidly changing and usually ambiguous conditions'.[42]

Resilience with meaning

The tendency to treat resilience as a technical problem diverts attention from the fact that the response of a community to a threat and its level of morale is influenced by its shared experience and values and the meaning attached to them. Communities that are bound together by a robust system of meaning are able to act with a sense of purpose in defence of their community and way of life. Shared meaning provides people with clear guidelines about what's expected of them in their interaction with members of their communities. Of course political leaders implicitly understand that the future of society is linked to its capacity to develop a sense of direction that can inspire the public. This sentiment is regularly expressed through statements that acclaim the need for a 'narrative' or clarity about society's values. However, such narratives or values cannot be invented. What governments can do is to encourage a cultural climate where people are able to freely exchange their views and develop their opinions on the basis of their experience. Current policies of social engineering that treat grown-ups as children directly undermine this project.

Elites who themselves do not feel particularly resilient are reluctant to bank on the resilience of their people. A resilience-led approach requires that people are treated as grown-ups. Learning to accept the threat of terrorism as 'normal' risk is crucial for confronting the problem. As long as it is defined as 'exceptional', its consequences regarded as 'incalculable' and its effects represented in science-fiction terms it will not be possible to deal with this threat. Such a perspective merely informs everyone about their vulnerability and says little about how they can gain resilience from engaging with this risk. Yet the human imagination possesses a formidable capacity to engage and learn from the risks it faces. As one American commentator writes:

> Great nations face great risks. That's life. Through its history, the United States endured early decades in which its very survival was in question, and then a horrific war over the preservation of the Union. What it suffered five years ago on 9/11 was terrible and unprecedented and paradigm-changing. But it does not mean, as current discourse seems to assume, that we need to live in fear and assume the worst forever.[43]

Throughout history humanity has learnt from its setbacks and losses and has developed ways of systematically identifying, evaluating, selecting and implementing options for reducing threats. Accepting the risk of terrorism as normal should not be interpreted as a call for passivity or resignation to the inevitable. On the contrary, precisely because it is seen to be normal, it represents a call for taking measures that can reduce risks, but also for accepting rather than being stupefied by areas of uncertainty.

Containing the threat of terrorism requires that the public learns to live with it. Experience indicates that this is easier said than done. Since an open society is vulnerable to serious loss of life from terrorists attacks, there is immense pressure for reacting to this threat with a vulnerability-led response and an overwhelming focus on security. However, such a response threatens to further inflate public anxiety. It can also serve as an invitation to further acts of violence. It is important to note that society can absorb occasional acts of terror but it can become easily disoriented if morale diminishes significantly. Instead of responding to the threat of violence through changing the way we live, it is preferable to affirm it and carry on as before.

One final point: Many of the influences that encourage a heightened sense of insecurity have emerged independently of the threat of terrorism. Terrorism has been waiting to happen a long time before 9/11. The dramatization of security has influenced the Western cultural imagination for many a decade. The rise of possibilitic thinking, the preoccupation with unknown unknowns and the dread of uncertainty are the product of a cultural imagination that has influenced many aspects of life. Moreover, the diagnosis of vulnerability as a condition of life is both logically and chronologically prior to the contemporary preoccupation of terrorism. These are influences that work towards the intensification of our sense of existential insecurity. Even if 9/11 never occurred and every Al-Qaeda operative was rounded up, these influences would continue to incite confusion and terror. In the end, terrorism will only be unmasked when we understand that the forces feeding it are not over there, but over here.

Notes

1. Fromkin (1975) p. 697.

2. Chapman (2002) p. 1.

3. Smil (2005) p. 227.

4. Parachini (2000) p. 1.

5. Ibid., p. 4.

6. Chapman (2002) p. 2.

7. See Furedi (2007a).

8. Sheppard, Rubin, Warman and Wessely (2006) p. 219.

9. Laqueur (1996) p. 25.

10. Cited in Mueller (2006a) p. 6.

11. See Bill Durodié and Simon Wessely, 'Resilience or Panic? The Public's Response to a Terrorist Attack', *The Lancet*, Vol. 360, no. 9349, 6 December 2002.

12. Fischer (2002) p. 123.

13. Tierney (2004) p. 28.

14. Webb (2002) p. 87.

15. See Gilbert (1998) pp. 12–13.

16. Quarantelli (1978).

17. Carr (1932) p. 211.

18. Kempe (2003) pp. 151–2.

19. Freud (1927) p. 21.

20. Webb (2002) p. 88.

21. Quarantelli (1954) p. 275.

22. Janis (1951).

23. Sheppard, Rubin, Warman and Wessely (2006) p. 223.

24. Drury and Cocking (2007) p. 9.

25. Ibid., p. 24.

26. Ibid., p. 27.

27. Turkel (2002) p. 74.

28. Dynes (2003) p. 19.

29. Cabinet Office (2003).

30. Waller (2001) p. 3.

31. See Waysman, Schwarzwald and Solomon (2001) for their work on Israeli prisoners of war and Joseph, Williams and Yule (1993), who note that in work with survivors of the Herald Free Enterprise disaster, they found that 'half rated their view of life as having changed for the better.'

32. Drury and Cocking (2007) p. 27.

33. Kendra and Wachtendorf (2002) p. 52.

34. Tierney (2004) p. 29.

35. Furedi (2007a).

36. Pupavac (2004) p. 5.

37. Joseph, Williams and Yule (1993) p. 278.

38. Waysman, Schwarzwald and Solomon (2001).

39. Han and Sugrue (2003) p. 30.

40. Ibid., p. 30.

41. Waller (2001) p. 5.

42. Dynes (2003) p. 9.

43. James Fallows, 'Act as if Mueller is Right', *Foreign Affairs Roundtable*, posted 7 September 2006.

Bibliography

Abbott, C., Rogers, P. and Sloboda, J. (2006) *Global Responses To Global Threats: Sustainable Security For The 21st Century*, Oxford: Oxford Research Group.

Abshire, D. (2002) *Lessons For The 21st Century: Vulnerability and Surprise, December 7, 1941, September 11, 2001*, Washington DC: Center For The Study Of The Presidency.

Aldrich, R. (2005) 'Whitehall and the Iraq War: the UK's Four Intelligence Enquiries', *Irish Studies in International Affairs*, Vol. 16.

Allison, G. (2006) 'The ongoing failure of imagination', *Bulletin of the Atomic Scientists*, Vol. 62, no. 5.

Altheide, D. (2002) *Creating Fear: News and the Construction of Crisis*, New York: Aldine De Gruyter.

— (2006) *Terrorism and the Politics of Fear*, Lanham: Alta Mira Press.

Appandurai, A. (2006) *Fear of Small Numbers; An Essay On The Geography Of Anger*, Durham NC: Duke University Press.

Aradau, C. and van Munster, R. (2005) *Governing terrorism and the (non-) politics of risk*, Political Science Publications, No.11/2003, Odense: Sysddansk Universitet.

— (forthcoming) 'In the name of politics: governing through risk', undated paper published online in 2005, forthcoming in *European Journal of International Relations*.

Atran, S. (2006a) 'A Failure of Imagination (Intelligence, WMDs, and "Virtual Jihad")', *Studies in Conflict & Terrorism*, Vol. 29.

— (2006b) 'The Moral Logic of Suicide Terrorism', *The Washington Quarterly*, Spring.

Barton, A. (1969) *Communities in Disaster: A Sociological Analysis of Collective Stress Situations*, New York: Ward Lock Educational.

Bauman, Z. (1992) *Intimations of Post-Modernity*, London: Routledge.

— (2006) *Liquid Fear*, Cambridge: Polity Press.

Beck, U. (2002) 'The Terrorist Threat; World Risk Society Revisited', *Theory, Culture & Society*, Vol. 19, no. 4.

— (2003) 'The Silence of Words: On Terror and War', *Security Dialogue*, Vol. 34, no. 3.

Bendle, M. F. (2005) 'The Apocalyptic Imagination and Popular Culture', *Journal of Religion and Popular Culture*, Vol. XI, Autumn 2005.

— (2006) 'Existential Terrorism: Civil Society and Its Enemies', *American Journal of Politics and History*, Vol. 52, no. 1.

Bergesan, A. and Han, T. (2005) 'New Directions for Terrorism Research', *International Journal Of Comparative Sociology*, Vol. 46, no. 1–2.

Berman, P. (2004) *Terror and Liberalism*, New York: W. W. Norton & Co.

Best, J. (1999) *Random Violence*, Berkeley, CA: University of California Press.

Better Regulation Commission (2006) *Risk, Responsibility and Regulation – Whose risk is it anyway?* London: Better Regulation Commission.

Betts, R. (1980–81) 'Surprise Despite Warning: Why Sudden Attacks Succeed', *Political Science Quarterly*, Vol. 95, no. 4.

Birkland, T. (2004) '"The World Changed Today": Agenda-Setting and Policy Change in the Wake of the September 11 Terrorist Attacks', *Review of Policy Research*, Vol. 21, no. 2.

Blair, T. (2006) *A Global Alliance for Global Values*, London: The Foreign Policy Centre.

Blick, A., Choudhury, T. and Weir, S. (2007) *The Rules of the Game: Terrorism, Community and Human Rights*, London: Joseph Rowntree Reform Trust.

Blum, A., Asal, V. and Wilkenfeld, J. (eds) (2005) 'Nonstate Actors, Terrorism, and Weapons of Mass Destruction', *International Studies Review*, Vol. 7.

Blumenthal, S. (2003) *The Clinton Wars. An Insider's Account of the White House Years*, New York: Penguin Books.

Bourke, J. (2005) *Fear: A Cultural History*, London: Virago Press.

Bracken, P. (2002) *Trauma: Culture, Meaning and Philosophy*, London: Whurr Publishers.

Bunn, M. and Wier, A. (2005) 'The Seven Myths of Nuclear Terrorism', *Current History*, April.

Burnett, J. and Whyte, D. (2005) 'Embedded Expertise and the New Terrorism', *Journal for Crime, Conflict and the Media*, Vol. 1, no. 4.

Busch, K. (2005) 'The Intelligence Community and the War on Terror: The Role of Behavioral Science', *Behavioral Sciences and the Law*, Vol. 23.

Cabinet Office (2003) *Dealing with Disasters* (3rd ed.), www.ukresilience. info/contingencies/dwd/index.htm.

Carr, L. J. (1932) 'Disaster and the Sequence-Pattern Concept of Social Change', *American Journal of Sociology*, Vol. 38.

Carr, M. (2006) *Unknown Soldiers: How Terrorism Transformed the Modern World*, London: Profile Books.

Carter, A., Deutch, J. and Zelikow, P. (1998) 'Catastrophic Terrorism: Tackling The New Danger', *Foreign Affairs*, November/December.

Chapman, C. (2002) 'A sceptical look at September 11th: How we can defeat terrorism by reacting more rationally', *Skeptical Inquirer*, September–October.

Clarke, L. (2003) (ed.) *Terrorism and Disaster: New Threats, New Ideas*. Research, Oxford: Elsevier.

— (2006) *Worst Cases: Terror and Catastrophe in The Popular Imagination*, Chicago: The University of Chicago Press.

Clarke, S. E. and Chenoweth, E. (2006) 'The Politics of Vulnerability: Constructing Local Performance Regimes for Homeland Security', *Review of Policy Research*, Vol. 23, no. 1

Cohen, W., Secretary of Defense (1997) *Annual Report To The President And The Congress*, April 1997 Washington DC: Department of Defense, www.dod.mil/execsec/adr97/toc.html, accessed 19 December 2006.

Coleman, J. (1976) 'Community Disorganization and Urban Problems' in Merton, R. K. and Nisbet, R. (eds) (1976) *Contemporary Social Problems*, New York: Harcourt Brace Jovanovich, Inc.

The Commission on the Intelligence Capabilities of the United States Regarding Weapons of Mass Destruction, *Report to the President of the United States*, 31 March 2005, Washington DC.

Cordesman, A. H. (2000) *Asymmetric Threats and Arms Control: The Impact of a Partial and Full Peace in the Middle East*, Washington DC: Center for Strategic and International Studies.

Cornish, P. (2007) *The CBRN System: Assessing the threat of chemical, biological, radiological and nuclear weapons in the United Kingdom*, London: Chatham House.

Crelinsten, R. D. (1998) 'The Discourse and Practice of Counter-Terrorism in Liberal Democracies', *Australian Journal of Politics and History*, Vol. 44, no. 1.

Cutter, S. (2003) 'The Vulnerability of Science and the Science of Vulnerability', *Annals of the Association of American Geographers*, Vol. 93 (1).

— (2005) 'The Geography of Social Vulnerability: Race, Class, and Catastrophe', discussion organised by SSRC on Understanding Katrina: Perspectives from the Social Sciences, www.understandingkatrina.ssrc.org/Cutter/, accessed 24 January 2006.

De Chesnay, M. (ed.) (2005) *Caring For The Vulnerable: Perspectives In Nursing Theory, Practice and Research*, Sudbury, MA: Jones & Bartlett Publishers.

Department of Defense (1997) *Report Of The Quadrennial Defense Review*, www.defenselink.mil/pubs/qdr/index.html, accessed 13 December 2006.

Department of Justice, Federal Bureau of Investigation (1999) *Project Megiddo*, Washington DC.

Doig, A. and Phythian, M. (2005) 'The National Interest and the Politics of Threat Exaggeration: The Blair Government's Case for War against Iraq', *The Political Quarterly*.

Drury, J. and Cocking, C. (2007) *The mass psychology of disasters and emergency evacuations: A research report and implications for practice*, Falmer: Department of Psychology, University of Sussex.

Durodié, B. (2004) 'Facing the possibility of Bioterrorism', *Current Opinion in Biotechnology*, Vol. 15.

— (2005) 'Cultural Precursors and Psychological Consequences of Contemporary Western Responses to Acts of Terror' in Wessely, S. and Krasnov, V. N. (eds.) (2005) *Psychological Responses to the New Terrorism: A NATO–Russia Dialogue*, IOS Press.

Durodié, B. and Wessely, S. (2002) 'Resilience or Panic? The Public's Response to a Terrorist Attack', *The Lancet*, Vol. 360, no. 9349, 6 December.

Dynes, R. (2000) 'The Dialogue between Voltaire and Rousseau on the Lisbon Earthquake: The Emergence of Social Science View', *International Journal of Mass Emergencies and Disasters*, Vol. 18.

— (2003) 'Finding Order in Disorder: Continuities in the 9-11 Response', *International Journal of Mass Emergencies and Disasters*, Vol. 21, no. 3.

Edwards, C. (2006) *The Case For A National Security Strategy*, London: Demos Report.

Ellin, N. (2001) 'Thresholds of Fear: Embracing the Urban Shadow', *Urban Studies*, Vol. 38, no. 5–6.

Falkenrath, R. (2004/5) '*The 9/11 Commission Report*: A Review Essay', *International Security*, Vol. 29, no. 3.

Ferguson, C. and Potter, W. (2004) *The Four Faces Of Nuclear Terrorism*, Monterey, CA: Center for Nonproliferation Studies.

Fischer, H. (2002) 'Terrorism and 11 September 2001: does the "behavioural response to disaster" model fit?', *Disaster Prevention and Management*, Vol. 11, no. 2.

Foxell, J. (1997) 'The Prospect of Nuclear and Biological Terrorism', *Journal of Contingencies and Crisis Management*, Vol. 5, no. 2.

Freedman, L. (2005) 'The Politics of Warning: Terrorism and Risk Communication', *Intelligence and National Security*, Vol. 20, no. 3.

Freud, S. (1927) *The Future of an Illusion*, New York: Doubleday.

Friedman B. and Sapolsky, H. (2006) 'You Never Know(ism)', *Breakthroughs*, Spring.

Fritz, C. E. (1996) *Disasters and Mental Health: Therapeutic Principles Drawn from Disaster Studies*, DRC Historical and Comparative Series no.10, Wilmington, DE: DRC.

Fromkin, D. (1975) 'The Strategy of Terrorism', *Foreign Affairs*, July.

Furedi, F. (2002) *Refusing to Be Terrorised: Managing Risk after September 11th*, Faversham: Global Futures.

— (2004) *Therapy Culture: Cultivating Vulnerability in an Anxious Age*, London: Routledge.

— (2005) *Politics of Fear: Beyond Left and Right*, London: Continuum.

— (2006) *The Culture of Fear Revisited*, London: Continuum.

— (2007a) 'Coping With Adversity: The Turn to the Rhetoric of Vulnerability', *Security Journal*, April.

— (2007b) 'From the narrative of the Blitz to the rhetoric of vulnerability', *Cultural Sociology*, Vol. 1, no. 2, April.

Gearson, J. (2002) 'The Nature of Modern Terrorism', *The Political Quarterly*.

Gilbert, C. 'Studying disaster: Changes in the main conceptual tools' in Quarantelli, E. L. (ed.) (1998) *What Is a Disaster?: Perspectives on the Question*, London: Routledge.

Grove-White, R. (2001) 'New Wine, Old Bottles? Personal reflections on the New Biotechnology Commissions', *The Political Quarterly*, Vol. 72, no. 4.

Haggerty, K. D. (2003) 'From Risk to Precaution: The Rationalities of Personal Crime Prevention' in Ericson, R. V. and Doyle, A. (eds) *Risk and Morality*, Toronto: University of Toronto Press.

Hall, V. H. (ed.) (2003) *Terrorism: Strategies for Intervention*, Binghamton, NY: The Haworth Press, Inc.

Hamm, M. (2004) 'Apocalyptic violence: The seduction of terrorist subcultures', *Theoretical Criminology*, Vol. 8, no. 3.

Han, H. and Sugrue, N. (2003) *Facing Fear Together: Mental Health and Primary Care in a Time of Terrorism-Blueprint Report*, Washington DC: Facing Fear Together.

Hardt, M. and Negri, A. (2005) *Multitude*, London: Penguin Books.

Hewitt, J. (1998) *The Myth of Self-Esteem: Finding Happiness and Solving Problems in America*, New York: St Martin's Press.

Hewitt, K. (1983) (ed.) *Interpretations of Calamity from the Viewpoint of Human Ecology*, Boston: Allen & Unwin.

HMSO (2006) *Intelligence and Security Committee Report into the London Terrorist Attacks on 7 July 2005*, Cm 6785, London: HMSO.

Homer-Dixon, T. (2002) 'The Rise of Complex Terrorism', *Foreign Policy*, January.

Horlick-Jones, T. (1995) 'Modern Disasters as Outrage and Betrayal', *International Journal of Mass Emergencies and Disasters*, Vol. 13, no. 3.

House of Commons (2006) *Report of the Official Account of the Bombings in London on 7 July 2005*, HC1087, London: The Stationery Office.

Huddy, L., Feldman, S., Taber, C. and Lahav, G. (2005) 'Threat, Anxiety, and Support of Antiterrorism Policies', *American Journal of Political Science*, Vol. 49, no. 3.

Janis, I. (1951) *Air War and Emotional Stress*, Santa Monica, CA: Rand Corporation.

Jenkins, B. (1999) 'Foreword' in Lesser, I., Hoffman, B., Arquilla, J., Ronfeldt, D., Zanini, M. and Jenkins, B. (1999) *Countering the New Terrorism*, Santa Monica, CA: Rand Corporation.

Jenkins, M. J. (2006) 'The New Age of Terrorism' in Kamien, D. (2006) (ed.) *McGraw-Hill Homeland Security Hand-book*, The McGraw Hill Companies Inc.

Jenkins, P. (2003) *Images of Terror*, New York: Aldine de Gruyter.

Jiang, B. (2002) 'Risk Management and the Office of Homeland Security's Antiterrorism Tasks', *The Online Journal of Peace and Conflict Resolution*, 4.2.

Johnson, R. (2002) 'Defending Ways of Life: The (Anti-) Terrorist Rhetorics of Bush and Blair', *Theory, Culture & Society*, Vol. 19 (4).

Johnston, P. and Santillo, D. (2006) *The Precautionary Principle: A Barrier to Innovation and Progress?*, Greenpeace Research Laboratories Discussion Paper 01/2006, University of Exeter.

Jones, D. M. and Smith, M. (2006) 'The commentariat and discourse failure: language and atrocity in Cool Britannia', *International Affairs*, Vol. 82, no. 6.

Jones, E., Woolven, R., Durodié, B. and Wessely, S. (2006) 'Public Panic and Morale: Second World War Civilian Responses Re-examined in the Light of the Current Anti-terrorist Campaign', *Journal of Risk Research*, Vol. 9, no. 1.

Joseph, S., Williams, R. and Yule, W. (1993) 'Changes in Outlook Following a Disaster: The Preliminary Development of a Measure to Assess Positive and Negative Responses', *Journal of Traumatic Stress*, Vol. 6, no. 2.

Kamien, D. (2006) (ed.) *McGraw-Hill Homeland Security Handbook*, The McGraw Hill Companies Inc.

Keith, S. (2005) 'Fear-mongering or fact: The construction of "cyber-terrorism" in the US, UK, and Canadian news media', paper presented at *Safety and Security in a Networked World: balancing cyber-rights and responsibilities*, Oxford Internet Institute, 8–10 September 2005, Oxford.

Kempe, M. (2003) 'Noah's Flood: The Genesis Story and Natural Disasters in Early Modern Times', *Environment and History*, Vol. 9.

Kendra, J. and Wachtendorf, T. (2002) 'Elements of Resilience in the World Trade Center Attack', preliminary report published by the Disaster Research Center, Newark, DE: DRC, University of Delaware.

King, N. B. (2003) 'The Influence of Anxiety: September 11, Bioterrorism and American Public Health', *Journal of the History Medicine*, Vol. 58.

Koch, R. and Smith, C. (2006) *Suicide of the West*, London: Continuum.

Kunreuther, H. and Michel-Kerjan, E. (2004) *Dealing with Extreme Events: New Challenges for Terrorism Risk Coverage in the US*, Philadelphia, PA: Center for Risk Management and Decision Processes, Wharton University of Pennsylvania.

Lacquement, R. A. Jr (2004) 'The Casual-Aversion Myth', *Naval War College Review*, Vol. 57, no. 1.

Lagadec, P. (2006) 'Crisis management in the Twenty-First Century: "Unthinkable" Events in "Inconceivable" Contexts' in Rodriguez, H., Quarantelli, E. and Dynes, R. (eds) (2006) *Handbook of Disaster Research*, New York: Springer.

Laidi, Z. (1998) *A World Without Meaning: The Crisis Of Meaning In International Politics*, London: Routledge.

Laqueur, W. (1996) 'Postmodern Terrorism', *Foreign Affairs*, Vol. 75, no. 5.

— (1999) *The New Terrorism: Fanaticism and the Arms of Mass Destruction*, New York: Oxford University Press.

Laver, H. (2005) 'Preemption and the Evolution of America's Strategic Defense', *Parameters*, Summer, 108.

Lawrence, B. (2005) (ed.) *Messages To The World: The Statements Of Osama Bin Laden*, London: Verso.

Leonard, M. and Small, A., with Rose, M. (2005) *British Public Diplomacy in the 'Age of Schisms'*, London: The Foreign Policy Centre.

Lesser, I., Hoffman, B., Arquilla, J., Ronfeldt, D., Zanini, M. and Jenkins, B. (1999) *Countering the New Terrorism*, Santa Monica, CA: Rand Corporation.

Lincoln, C. E. (1960) 'Anxiety, Fear and Integration', *Phylon*, Vol. 21, no. 3.

Linenthal, E. T. (2001) *The Unfinished Bombing: Oklahoma City in American Memory*, New York: Oxford University Press.

Lipschutz, R. D. (1999) 'Terror in the Suites: Narratives of Fear and the Political Economy of Danger', *Global Society*, Vol. 13, no. 4.

Lipschutz, R. D. and Turcotte, H. (2004) 'Wild in the Streets: The Political Economy of Threats and the Production of Fear', unpublished chapter.

Lustick, I. S. (2006) *Trapped in the War on Terror*, Philadelphia, PA: University of Pennsylvania Press.

Luttwak, E. (1995) 'Toward Post-Heroic Warfare', *Foreign Affairs*, Vol. 74, no. 3

MacIntosh, J. P. and Hills, M. 'The Psychology of Future Warfare: Asymmetric Risk and Decision-Taking' in Campen, A. and Dearth, D. (2000) *Cyberwar 3.0: Human Factors in Information Operations and Future Conflict*, Fairfax, VA: AFCEA International Press.

Mandel, D. (2005) 'Threats to Democracy: A Judgment and Decision-Making Perspective', *Analyses of Social Issues and Public Policy*, Vol. 5, no. 1.

Mannheim, K. (1960) *Ideology and Utopia*, London: Routledge, Kegan and Paul.

Martin, G. (2004) (ed.) *The New Era of Terrorism: Selected Readings*, London: Sage Publications.

May, E., Zelikow, P. and Falkenrath, P. (2005) 'Correspondence; 'Sins of Commission? Falkenrath and His Critics', *International Security*, Vol. 29, no. 4.

Mclean, C. and Patterson, A. (2006) 'A Precautionary Approach to Foreign Policy? A Preliminary Analysis of Tony Blair's Speeches on Iraq', *British Journal of Politics and International Relations*, Vol. 8.

Meeuf, R. (2006) 'Collateral Damage: Terrorism, melodrama and the action film on the eve of 9/11' *Jump Cut*, no. 48, Winter.

Meyer, G., Folker A. P., Jorgensen, R. B., Kyare von Krauss, M., Sandoe, P. and Tveit, G. (2005) 'The factualization of uncertainty: Risk, politics and genetically modified crops – a case of rape', *Agriculture and Human Values*, Vol. 22.

Miller, J., Engelberg, S. and Broad, W. (2001) *Germs, Biological Weapons and America's Secret War*, New York: Simon & Schuster.

Mills, C. W. (1959) *The Sociological Imagination*, New York: Oxford University Press.

Mitchell, J. K. (2003) 'The fox and the hedgehog: Myopia about homeland security in US policies on terrorism' in Clarke, L. (ed.) (2003) *Terrorism and Disaster: New Threats, New Ideas*, Oxford: Elsevier.

Mockaitis, T. (1990) *British Counterinsurgency 1919–60*, Houndmills, Basingstoke: The Macmillan Press.

Moore, M. (2003) *Dude, Where's My Country?* New York: Warner.

Mueller, J. (2005a) 'Simplicity and Spook: Terrorism and the Dynamics of Threat Exaggeration', *International Studies Perspectives*, Vol. 6, no. 2.

— (2005b) 'Six Rather Unusual Propositions about Terrorism', *Terrorism and Political Violence*, Vol. 17.

— (2006a) 'Is There Still a Terrorist Threat?: The Myth of the Omnipresent Enemy', *Foreign Affairs*, September/October.

— (2006b) *Overblown: How Politicians and the Terrorism Industry Inflate National Security Threats, and Why We Believe Them*, New York: Free Press.

Mueller, K. (2000) 'Politics, Death, and Morality in US Foreign Policy', *Aerospace Power Journal*, Summer.

van Munster, R. (2005) *Logics of Security: The Copenhagen School, Risk Management and the War on Terror*, Syddansk Universitet, University of Southern Denmark: Political Science Publications.

Mythen, G. and Walklate, S. (2006) 'Criminology and Terrorism, Which Thesis? Risk Society or Governmentality? *British Journal of Criminology*, Vol. 46.

The National Security Strategy of the United States of America, September 2002, Washington DC: The White House, www.whitehouse.gov/nsc/nss.pdf.

Neumann, P. and Smith, M. (2005) 'Missing the Plot? Intelligence and Discourse Failure', *Orbis*, Winter.

Noji, E. K. (2005) 'Disasters: Introduction and State of the Art', *Epidemiologic Reviews*, Vol. 27.

Nolte, W. (2004) 'Keeping pace with the revolution in military affairs', *Studies in Intelligence*, Center for the Study in Intelligence, Central Intelligence Agency, 48 (1), 9.

Nye, J. (2004) 'The Decline of America's Soft Power', *Foreign Affairs*, May/June, Vol. 83, issue 3.

O'Hanlon, M. (2000) *Technological Change and the Future of Warfare*, New York: Brookings Institute Press.

Omand, D. (2005) 'Countering International Terrorism: The Use of Strategy', *Survival*, Vol. 47, no. 4.

Parachini, J. (2000) *Statement of John V. Parachini, Centre for Nonproliferation Studies, Monetary Institute of International Studies, Before the House Subcommittee on National Security, Veteran Affairs, and International Relations. Combating Terrorism: Assessing Threats, Risk Management, and Establishing Priorities*, 26 July.

— (2001) *Combating Terrorism: Assessing The Threat Of Biological Terrorism. Before the House Subcommittee on National Security, Veteran Affairs, and International Relations, Committee on Government Reform, US House of Representatives,* 12 October.

Parkin, D. (1986) 'Toward an Apprehension of Fear' in Scruton, D. L. (ed.) (1986), *Sociophobics: The Anthropology of Fear,* Boulder, CO: Westview Press.

Pupavac, V. (2002) 'Traumatizing children: war and trauma risk management', paper given at The Society for the Study of Social Problems, 52nd Annual Meeting, Chicago.

— (2004) 'Psychosocial Interventions and the Demoralisation of Humanitarianism', *Journal of Biosocial Science,* Vol. 36.

Quarantelli, E. L. (1954) 'The Nature and Conditions of Panic', *American Journal of Sociology,* Vol. 60.

— (1978) (ed.) *Disasters: Theory and Research,* London: Sage Publications.

Quarantelli, E. and Dynes, R. R. (1977) 'Response to Social Crisis and Disaster', *Annual Review of Sociology,* Vol. 3.

Quarantelli, E., Lagadec, P. and Boin, A. (2006) 'A Heuristic Approach to Future Disasters and Crises: New, Old, and In-between Types', in Rodriguez, H., Quarantelli, E. and Dynes, R. (eds) (2006) *Handbook of Disaster Research,* New York: Springer.

Quille, R. (1998) 'The Revolution in Military Affairs and the UK', *International Security Information Service Briefing,* no. 73, December.

Rasmussen, M. V. (2002) '"A Parallel Globalization of Terror": 9-11, Security and Globalization', *Cooperation and Conflict: Journal of the Nordic International Studies Association,* Vol. 37, no. 3.

Record, J. (2002) 'Collapsed countries, casualty dread, and the new American way of war', *Parameters,* Summer.

— (2005–06) 'Why the Strong Lose', *Parameters,* Winter.

Richelson, J. (2002) 'Defusing Nuclear Terror', *Bulletin of Atomic Scientists,* Vol. 58, no. 2.

Riezler, K. (1944) 'The Social Psychology of Fear', *The American Journal of Sociology,* Vol. 49, no. 6.

Rodriguez, H., Quarantelli, E. and Dynes, R. (eds) (2006) *Handbook of Disaster Research,* New York: Springer.

Rose, G. (1999) 'It Could Happen Here: Facing the New Terrorism', *Foreign Affairs,* March/April.

Rosenbaum, D. (1977) 'Nuclear Terror', *International Security,* Vol. 1, no. 3.

Runciman, D. (2006) *The Politics of Good Intention,* Princeton, NJ: Princeton University Press.

Scheid, L. T. and Horwitz, A. V. (1999) 'The Social Context of Mental Health', in Horwitz, A. V. and Scheid, T. L. (1999) (eds) *Handbook for the Study of Mental Health: Social Contexts, Theories and Systems,* Cambridge: Cambridge University Press.

Schmid, A. (2005) 'Terrorism as Psychological Warfare', *Democracy and Security,* Vol. 1.

Schmid, A. and Jongman, A. (1988) *Political Terrorism: A New Guide to Actors, Authors, Concepts, Data bases, Theories, and Literature,* New Brunswick, NJ: Transaction Books.

Scruton, D. L. (ed.) (1986) *Sociophobics: The Anthropology of Fear,* Boulder, CO: Westview Press.

Seligmann-Sliva, M. (2003) 'Catastrophe and representation: History as trauma', *Semiotica,* Vol. 143.

Sheppard, B., Rubin, J., Warman, J. and Wessely, S. (2006) 'Terrorism and Dispelling the Myth of a Panic Prone Public', *Journal of Public Health Policy*, Vol. 27.

Simon, D. (1995) *Social Problems and the Sociological Imagination: A Paradigm for Analysis*, New York: McGraw-Hill.

Slovic, P. (2002) 'Terrorism as Hazard: A New Species of Trouble', *Risk Analysis*, Vol. 22, no. 3.

Smil, V. (2005) 'The Next 50 Years: Fatal Discontinuities', *Population and Development Review*, Vol. 31, no. 2.

Smith, H. (2005) 'What costs will democracies bear? A review of popular theories of casualty aversion', *Armed Forces & Society*, Vol. 31, no. 4.

Sparks, C. (2003) 'Liberalism, Terrorism and the Politics of Fear', *Politics*, Vol. 23, no. 3.

Spencer, A. (2006) 'Questioning the Concept of "New Terrorism"', *Peace, Conflict and Development*, Issue 8.

Spiegel, L. 'Entertainment Wars: Television Culture after 9/11', *American Quarterly*, Vol. 56. no. 2.

Sprinzak, E. (1998) 'The Great Superterrorism Scare', *Foreign Policy*, Autumn.

— (2000) 'Rational Fanatics' *Foreign Policy*, September/October.

— (2001) 'The Lone Gunmen', *Foreign Policy*, November.

Steele, R. D. (1998) 'The Asymmetric Threat to the Nation', *Defense Daily Network*, www.defensefaily.com/reports/takedown.htm.

Steinbruner, J. (2005) 'Terrorism: Practical Distinctions and Research Priorities', *International Studies Review*, Vol. 7.

Sterba, J. (2003) (ed.) *Terrorism and International Justice*, Oxford: Oxord University Press.

Stern, J. (2004) 'Fearing Evil', *Social Research*, Vol. 71, Winter.

Stern, J. and Wiener, B. J. (2006) 'Precaution Against Terrorism', in Bracken, P., Gordon, D. and Bremmer, I. (eds) (2006) *Managing Strategic Surprise: Lessons from Risk Management and Risk Assessment*, Cambridge: Cambridge University Press.

Summerfield, D. (2001) 'The invention of post-traumatic disorder and the social usefulness of a psychiatric category', *British Medical Journal*, no. 322, 13 January.

Suskind, R. (2006) *The One Percent Doctrine: Deep Inside America's Pursuit of its Enemies Since 9/11*, New York: Simon & Schuster.

Thomas, T. L. (2001) 'Deciphering Asymmetry's Word Game', *Military Review*, Vol. 81, no. 4.

Tierney, K. (2004) *Collective Behavior in Times of Crisis*, Paper prepared for the National Research Council Roundtable on Social and Behavioral Sciences and Terrorism, Meeting 4, 'Risk Communication for Terrorism', Washington DC, 30 January 2004.

Tucker, Jonathan (2000) (ed.) *Toxic Terror: Assessing Terrorist Use of Chemical and Biological Weapons*, Cambridge, MA: MIT Press.

Tulloch, J. and Lupton, D. (2003) *Risk and Everyday Life*, London: Sage Publications.

Turkel, G. (2002) 'Sudden Solidarity and the Rush to Normalization: Toward an Alternative Approach', *Sociological Focus*, Vol. 35, no. 1.

Untitled (2000) 'American and the New Terrorism: an exchange', *Survival*, Vol. 42, no. 2.

Vasterman, P., Yzermans, J. and Dirkzwager, A. (2004) 'The Role of the Media and Media Hypes in the Aftermath of Disasters', *Epidemiologic Review*, Vol. 27.

Victoroff, J. (2005) 'The Mind of the Terrorist: A Review and Critique of Psychological Approaches', *Journal of Conflict Resolution*, Vol. 49, no. 1.

Walker, S. (2001) 'Regulating against Nuclear Terrorism: The Domestic Safeguards Issue', *Technology and Culture*, Vol. 42, January.

Waller, M. A. (2001) 'Resilience in Ecosystemic Context: Evolution of the Concept', *American Journal of Orthopsychiatry*, Vol. 71, no. 3, July.

Waugh, W. (1986) 'Integrating the policy models of terrorism and emergency government', *Policy Studies Review*, Vol. 6.

Waysman, M., Schwarzwald, J. and Solomon, Z. (2001) 'Hardiness: An Examination of its Relationship with Positive and Negative Long Term Changes Following Trauma', *Journal of Traumatic Stress*, Vol. 14, no. 3.

Webb, G. (2002) 'Sociology, Disasters, and Terrorism: Understanding Threats of the New Millennium', *Sociological Focus*, Vol. 35, no. 1.

Westgate, K. N. and O'Keefe, P. (1976) *Some Definitions of Disaster*, University of Bradford, Disaster Research Unit, Occasional paper no. 4.

Weiland, K. (2005) *Breeding Insecurity: Global Security Implications of Rapid Population Growth*, Washington DC: The Population Institute, 21st Century papers, no. 1.

Weinberg, L., Pedahzur, A. and Hirsch-Hoeffler, S. (2004) 'The Challenges of Conceptualizing Terrorism', *Terrorism and Political Violence*, Vol. 16, no. 4.

Wessely, S. (2005) 'Risk, psychiatry and the military', *British Journal of Psychiatry*, no. 186.

Wilkins, L. T. (2001, originally published in 1964) *Social Deviance: Social Policy, Action and Research*, London: Routledge.

Wilkinson, P. (1974) *Political Terrorism*, New York: Macmillan.

Wisniewski, J. (2004) 'Strategic Surprises for a New Administration', *Schlesinger Working Group Report, Fall 2004*, Washington DC: Institute for the Study of Diplomacy, Georgetown University.

Wynne, B. (2002) 'Risk and Environment as Legitimatory Discourses of Technology: Reflexivity Inside Out?', *Current Sociology*, Vol. 50, no. 3.

Zanders, J. P. (1999) 'Assessing the Risk of Chemical and Biological Weapons Proliferation to Terrorists', *The Nonproliferation Review*, Autumn.

Zenko, M. (2006) 'Intelligence Estimates of Nuclear Terrorism', *The Annals of the American Academy of Political and Social Science*, September, no. 607.

Zimmermann, D. (2003) 'The Transformation of Terrorism: The "New Terrorism", Impact Scalability and the Dynamic of Reciprocal Threat Perception', *Zürcher Beiträge zur Sicherheitspolitik und Konfliktforschung*, no. 67.

Zulaika, J. (1998) 'Tropics of Terror: from Guernica's Natives' to Global "Terrorists"', *Social Identities*, Vol. 4, no. 1.

— (2003) 'The Self-Fulfilling Prophecies of Counterterrorism', *Radical History Review*, Issue 85, Winter.

Index